GRANTA

GRANTA 89, SPRING 2005
www.granta.com

Granta, 2–3 Hanover Yard, Noel Road, London N1 8BE
Tel 020 7704 9776 Fax 020 7704 0474
email for editorial: editorial@granta.com

Granta US, 1755 Broadway, 5th Floor, New York, NY 10019-3780, USA

TO SUBSCRIBE call 020 7704 0470 or e-mail subs@granta.com
A one-year subscription (four issues) costs £26.95 (UK), £34.95 (rest of Europe) and £41.95 (rest of the world).

Granta is printed and bound in Italy by Legoprint. The paper used in this publication meets the minimum requirements of American National Standard for Information Sciences—Permanence of Paper for Printed Library Materials, ANSI Z39.48-1984.

Granta is published by Granta Publications.

Design: Slab Media.

Front cover: 'Coming from the Mill' by L. S. Lowry (1930), oil © The L. S. Lowry Collection, Salford
Back cover: Taken by Mitchell and Kenyon, 1900 © British Film Institute; Taken by Alec Soth, 2004

ISBN 0-903141-75-2

Kazuo Ishiguro
Never Let Me Go
By the author of
The Remains of the Day and When We Were Orphans
ff
ff

THE FACTORY

Motley Notes

Perhaps the most famous factory in recent literature is Newark Maid Leatherware in Newark, New Jersey. It made ladies' gloves—very good ones. Newark Maid, according to the company's historian, became 'one of the most respected names in ladies' gloves south of Gloversville, New York, the center of the [American] glove trade'. Lou Levov, its energetic founder, started off small in the 1920s and then bought an old umbrella factory on the corner of Central Avenue and 2nd Street. Levov employed hard-working Germans and Italians (and eventually black Americans), and thanks to his ambition and his workers' skill—which was immense in this small matter of cutting and sewing leather—the company prospered. It had two lucky breaks. In the Second World War it got the order—a very big order indeed—for 'a black, lined sheepskin dress glove' from the Women's Army Corps; and then it got the Bamberger account, which meant a great deal as Bamberger's was then the finest department store in New Jersey.

The Newark Maid brand still exists, but its Newark factory doesn't. It closed in 1973 when production moved offshore, first to Puerto Rico and Czechoslovakia, and then, when Puerto Rico got too expensive and Eastern Bloc bureaucracy too troublesome, to the Philippines, to Korea and Taiwan, always looking for cheaper labour (but trying not to forget quality), until in ended up in China. In this way, the story of Newark Maid is a very ordinary story: the ending in China is almost inevitable, you might say. And gloves are only gloves, pieces of leather stitched with thread, not the fashion they once were (in the elder Levov's day they were essential items for the well-dressed woman): it can hardly matter where they are made.

To quote the company history again, it was Lou Levov's son, Seymour 'Swede' Levov, who made the decision:

> Virtually the whole industry had moved offshore: the unions had made it more and more difficult for a manufacturer to make any money, you could hardly find people to do that kind of piecework anymore, or to do it the way you wanted it done, and elsewhere there was an availability of workers who could be trained nearly to the standards that had obtained in the glove industry forty and fifty years ago.

The decision, though it was his to take, saddened Seymour Levov. He told his historian (whose name is Skip Zuckerman) about his delight in the business of glove-making, about the knowledge and dexterity that had now quit America:

> Takes great skill to cut a glove right. Table cutting is an art. No two skins are alike. The skins all come in different according to each animal's diet and age, every one different as far as stretchability goes, and the skill involved in making every glove come out like every other one is amazing. Same thing with the sewing. Kind of work people don't want to do anymore... Glove sewing is a tremendously complicated procedure. If you want to make a better glove, you have to spend money and train workers. Takes a lot of hard work and attention, all the twists and turns where the finger crotches are sewn—it's very hard.

Equally saddening to Levov was the fate of Newark itself, a city that had once made so many things: water coolers, fire alarms, corsets, pillows, pen points. Now the place 'broke his heart'. It had become 'the worst city in the world...the car-theft capital of the world'. Once 'there was a factory where somebody was making something down every side street'. Now there was 'a liquor store in every street—a liquor store, a pizza stand, and a seedy storefront church. Everything else in ruins or boarded up'.

These facts and opinions—this history—appear in Philip Roth's great novel, *American Pastoral*, published in 1997. It's fiction: Roth made it up. But though the particulars are Roth's creation and apply only to one small part of the USA, anyone who lived through the last thirty years of the twentieth century in many other parts of Europe and North America will attest to the wonderful persuasiveness and wider application of them. Greenock, Pittsburgh, Blackburn, towns on the Tyne and towns in the Ruhr, all once upon a time with their factories and their Levovs (not necessarily Jewish, not necessarily in gloves) and now coping, for better or worse, with the death of that way of working and living.

In his book, *The First Industrial Nation*, the historian Peter Mathias describes how what he calls 'the first genuine factory' was erected on the River Derwent at Derby in 1719. It prepared silk yarn for weaving, was six storeys high, and employed three hundred people, mainly women and children, to re-knot the silk threads when they broke; 'light work in terms of physical exertion,' writes Mathias, 'but demanding very high standards of attention.' Its factory-ness was expressed in its size, its large number of workers, and the non-human source of its energy: a water wheel in the river was connected to enough shafts and spindles to perform 25,000 industrial movements. Towards the end of the eighteenth century, when James Watt's rotary steam engine began to replace water as the power source in textile manufacture, the country went 'steam mill mad'. By 1816, the year after Waterloo, a large cotton spinning mill might employ more than 1,500 workers, most of them doing the same repetitive tasks in a new kind of world which obeyed the speed of the machine and the laws of the clock.

What was it like to work in such a place? Writers such as Dickens and Mrs Gaskell gave accounts, and factory life also appears in the work of a few twentieth-century novelists, mainly to exemplify the class struggle or poverty and boredom (there was no thought that factory work might disappear and there has never been much literary interest in how things are made—Roth's description of glove-making is striking partly because of its rarity). The plain documentary is usually the best source of information. Here is one from a woman, the daughter of a miner, who started work in a linen mill in Dunfermline, Fife, 1921:

> I left school at fourteen and had to find a job. There was some talk of a job in a shop in Cowdenbeath. I can't remember what happened but I remember going with my mother to Mathewson's factory in Dunfermline and starting there as a message girl in the Service Room where the linen cloth was examined after it was

brought off the looms. My job was to go into the weaving shed and tell the weaver she was wanted if there were faults in her cloth. I was never very welcome. I had lots of other errands, bringing up drinking water every morning in a watering can and filling up a big jar with a tinnie at the side for drinking, not very hygienic and a bit crude. The young apprentices in the Mechanic Shop used to tease me a lot when they saw me, they used to drop pieces of coal in the water and I had to go back and fill up my can again.

After a year at this I was promoted and had to stand at a table and examine the cloth and look for faults. We were called cloth pickers.

Sometimes I was on the folding machine, which folded the cloth into bundles ready to be sent to the bleachworks to be bleached white; it was cream before. They made lovely linen tablecloths and napkins and we got faulty ones quite cheap. I used to buy tablecloths made for the P & O line, big cloths for only 4s 6d with the name cut out—we could easily patch it with odd scraps of linen. We also wove tablecloths for the Lyons cafés, white with a yellow border with lions in the border. I did have plenty of linen in my bottom drawer when I got married, I never had to buy a dish towel for years.

We used to travel to work in the tram car, quite a few of us travelled together. There was no other work, then, in a mining village, there was only going into service, [though] some girls used to work on the pit head, coarse dirty work standing on a conveyor belt picking up stones and rubbish from the coal. That was dying out by the time I started to work so most of the girls had to travel to Dunfermline. We could buy a weekly ticket in the factory which cost us two shillings for the six days. The trams were always full and often we had to sit upstairs, which was open top. Fine in the summer, but bitterly cold in the winter especially if it snowed.

When I started at the factory my wage was seventeen shillings a week paid fortnightly. After a few weeks it was dropped to ten shillings weekly. It was some Truck Act that caused it. Not much left to take home after paying for tram tickets, etc.

The woman who wrote that was my mother. She wrote it when she was ninety, a year or two before she died. She and my father often talked about 'the factory' as though there were only one of them, though my father, throughout his life, worked in many. That may be because they met at this particular factory, Mathewson's, where my dad served his apprenticeship in the Mechanic Shop.

Thirty years later I went to school in the same town: Dunfermline, where Andrew Carnegie's father had worked as a handloom weaver until he migrated with his family to America in the 1840s. At that time, new steam-driven factories like Mathewson's were destroying the cottage industry of handloom weaving—the Carnegies fled poverty and unemployment—but though the factories were built strongly of stone and looked permanent (one of them had its buildings linked with a copy of the Bridge of Sighs) their usefulness was measured only in decades. Several of them were dead and demolished by the 1930s, early victims of Scotland's long industrial decline.

During our school lunch-hours in the late 1950s, a group of us would sometimes amuse ourselves by crossing the playing fields and following a small river that ran through a culvert under the railway, to emerge by the side of what had been a square reservoir, now empty of water and full of weeds. There were stone walls, broken and overgrown, all around. Eventually I realized that this had been Mathewson's, The Factory: the site of the romance between mechanic and cloth picker that started the chain of events that caused the birth of the being with the following name: *Ian Jack*

GRANTA

MADE IN CHINA

Isabel Hilton

CHIEN-CHI CHANG/MAGNUM PHOTOS

1. The comfort of inefficiency

In the early 1970s, I went to China to study. My subject was meant to be Chinese literature of the twentieth century, but the timing was unfortunate: the Cultural Revolution was still unfolding and Mao's wife, Jiang Qing, had banished or otherwise disposed of the authors and the writing that interested me. Literature had gone to ground and in its place were the collectively produced works—a handful of 'reformed' operas and a ballet—on which Jiang Qing decreed that all of China's future creative efforts were to be modelled. It made for dull evenings in the theatre and desperate days in the classroom, which made me all the more receptive to another proposition in vogue in China at the time: that intellectuals, never a category highly valued by Mao, should drop their books and go and learn from the heroes of the Chinese Revolutionary state—the workers, peasants and soldiers.

Since I was a foreigner, learning from the soldiers was unlikely to be permitted. Workers and peasants were an easier proposition. After a prolonged series of meetings, the authorities at Fudan University in Shanghai agreed that the handful of foreign students then studying there might be permitted to work in suitable factories. I had some idea of what a Chinese factory was like. In Beijing the year before I had spent a tedious week in an electrical components factory winding copper wire around wooden bobbins, 'repairing' objects whose function I never understood. And, like anyone who visited China at the time, I had been taken round dozens of factories, visits that invariably began with an inaccurately named 'brief introduction'. We would sit around long brown varnished tables set out with saucers of sweets and lidded tea mugs—and, if we were lucky, red packets of dry but faintly vanilla-flavoured cigarettes—and hear the standard story of the factory's evolution from locus of alienated labour and capitalist exploitation to fully mobilized revolutionary production unit in which the people—proletarians in the dictatorship of the proletariat—were both workers and masters. I would note down production figures that had little meaning for me or, as it turned out, for anybody else, before being taken on the obligatory tour of the workshops. The factory had replaced the temple or the palace—all closed if not destroyed—as the officially favoured destination for visitors to China and for years I treasured a postcard that was captioned, with disarming frankness, AMMONIA AND UREA FACTORY, WUHAN.

Visiting a factory was one thing; working in one quite another. It didn't take long to understand that the arrival of students—especially foreign students—in a factory caused a headache for management: what could we do that would satisfy the political form without inflicting too much damage on production? Different managers solved the problem in different ways. In the depths of the Shanghai winter—a long dank affair unrelieved in those days by any central heating—I was sent to a custard cream factory, selected by the literature department at Fudan because the workers were particularly enthusiastic about Jiang Qing's model operas and had formed a cultural troupe of their own to sing them. I whiled away my days there in a steady blast of warm air, watching a slow river of hot biscuits emerge from the oven and head for the packers. I was meant to be looking for misshapes but I doubt that anyone took me seriously as quality control. Then, in a Shanghai cotton factory, I worked in the spinning shop. The machines still carried the brass plates that said they were made in Massachusetts. They were jammed close together and when the workshop was running at full tilt the noise was deafening. It looked effortless and satisfying: the threads spun almost too fast to see and the thread pouring on to the bobbins seemed to bulk out by magic. But I soon learned to give the machines I was supposed to be running a wide berth. Any attempt on my part to imitate my supervisor—a patient woman in her thirties whose dexterity had clearly taken some years to acquire—ended in a tangle of broken threads. She would have to stop the ancient machines and re-thread them. It was in this factory that I had an abiding lesson in the role of performance in the daily life of the Chinese Revolution. On our last morning we were told to tidy the workshop for some foreign visitors. That afternoon, as the foreign visitors in question, we were solemnly shown around the same workshops.

I grew attached to the workers assigned to supervise me in my brief industrial career. Unlike the bureaucrats who fretted over our visits, they were refreshingly free of political jargon. Invariably an old worker would be pushed forward to give a dramatic account of the horrors of life before the Revolution, when workers were ground beneath the heel of capitalism, and yet most of the factories I visited or worked in did not appear to have changed much since 1949. The difference lay in official perception. Before 'liberation' the workers were the exploited proletariat. After liberation, they were the masters of the state. Their factories might have been as dirty and dangerous as ever, but now, in theory, the workers were the bosses.

Their journey to this theoretical position had not been swift or simple. Mao's revolutionary movement had an ambivalent attitude to the industrial working class. In the 1920s, under Soviet tutelage, the Chinese tried to follow Marx's prescription and lead a workers' revolution. The difficulty was that China barely had a proletariat. China's workshops had produced textiles and porcelain for thousands of years, but the first modern factory in China had been the Jiangnan Arsenal, set up in Shanghai in 1865 as the decaying Qing dynasty tried, unsuccessfully, to respond to the aggression of a technologically superior West. By the 1920s Shanghai had some modern textile mills, mostly foreign-owned, and there were a few factories in Canton, but the industrial working class was still tiny as a proportion of China's total population—about 2 million at the beginning of the twentieth century—mainly employed in railways, mining, textiles and shipbuilding. The economy, overall, was in steep decline: according to some economists, between 1820 and 1952, when world economic output rose eightfold, China's gross domestic product fell from one-third to one-twentieth of total world production, and her income per head shrank from the world average to a quarter of the average.

Stalin, however, believed that the Chinese revolution would be made in alliance with the Guomindang, the Nationalist Party, using the muscle of the urban proletariat. Stalin had cut his political teeth organizing strikes in the oil industry in Baku and shared Marx's contempt for the peasantry. In China, the Nationalist Party's early attempts to fulfil his prescription ended in disaster. As early as 1926, Mao had argued that the Chinese revolution should be made not by the urban working class but by a peasant guerrilla army led by the Communist Party. In the 1930s, as the argument persisted inside the Communist Party itself, he wrote of China, 'a few modern industrial and commercial cities coexist with a vast stagnant countryside; several million industrial workers coexist with several hundred millions of peasants and handicraftsmen labouring under the old system.' In 1949 the People's Liberation Army—largely made up of peasants—finally took Beijing.

The peasants' success did not prevent Mao from repeating most of

Stalin's catastrophic prescriptions for building the perfect society. Stalin sent teams of advisors from the Soviet Union with blueprints for industrial plants and built factories all over the country. After Stalin's death, China and the USSR fell out and Mao decided to go it alone. By the time I got to China in 1973, China's industrial output had still not recovered from the Cultural Revolution that had begun in 1964, or from the protracted struggle for power between Mao and his long term opponents in the Party, who had tried to oust him in the early 1960s. Isolated and shorn of formal power, Mao called on China's young to attack existing authority, including Party authority, to carry the revolution forward. Schools, universities and factories were all thrown into the upheaval. The result was several years of chaos that had, by the time I arrived, settled into a narrow, exhausted ideological orthodoxy. The Red Guards had been sent off to the countryside, the Party had been broken and would be rebuilt from the ground up and the prevailing mood was fear of political transgression.

There were shortages of everything. Basic goods—oil, rice and cotton cloth—were rationed and a bicycle was a scarce luxury for which a citizen might wait for years. Maoism was a popular pose for students all over Western Europe, but after twenty years of Mao's prescriptions, China's economy was smaller than Belgium's and pig bristle loomed large in the table of its major exports.

China was closed, hostile and xenophobic and foreigners were rare enough to cause a minor commotion in the streets. Foreign governments occasionally organized trade fairs and businessmen would set up their stalls and wait for orders. By day, tame and polite crowds of Chinese would turn up: you could, one exhibitor told me, order any number of visitors you wished. By night, so the foreigners complained, other less tame Chinese would arrive and methodically dismantle the equipment piece by piece, trying to capture its secrets. The only foreigners I met who had succeeded in selling anything of note to the world's largest nation in those years were a stoic Scotsman who had spent months honing his forehand on the British Embassy tennis court while waiting for the Chinese to buy his military aircraft, and a group of mining engineers from Derby who had appeared one day in Beijing. They were intimidatingly tough, with massive forearms and fewer than the usual complement of fingers. They had spent several weeks in a Chinese coal mine in Henan, living off a cache of imported tins of baked beans, installing mining equipment. They did not expect it to last, they told me. The locals, inspired by Mao's teachings on self-reliance, insisted on making 'improvements'.

Mao's version of self-reliance had brought Chinese industrial production almost to a standstill, and yet, according to the state's official story, the workers were masters of the country. The factory existed not merely to produce things: it was the unit through which the wider community was organized, the means by which the state distributed welfare and the instrument through which unemployment was kept to a minimum. Through it, the Party could reach individuals and their families, to keep them ideologically in line and to mobilize them when necessary for national effort. The factory was both a unit of production and an arm of the state.

Unlike the peasants, factory workers had regular hours and were paid regular wages. They were housed by the factory; when they were ill, the factory clinic attended to them; their children were taken care of in factory crèches and, when the time came, could expect to work in a factory while their parents retired on factory pensions. The factory was both a world of labour and the centre of social and cultural life. It was run by the Party, the workers were told, on behalf of the people. It was a place that many of my Chinese fellow students would gladly have accepted as a lifelong assignment.

And now, thirty years later? I remembered what one worker, Mr Wu, had told me a few months previously, in the autumn of 2004. 'In China,' he said, 'it is a death sentence to be a worker.' Of course, he was generalizing from the particular: but understandably, the particular being himself.

2. Mr Wu tries to breathe

I had first heard of Wu in the office of the Christian Industrial Committee in Hong Kong. My introduction to him was his chest X-ray, one of several that CIC activists were mounting on to posters to use in a demonstration that weekend. The biggest jewellery fair in the world was about to open in Hong Kong and the activists wanted to use the occasion to embarrass a Hong Kong businessman—Wu's former employer.

To meet Wu, rather than a picture of his lungs, I travelled about fifty miles north to the town of Huizhou, across the border that encloses Hong Kong and its neighbouring New Territories, which together formed Britain's last significant imperial possession until their return to China in 1997. When I first crossed that border in 1974, passengers from China would get off the train at the final station of Lo Wu and walk across a simple wooden bridge. At the Chinese end of the bridge, severe-looking Chinese soldiers would scrutinize the departing travellers' documents. At the other end, in a hut flying the Union flag, Hong Kong customs officers would do the same. Behind the traveller from China were austerity, exhortation by loudspeaker and material shortages; ahead, the unimaginable abundance of the Crown Colony's shops and markets. The passengers crossed the bridge in a rural silence broken only by the sound of their own footsteps, the scraping of luggage on the wooden boards and, in the distance, the soft chattering of ducks being herded to a pond by a Cantonese peasant. It was one of those Cold War crossings, on the frontier between two implacably hostile worlds.

Today, a city of nearly five million people, Shenzhen, sits at the border. The hinterland behind Shenzhen, the Pearl River Delta, is the heart of the fastest growing industrial zone in the world, the Chinese province of Guangdong. This is the landscape that produces two-thirds of the world's photocopiers, microwave ovens, DVD players and shoes, more than half of the world's digital cameras and two-fifths of its personal computers. Guangdong's business is to make things. It sucks manufacturing from Europe and North America and other economies with high wage rates, cheapens it, increases it, then ships it by container to overseas markets. The factories here bear no relationship to the ones I knew thirty years ago in Shanghai. It is as different as Manchester in the 1840s was from rural England in the eighteenth century and to come here is to feel a little of what Friedrich Engels felt when he set out to describe Manchester, the world's first uncompromisingly industrial city. Here too, the visitor marvels at the industrial energy and is appalled by the degrading conditions in which the workers live. 'In this place,' as Engels put it, 'the social war, the war of each against all, is here openly declared.'

My rendezvous with Mr Wu was a curve in the road just in front of the municipal park in Huizhou. I took a taxi and waited inside it. It wasn't my first trip to Huizhou and I'd come to prefer it by night. During the day, the air is visible—a yellow-grey haze that

N
W
E
S
0
100
200
300 miles
Beijing
CHINA
Yellow Sea
Xianyang
SHAANXI
SICHUAN
Yangtze River
Shanghai
GUANGDONG
Guangzhou (Canton)
Pearl River Delta
Shenzhen
Hong Kong
TAIWAN
South China Sea
JOHN GILKES

makes the buildings of the Pearl River Delta shimmer like an optical illusion but unfortunately does not quite disguise them. In the dark, the tawdry architecture—cheap hotels, box-like factories, high-rise workers' dormitories, kitschy monuments—becomes a nightscape of coloured lights that might be mistaken for urban glamour. As I waited for Mr Wu in my taxi, the smog laying down a furry deposit in my throat, I tried to remember how the Pearl River Delta had been when I first travelled through it thirty years before. I remembered low green hills and valleys that were flat, wet and wide, with women in hats that looked like old-fashioned lampshades bent double over flooded paddy fields. Picturesque; agricultural; the ancient (and back-breaking) labour of planting, replanting, and harvesting rice.

When had it begun to change? In fact, not long after I first saw it. In 1976, Mao died and his widow was swiftly arrested. By 1979 her old enemy, Deng Xiaoping, was moving China in a new direction. Deng was, as Mao had always maintained, a man bent on taking the capitalist road. Unlike Mao, he had travelled—as a young man he had worked in the Renault factory in France—and he wanted to liberalize China's economy and open it up to the world. He rationalized the labyrinthine and bureaucratic foreign trade system and gave the southern provinces of Guangdong and Fujian the freedom to pursue their own foreign trade and investment without having to go through Beijing. In 1980 he set up four Special Economic Zones for foreign investors, three of them in Guangdong. Hong Kong and Taiwanese businesses began to set up factories, encouraged by the tax breaks and the fact that labour costs in Hong Kong were eight times as high. Across the world, an old dream began to stir in the heads of businessmen—that their companies might sell into what was potentially the biggest market in the world. What they had still to discover was that China would put many of them out of business.

The economy of the Pearl River Delta began to grow. In the nine years from 1985 to 1994, the value of Guangdong's exports went from 2.9 billion dollars to 50 billion dollars. By the early 1990s, the province was producing a quarter of China's exports. Peasants who had sweated all their lives wringing three harvests a year from their small fields became suddenly rich enough to retire and play leisurely games of cards when their land was bought and built on. At Shenzhen—one of the first Special Economic Zones—the streams where once they had raised their ducks turned black. The old railway bridge at Lo Wu, once the frontier between capitalism and communism, was swallowed up by a new railway station and forgotten.

More and more factories moved in from Hong Kong, Korea and Taiwan, looking for labour to produce the goods that would feed their existing export markets—looking for men such as Wu.

He eventually arrived at our meeting place on the back of one of Huizhou's many motorbike taxis. He was a tall man in his thirties dressed in a shirt and football shorts, with flip-flops on his feet. He spoke with a strong Sichuan accent and his voice rattled slightly in his throat. He climbed into the front seat of the cab and began to tell his story.

He was the middle child of five siblings. His parents struggled to support the family by growing vegetables on a small plot of land in the hills of Sichuan, about 1,500 miles to the north-west of Huizhou. Convention says that Chinese peasants are deeply attached to their land, and in some senses that may be true. But more than 200 million of them have left rural life in the last twenty years, driven out by poverty and the lack of any prospect of a life other than the physical labour of their parents and grandparents. Where Wu grew up, life was implacably hard. 'We live in the mountains and there's no good road,' he said. 'Everyone grows grain and vegetables. You have to sell most of the grain to the state and you eat what's left. You are growing the same things as your neighbours so there's nobody to sell your vegetables to. You can eat, after a fashion, but you never have any cash.' What cash there was went mainly in taxes; peasants pay at higher rates than city dwellers, even though city dwellers have more money. The government reasons that discontent is more dangerous in the cities than in the countryside and it is therefore better to keep the cities happy at the peasants' expense. As a result, some rural families work all year for barely 800 yuan in cash, or less than one hundred dollars. Factories, for such a family, held the key to the future. If a son or a daughter could get a job in a factory, he or she might be able to earn a hundred dollars in a month.

His younger brother had left home before him but Wu was bright and stayed on to finish high school and marry a village girl. Finally, in 1989, when he was twenty-one, the family clubbed together to buy him and a young cousin the cheapest train tickets available for the long

HIROJI KUBOTA/MAGNUM PHOTOS

journey to Shenzhen. He was part of a new mobility. For forty years, peasants had been nailed to the land by a system of residence permits—the *hukou*. Only someone born in the city had a city dweller's *hukou*. Without it, you had no access to food rations, housing, schools, or health services. However grim life in the village might be, most Chinese had no choice but to live and die there. But by the time Wu set off, though the police could still arrest a migrant peasant and ship him back home, the new factories in the south saw to it that if a migrant had a factory job, the police would leave him alone.

Wu and his cousin boarded their train on June 3, 1989. They had no idea that, nearly 2,000 miles away in Beijing, a confrontation between an old Party leadership and thousands of young university students was about to reach a violent and bloody climax. Just before midnight that night, as Wu and his cousin tried to sleep on their wooden train seats, Deng Xiaoping unleashed the People's Liberation Army on the student protesters in Tiananmen Square. By morning the shock waves had reached Sichuan. The railway track swarmed with students and the train was delayed. By the time it arrived in Shenzhen, two days late, both boys were faint with hunger. They had no money to spare and no food. They didn't know what the trouble was about and didn't care.

Today about 2.5 million people live in the 112 square miles of Shenzhen's Special Economic Zone and as many more in the area around it. To get to Huizhou from Shenzhen I had battled along motorways choked with container lorries. But in 1989 Shenzhen was still in its adolescence, an awkward, half-formed city where fields were still visible between the new buildings. The paved roads ended abruptly at the edge of the town. 'I wasn't that impressed,' Wu said. 'Back then it wasn't as developed as now. The houses weren't that different from where I had come from. There were still fields, still farms.' Getting a job proved simple. After a couple of nights in his little brother's factory dormitory, Wu paid a deposit of thirty yuan, lent to him by his brother, to the Lucky Gem Factory and was taken on. A factory ID came with it so he could move about without fear of arrest.

The factory was in Bailijun Village in Pingfu County, near Shenzhen. Its Hong Kong owner had moved his business here in 1984 but it was still a relatively makeshift affair. He employed around 200 workers to turn out semi-precious jewellery for the lower end of the international market. There were local regulations, including health and safety laws, but nobody bothered to enforce them. The boss was often around on the factory floor. 'He didn't even have a car in those days,' Wu said. 'By 1993 he had four—one of them was a Mercedes Benz.'

Wu was earning a hundred yuan a month and spending sixty on his living expenses. At first he planned to make money for a few years then return to the village, but gradually he got used to urban life. In 1992 his wife joined him. They lived apart for the first two years, each in a crowded dormitory room shared with eight to ten other workers, before the factory gave them permission to live together. They had left their two children behind in the care of Wu's parents. They saw them only once every couple of years, after they'd saved up the time and money for the journey home. In the meantime they wrote to them. Each reply took a month to arrive.

Wu had been happy enough in his job. He operated a machine that cut and ground semi-precious stones, twelve hours a day, seven days a week. In the low season, he had two days off a month. In the busy season, he was lucky to get one. Wu did not find the conditions particularly onerous. He was young and anyone who had grown up in a peasant household in Sichuan was prepared for hard work. What mattered most was how much he had left at the end of the month to send back to his family. As the factory grew, more of his extended family made the long train journey down to Shenzhen. By the end of his time there were fifty cousins, uncles, brothers and in-laws working for Lucky Gem. Over the ten years he worked there the company grew to more than one thousand workers and in 1997 it moved out to Huizhou to escape Shenzhen's rising rents.

As Wu was telling me some of this, we were driving to meet other former employees of the Lucky Gem factory. We turned off the main road and eventually down a dirt track that ended in a warren of little streets, broken pavements and haphazard buildings. A few of them were whitewashed and had red-tiled roofs; the remaining evidence of a previous, more innocent landscape, now jostling for space with concrete barracks which had been hastily erected by local farmers who had seized the chance to make money. One of these barracks—a five-storey building with an open sewer at its feet—was where Wu now lived. His wife had moved back to Sichuan.

We climbed a bare concrete staircase, turned along a dark

concrete corridor and into a large room furnished with a bed, a table and two child-sized plastic stools. Wu sat on the floor, his head tilted back against the wall to keep his long hair out of his eyes. I perched on one of the stools. A small plastic mirror dangled from a coat hanger that hung from a nail in a wall. Electric wiring led across the ceiling to feed a neon strip light. The open windows were covered with an insect screen of wire mesh, but despite this access to the air outside, the atmosphere in the room was damp and fetid, stirred rather than cooled by two small electric fans. A pack of cards, its edges black with use, sat on the table.

Other workers paused in the doorway to stare at me as Wu's friends arrived. One by one they slipped off their flip-flops in the doorway and sat on the floor or on the bed, waiting to tell their stories. A flimsy sheet of paper was handed round. The men listed their names for me and the villages they came from. They were all peasants from Sichuan. They were all married with children, and they were all bound for an early death.

The men who crowded into Wu's room no longer worked for Lucky Gem. Wu pointed to a small man who, like the others, had slipped off his sandals at the door and who was now sitting barefoot on the concrete floor, leaning against the wall, his legs stretched out in front of him. His face was pale. Liu Huaquan, Wu said, was the first to fall ill. Liu acknowledged Wu's introduction with a smile—a perverse pride in being the first one afflicted. It was 1999 when his symptoms—breathlessness and coughing—first appeared. They were diagnosed as tuberculosis and for two and half years he paid 300 yuan a month—nearly half his wages—for treatment. But his health continued to worsen and when he finally sought a second opinion at the Guangzhou Occupational Diseases Centre, he was told he had silicosis.

'I had never heard of it,' Liu said. 'They said it was an occupational disease and I shouldn't work any more. They said I should get compensation from the factory. I wanted to work. I still do. I have a wife and two children. But now they ask you for a health certificate and I can't get a job anywhere.' His weight had dropped from 121 pounds to ninety and he could barely climb the stairs. Silicosis is incurable, but the right treatment can slow the disease's progression. Liu had received some compensation from a social insurance fund but he could not spend the money on the treatment that might slow his decline because he fears that his wife and children would be left destitute. His only hope was somehow to force the factory to compensate him. 'I never thought this was going to happen,' he said. 'I thought I would work for a while, then go home and set up a business.'

On the bed in Wu's room one of the men had fallen asleep and was beginning to snore.

Silicosis: quarry workers get it, miners get it (in Britain, though few coal mines survive, the benefits paid to former coal miners who have silicosis make the government's compensation scheme one of the largest in the world). The disease results in inflammation and scarring of the lungs caused by the inhalation of mineral dust, the kind of dust that was flying up from the cutting and polishing machines at the Lucky Gem factory. After Liu was diagnosed, the others realized, one by one, that they were also sick. Each man visited the Guangzhou Occupational Diseases Centre and there was handed his own death sentence. All told, forty-five workers from the Lucky Gem factory were diagnosed with silicosis.

They had tried to sue the owner, but the court in Shenzhen had refused to take the case on the grounds that the factory had moved to Huizhou. In Huizhou, the court heard the case and ruled in favour of the workers, but made no order of compensation on the grounds that it did not know how much an early death from silicosis was worth.

They had been fighting for three years. They had lobbied local officials, and then twenty-five of them had gone to Beijing to petition the government, just as people have always done in China, seeking justice from a righteous emperor for the wrongs inflicted by local officials. Liu said, 'We went to Beijing, to the Health Ministry. They told us there was a law but they were not responsible for implementing it. They said we needed to get the attention of the government.' They tried to get the attention of the government through publicity, a tactic that sometimes works in today's China. They invited a hard-hitting programme on China Central TV which had run stories like theirs in the past to visit them, but the producers turned them down. They tried local government, only to be told that the Lucky Gem boss was an important local investor. Six months before I'd met him, Wu had even been to see the boss himself.

'I explained our situation. About how the disease moves from one stage to another and how we will die quickly if we don't control the progression. He told me I would die even sooner if I didn't get out of his sight. Now the security guards don't let us past the gate.'

I asked them who they blamed. They shrugged. The factory owner was in league with the local authorities. That was how things were. They were *nongmingong*, they said, peasant workers. They had no status. It was normal to be badly treated. The man on the bed woke up and chipped in. 'All factories in this industry are the same,' he said. 'The only difference is the big ones can afford to install the proper equipment. The buyers come and inspect the factory because they have codes of conduct, but the workers are told to lie. If they don't, they lose their jobs.' For nearly ten years they had worked in thick dust with no protection. They didn't even seem angry.

As I left, I asked Wu to show me the Lucky Gem factory, less than a quarter of a mile away. We drove cautiously past it, trying to avoid the notice of the security guards. Wu directed us to the back where he pointed out the third-floor windows behind which he used to work. Thick dust caked the glass and lay in drifts across the window ledges. I asked Wu and some of his old colleagues in the car how they thought the government viewed factory workers in China. Wu looked at me as though I had descended from Mars. It was then that he said, 'In China, it is a death sentence to be a worker.'

3. Strike!

While Deng's reforms were promoting new factories in the south of China, the central exchequer wrestled with the problem of what to do with the thousands of factories it already had in the rest of the country: the old steel and textile mills, the obsolete light industrial plants built for political reasons, far from any markets or easy transport, the armaments factories hidden in deep valleys in the west of the country to keep them out of reach of Japan's bombers in the Second World War. Most of them were the industrial legacy of Chairman Mao's workers' paradise. Deng's new market philosophy was to blow through this rickety landscape like a typhoon.

From the moment that Deng began to move China towards the market, the character of the Chinese factory began to change. The balance sheet might be improved if the burden of the factory's social obligations and surplus labour was shed, but how could this be squared with the state's ideology? In 1979 Deng made a gesture to Marxist theory by announcing that China was not, after all, in the advanced stage of socialism but in the primary stage. Having said this, the way was open for factory workers to be switched from employment arrangements that offered lifetime security to fixed-term contracts with reduced or non-existent welfare provisions. By the early 1990s, the government was talking about bankruptcy and closing unprofitable enterprises.

For China's factory workers, the shift was cataclysmic. Since 1990, 30 million of them have been laid off from state-owned enterprises with a pay-off of 200 yuan (less than thirty dollars) for every year of service, and no continuing medical insurance or pension. If they wish to stay in their factory housing, they must find the money to buy it. Once a privileged elite, they are now near the bottom of the heap. Their factories, once the centre of their lives, have been stolen from them.

One day last October, I found myself in Xianyang, an ugly town in Shaanxi Province in northwest China, more than 1,500 miles from the Pearl River Delta and not far from its better-known sister city, Xi'an. Xianyang is a city of textile factories set up in the Communist days, a run-down place in which the old industrial mores and the social contract that went with them are still remembered. Turning the corner of a street, I walked straight into a strike. In China—still known as a People's Republic—there is no right to strike. In the old days it was argued that industrial action was a counter-revolutionary act under the dictatorship of the proletariat. Today, the prohibition is the bald expression of a fearful, authoritarian state that dares not allow its aggrieved industrial workers the right to organize. There they were, several hundred workers in the centre of Xianyang. Most were women. They sat in two semicircular arcs to either side of a factory entrance gate over which hung a large sign that read TIANWANG TEXTILE COMPANY. Smaller, hand-lettered signs below it proclaimed PROTECT WORKERS' RIGHTS and GIVE US BACK THE FUNDS WE WORKED HARD FOR.

A cheerleader with a megaphone was leading a chant that, as I watched, gave way to a playful rendition of the childish Maoist anthem of the Seventies—'I love Beijing's Tiananmen'—and then moved on to the 'The Internationale'. Uniformed and plain clothes police stood by, waiting for an identifiable transgression that would permit them to use force against a group of female factory workers who were unhelpfully singing socialist and patriotic songs.

Someone tugged at my sleeve and pulled me down on to a stool. 'Are you a reporter?' a woman whispered. I nodded. She smiled and the word passed down the line. They had been there a week, they told me, and the Chinese press had not reported a word. (The Chinese press is often forbidden to report industrial disputes by a government that is terrified that isolated brush fires might become a major conflagration.) Soon pieces of paper were being furtively stuffed into my hand and my pockets. Later, when I smoothed out the crumpled pages, I found a series of poems and a complete text of 'The Internationale', along with a statement of the workers' complaint. A young woman was slowly peeling an apple. She handed it to me.

Another woman offered a clean tissue as she began to explain their grievances. Their factory had been sold, she said, and new contracts had been issued to the workers that would slash their wages and remove their pensions. Experienced workers were being asked to accept a probationary period at less than a quarter of their normal salary and nobody knew whether they would have a job at the end of it. When they had seen the contracts, all 7,000 of them had downed tools. Now they had resolved not to give in until their grievances were addressed.

The police were pressing in, pushing the bystanders at the back of the crowd until they began to fall over the stools. Had the police tried to disperse them? I asked. She shook her head. 'They haven't touched us,' she said. 'Two nights ago they were getting ready to attack. Several bus loads of police were came with water cannon but someone ran to the dormitories and woke everybody up. Thousands of people turned out and the police backed off. They call us names, though. They call us troublemakers and falungong.'

Falungong is the name of a religious movement that has been savagely persecuted by the Chinese government since 1992, when several thousand falungong practitioners staged a peaceful protest around Zhongnanhai, the part of the former imperial palace in Bejiing that houses the Communist Party leadership. Since then, according to falungong practitioners, more than a thousand of them have been tortured to death. The word falungong in the mouth of the police was a naked threat.

Suddenly a well-dressed woman squatted down in front of me. 'Where are you from?' she asked in English. I told her. She took hold of my arm and tried to pull me up. 'Come with me,' she said. 'I want to talk to you.' A woman striker had hold of my other arm and pulled me down, equally insistently. 'You can say what you want here,' the striker said. The crowd agreed. The other woman had exhausted her English and continued in Chinese. 'What do you think of this? Do you think this is the way to solve a problem in a factory?' She was leaning into my face. 'Would this be allowed in your country? People causing chaos like this?'

The strikers were getting angry and a few began to shout. 'Who's causing trouble? We're not causing trouble!' As abruptly as she had arrived, the woman gave up. She dropped my arm, stood up and elbowed her way angrily through the onlookers. Within seconds she was out of sight. The incident made people restless. 'It's not safe here,' my neighbour said. 'We'll find people for you to talk to but not here. The police are watching you.'

A new cheerleader, a man in his late thirties, had taken the megaphone and was leading a series of chants. Suddenly there was a commotion as a large flat basket carried by two old ladies made its way to the front of the crowd. A cheer went up as the basket was handed round. It contained *baozi*—steamed dumplings, stuffed with pickled cabbage. One was thrust into my hand and I split it with my neighbour. It was growing dark and I was grateful for the dumpling's steamy tang. The cheerleader was improvising a chant of thanks for the old women. 'Thank you, retired workers!' he sang. 'We learn from you, retired workers.' The crowd laughed. My neighbour nudged me. 'Look, she's crying,' she said. 'She worked in this factory her whole life.' The two old women held on to each other's arms, tears running down their cheeks.

Someone else said it wasn't safe for me to stay, so I stood up and edged my way to the fringe of the crowd and set off back to my hotel, along a wide pavement that was busy with people going home at the end of their day. There were familiar Chinese sights. A large banner announced the XIANYANG IDEAL HOME EXHIBITION. A few plastic tables had been set out on the pavement and some dusty helium balloons were straining against their strings. Street vendors peddled fruit and small items of hardware. On the other side of the road, in the gathering dusk, about twenty men squatted on the ground as they had all day. Some had set out the tools of their trade—screwdrivers, saws—in front of them. One man had a long handled paint roller and a bucket slung on the handlebars of an old bicycle. They were the unemployed touting for odd jobs: their few tools advertised their skills.

Three women from the crowd at the factory gate fell into step with me, and began to talk about their lives in the factory and their strike. There are hundreds of thousands of strikes in China every year: in Shenzhen alone there were 41,000 labour disputes in the first six months of 2004. Most, though, are relatively short affairs. In the largely foreign-owned factories of the south, they are mainly disputes about working conditions. Elsewhere, in the dying state-owned enterprises, they are protests against what the workers see as the theft of their livelihood and patrimony as a result of the economic reforms. The Chinese press rarely mentions strikes unless to report a satisfactory resolution: reporting ongoing disputes can land a newspaper in severe trouble. The government's strategy for containing unrest is to keep disputes isolated and compartmentalized. Talking to a foreign journalist about such things can lead to a charge of leaking state secrets.

Still, the women talked. The factory, they told me, used to be called the Xibei No. 7 Cotton Factory. It had been a successful state enterprise—a model factory, they said, with modern machinery—and they were proud to work there. Then came the economic reforms. Three years ago the factory was restructured: all the employees were instructed to buy shares—4,000 yuan's worth for the workers, 8,000 for middle managers and 16,000 for senior managers. Then, early in 2004, the municipal government decided to sell the company to Huaren, known in English as China Resources Enterprise, a conglomerate registered in Hong Kong but owned by the Chinese government. The workers were summarily instructed to sell their shares back to the company at a profit of twenty-five per cent.

The management and the workers both resisted the sale at first. 'They undervalued it. It was worth 500 million yuan but they valued it at 156 million then sold it for 80 million to Huaren,' one woman explained. 'At first Huaren promised to invest so we could buy new machines but then they withdrew the offer of investment. Our factory director decided against the sale and he was fired. The next director, a woman, agreed to the sale after they promised she would stay director. Once the sale went through, she was fired. Then they broke the workers up into small groups and bullied them until they agreed.' After the sale went through, the new labour contracts were announced—contracts that put experienced workers on probation for their jobs at drastically reduced salaries.

'We are not asking for much,' said one of my companions. 'We just want to live with dignity.'

Later that night, I opened my hotel door to a group of three men who smiled at me, nervously. They had come, they told me, to give me more details. They asked me not to use their names. One was a party member and a manager in the factory. A friend of his, he told me later, had served fifteen years in prison for talking to a foreigner about problems in another factory. But there was one point he wanted me to understand. China Resources was owned by the Chinese state. If the workers at Tianwang were still employees of a state-owned enterprise, then their pensions and other provisions could not legally be taken away. If they had been moved into the private sector, then they were entitled to compensation. 'Nobody will answer this question,' he said. 'Are we now a state-owned or a private enterprise?'

A second man had been an engineer in the factory. He sat on the edge of the bed and calmly expressed a profound anger. 'I used to think that the West's talk of human rights was just hypocrisy,' he said. 'But now I think that America is right. Workers have no rights here. They beat people up. They lock people up. There's a woman worker who went to ask about the new contracts and they beat her up so badly she is still in hospital. In the past we might have been backward but we still had food to eat. Now China is so corrupt. The government is so corrupt.' It was already hard, he said, to live on his wage of 700 yuan. 'Now they're talking about cutting it back. The cadres go on getting richer. There's corruption at every level. If you want anything here, you have to bribe somebody. I was invited to join the Party,' he continued. 'But I refused because of Tiananmen. In 1989,' he said, 'the students were asking for an end to corruption and I agreed with them. When it was suppressed I was shattered. I didn't go to work I was so upset. But I didn't do anything. This time, they can kill me but I won't move.'

Over the past two decades, millions of workers in state enterprises have found themselves at similar crossroads. In Xianyang, 2,000 workers from the town's Shaanxi No. 2 Woollen Factory blocked the centre of the city in July 2004 in protest at the loss of pensions and benefits. In the rust belt, the old heavy industrial zone in the north-east, it has often become violent. In Liaoning in 2002, tens of thousands of workers protested for weeks in a major dispute that ended with long prison sentences for the leaders.

The next day I could sense that the Xianyang police were still watching me. In daylight, on the street, they were constrained by the fact that the workers, in turn, watched them. At night, in the privacy of the hotel, it might be a different matter. I decided to withdraw to neighbouring Xi'an, a city full of tourists who come to wonder at Qin Shi Huang Di's terracotta army. There in a bookshop I watched young students and former factory workers browsing the shelves for clues to survival in the market economy. There were rows of management manuals and self-help books that promised to deliver mastery of a world whose contours the workers at Tianwang no longer recognized. The how-to books were mostly pirated editions in Chinese. They carried the original English title on the cover, for added cachet. English meant business and success. Heads were bent over pirated copies of *Who Moved My Cheese?*, *The University of Success*, *Thinking Caps and Action Shoes* and, more puzzlingly, *Doing the Person is Worked by Means to Depend the Wrist*.

Back on the street, I watched a middle-aged man slowly dip a paintbrush into a pot of vermilion paint and methodically paint a long message of protest on the window of a clothes shop. WE DEMAND THE MINIMUM, he wrote, in characters so regular that I wondered if, in happier times, he had been the man who did the notices announcing price reductions or the arrival of new lines. The shop door was locked but I could see some staff inside, looking out through the scarlet protest. Outside on the pavement were the unmistakable signs of a small picket—a few chairs and a wooden box on which was perched a thermos flask and four cups of tea. Three people sat on a bench—a young man, a stylishly dressed woman in her twenties and a man in middle age. I asked them what the trouble was. The middle-aged man snapped back, 'This is an internal Chinese matter. It is a secret.'

I laughed. 'I don't think a clothes shop is a matter of national security,' I said. The young woman giggled. 'You're right,' she said.

'He's being ridiculous. Besides, I have the right to talk to anyone I want.'

An old man in a ragged jacket had stopped to listen. Now he chipped in on her side. 'You can't push us around any more,' he said, to nobody in particular. Not part of the clothes-shop protest, he was just an angry old man. He began a long harangue. He was the same age as Lei Feng, he announced, and he had the same values. I looked at him, astonished to meet anyone in China who still believed that Lei Feng had really existed. Lei Feng was invented in the late Sixties as an exemplary character to try to re-instil moral values into a younger generation that had gone wild in the Cultural Revolution. His life story touched all the holy sites of the Revolution. He was born near Mao's own birthplace in Hunan Province. When he was still a child, his mother hanged herself as a result of their wicked landlord's cruelty (perhaps a hint of sexual crime here) and the orphaned Lei Feng poured his love into the Party. He joined the army where he became a model of selflessness, secretly darning his comrades' socks all night and by day reading the *People's Daily* aloud on the bus, for the benefit of the illiterate. This model soldier handily kept a detailed record of his selfless acts and his fervour for the Revolution in his diary. It was to this intimate journal that he confided his inmost desire—to be a 'rustless screw' in the Revolutionary machine.

On a visit to his 'birthplace' in the Seventies, at the height of Lei Feng fever, I overheard a French fellow student ask Lei Feng's 'uncle' when he had last seen Lei Feng. 'Who?' the bewildered peasant replied, surprised by an encounter with a foreigner who could ask his own questions. According to the official legend, Lei Feng's career had been brutally cut short when a fellow soldier reversed into a telegraph pole which fell on Lei Feng's head, tragically killing him. I sometimes wondered if the absurdity of this conclusion to his story was not a sign that even the inventors of Lei Feng were not immune to the exasperation their creation inspired in so many others. By meeting this unusual end, Lei Feng was officially described as having 'sacrificed himself' for the fatherland. After his death, of course, his diary was 'discovered' and formed the text of the 'learn from Lei Feng' campaign—one of the longest running campaigns in revolutionary China.

As China grew more capitalist in habit in the Nineties, Lei Feng became too preposterous even for those who longed for the purity of motive of the lost golden age of Maoism. But now, here on the streets of Xi'an, was someone who had modelled his behaviour on Lei Feng and still believed in him. He had been a Party member all his adult life, the old man was telling me, and a soldier in the People's Liberation Army in his youth. He had sent both his children to the army, to carry on the glorious family tradition of defending the Revolution. But the Revolution had let him down. His children had no jobs and he had no pension. He had torn up his Party card. After a lifetime of licensed Revolutionary fervour, he had finally become a rebel. Now it was the Communist authorities who were behaving like Lei Feng's childhood landlord and the workers were out on the streets, demanding the basic guarantees the Revolution was supposed to have given them. He was out there with them, I felt, not because he had any personal interest in their particular cause, but because they offered him a hook on which to hang all his own disappointment and rage.

The strikers at the Tianwang textile factory had also expressed their indignation in terms of betrayed idealism as they chanted the slogans of the Revolution and sang 'The Internationale'. Their solidarity with each other, for as long as they could maintain it, was the last expression of a shared belief that Revolutionary China had, indeed, belonged to the workers and peasants. Now they didn't know when they had been betrayed. Had it never been real, their ownership? Or had it once been real and now was real no longer? These things could be debated. An incontestable truth, on the other hand, was that someone had stolen the factory they thought of as theirs, banishing them to the outer edge of a society that showed no sign of making room for them.

Over the past ten years it is an experience that has been repeated all over China.

4. The Hogwarts Express in Factory No. 6

China fever is a recurring illness among Western traders and businessmen: there have been periodic outbreaks since the eighteenth century. The symptoms include an irrational conviction that the number of people in China can be translated directly into the size of the profits of any business established there. Businessmen have dreamed of the fortunes to be made by selling every Chinese housewife a piano, or adding a foot to the shirt tail that each Chinese man was imagined to wear. Very few such fortunes have ever been made, but in the 1980s and 1990s, in the wake of Deng's economic reforms, hope continued to triumph over experience.

Foreign investors combed through China's industrial plant, looking for promising joint ventures. Large sums of money were lost in the rush to form partnerships that were meant to open China's internal market to foreign companies but which usually left the foreign investor bemused, wondering where his money had gone. Still the money poured in: for more than two decades, China soaked up the lion's share of the world's overseas investment, an infusion that fuelled a massive building boom and rapid, if uneven, economic growth. China's major cities were remade and its banks plundered for capital. Speculation was reckless. Local officials grew rich through bribery.

But China's domestic market was—then at least—the wrong target. Rather than consumers, the best thing China had to offer the foreign investor was cheap, attentive and disciplined producers. The difference in wages between China and the old industrialized world was huge: a worker in Britain earning, say, £1,200 a month could be substituted by a Chinese worker earning the equivalent of £30 a month. The reduction in price offered a startling competitive advantage in the international market, even when transport costs were taken into consideration. China also offered tax concessions, a fairly stable political environment, an apparently inexhaustible supply of workers and local officials who were happy to waive the rules in favour of profits. Goods made in China need not be *for* China: China could be the factory for the world. Hong Kong businesses were the first to take advantage of this—by 2002, nearly 60,000 Hong Kong factories had moved into Guangdong Province, where they employed 11 million people—but in the 1990s factories in Europe and the United States also began to close their gates and move their production to China. It began with shoes and toys. A little English company called Hornby is a typical example of that movement, and an interesting demonstration of how the manufacture of objects (in this case, model trains) can be so easily separated from the audience that buys them and the culture that invented and nourished them.

The firm was founded in 1907 by Frank Hornby, a butcher's clerk from Liverpool with a Victorian enthusiasm (he was born in 1863) for engineering and self-improvement. He invented Meccano (the name comes from Mechanics-Made-Easy), construction kits of metal strips and screws from which children could assemble little bridges, cranes, ships and houses. Meccano became one of the most popular boys' hobbies in Britain and the British Empire, made Hornby a millionaire, and allowed the company to diversify into other branches of model-making. In 1920, Hornby produced its first clockwork train and in 1925 its first electric one—models, which as they developed over the next seventy years, grew in their sophistication and verisimilitude; they looked like the real thing, as observable in British railway stations and emerging from British tunnels, past as well as the present. The livery of their Edwardian carriages was correct, the wheel arrangements of their 1950s locomotives were correct, the pattern of rivets on their boilers faithfully reproduced. None of this was unique: other companies in other countries—especially in Germany and the US—made beautifully accurate model trains. But, like Hornby's, their models reflected national engineering traditions. A German model looked like a German train, and that was the point because the market was Germany and its fussy German hobbyists, who wanted to see recreated the Rheingold Express, circa 1965. It seemed unlikely that such miniature, intricate and highly culturally specific products could be 'globalized' like a soft toy bear or a training shoe. Surely a worker would need to bring to the making of such an object some local knowledge, some understanding of its appeal?

Then in the early 1990s another model train maker called Bachman (originally an American company, now owned in Hong Kong) began to make miniature British locomotives. In the shops, they were priced the same as Hornby's, though they were made in China. And, as Hornby could not help but notice, the quality was 'demonstrably better'. Hornby was struggling to survive by this time and made the obvious decision. In 1995, it closed its factory in Margate, Kent, cut the Hornby workforce in Britain from 550 to 110, and moved production to China.

The quality of its models didn't suffer—if anything, the reverse—and five years later it was able to buy up other model-makers who hadn't made the move in time. In 2004 the company expanded again by purchasing the leading model train-maker in Spain and the assets of a defunct Italian model-maker. Both countries will in future be supplied from the factory in China. But who owns the factory? Not Hornby.

Like many much bigger and truly international brands—Nike and Reebok, for example—it has become a company that 'doesn't do stuff', that is, it makes nothing. Instead it concentrates on brand management and marketing. It negotiates a price with its Chinese contractor, sends the designs of what it wants made to the contractor at his factory near the town of Dongguan in Guangdong, and waits for the results to arrive in England by container. Hornby has no share in the Dongguan factory although it now depends on it entirely for its products. You might say that the only manufacturing secret that Hornby still truly owns is the name of its Chinese partner. This became clear when, in England, I asked if I could see the Hornby factory, to which Hornby agreed provided that I neither identified the factory nor Hornby's agent. And so, in the lobby of one of Hong Kong's smarter hotels, I met my guide, Mr Wang, who worked for the company I now can't name.

Together we took the ferry to Shenzhen. Across the harbour, the familiar outline of Hong Kong's skyscrapers was fuzzy and indistinct, shrouded in pollution that had blown down from the factories of the Pearl River Delta. Mr Wang explained that his company had begun as a manufacturer of cheap toys in Hong Kong in 1973, having been founded by a man who later became known as 'the godfather of the model train industry' after he went into business with an American partner in the early 1980s. In 1981 the proprietor opened his first factory in Dongguan, but in those days, as Mr Wang said, foreign manufacturers were still competitive. 'We were supplying components but they were still doing the assembly and the decoration.' Gradually, Mr Wang's company grew in its expertise, so that when its foreign clients wanted to move the entire manufacturing process to China, very few mysteries about the techniques of production and assembly remained for the Chinese to unravel. They had moved from components suppliers to makers of finished objects, a move up the value chain made by many other companies in Guangdong.

With seventy major clients, Mr Wang and his colleagues now produce a very large—but necessarily unquantifiable—percentage of the world's model trains. Rivals in the marketplace they may be, with their different logos and little locomotives, but their stuff is made in the same place by the same workers. 'Hornby do get a bit anxious about the competition,' said Mr Wang. 'But we say we are open to anyone who wants to manufacture here. They try to keep our name a trade secret and they worry about their own trade secrets leaking.' He said that his company tactfully separated the most obvious rivals into different buildings on their site.

And what about Mr Wang, I wondered. Had he been a Hornby boy himself, tearing the wrapping off a box to discover a miniature Flying Scotsman? Mr Wang shook his head. 'These are very expensive models. They are not for children, most of the people who buy them are in their forties.' Mr Wang, it was clear, was in business, not in the business of passion. We got off the ferry and into a people carrier and drove for forty minutes though the familiar pollution—grey smog and black rivers—until we reached a large factory compound. As the gates swung open, Mr Wang pointed out a small Hornby logo on the wall. We parked and he led the way up a broad staircase, indicating another Hornby sign in the stairwell. I found myself wondering if these signs were interchangeable—today (for me) Hornby, tomorrow (for someone else) some other brand, and if Mr Wang was like the ferry captain played by Alec Guinness in *The Captain's Paradise*, a man with a wife in Gibraltar and a mistress in Tangiers who switched the pictures in his cabin from one to the other as he steamed across.

I had checked the company out in Hong Kong, to be told that it had several factories but the one that visitors were always shown was Factory Number 6. I asked Mr Wang which factory we were in. 'Number 6,' he replied. The factory could produce about 4,000 items a day, he told me. Whether it did depended, among other things, on the electricity supply. The previous year all the factories in the district had suffered day-long power cuts so over the winter the factory had been one of the investors in a village power plant. This year Mr Wang had had only five days guaranteed supply every week from the province but he had made up the rest with two days guaranteed supply from the village. So far, it had worked.

In the workshops, young women in uniform green shirts sat at long tables trimming the surplus from the plastic bodies of miniature carriages and wagons. Further on, more similarly dressed young women were examining a locomotive—a Harry Potter Hogwarts Express—for flaws. (This engine has worked miracles for Hornby's profits). Mr Wang explained the production process as we passed through the design department where a dozen young men in black

T-shirts were rendering the designs into specifications. A model train, Mr Wang said, can have 140 different parts. I passed pallets of Scalextric cars, and young women carefully spraying the white edges on to tiny motorbikes. At another table, they were bent over antique teak rolling stock. Further along, yet more of them were finishing off a British Railways buffet car. 'Do you know where these go to?' I asked. 'America,' one of them replied. The line supervisor grinned. 'England,' she said. The others looked bored. It was a matter of no interest. Why would it be?

Back in Mr Wang's office, he told me that it was normally against the factory rules for the workers to speak to strangers. I asked if I could visit the workers' dormitories. Mr Wang politely refused. It was not his department, he said. He had no authority over the dormitories. His demeanour told me my visit was over. I thanked him and left Factory Number 6. Perhaps I had seen the real thing. Or perhaps Factory Number 6 was a sort of Potemkin factory completely unlike the darker reality of Factories Numbers 1 to 5. In industrial China, as a woman I shall call Jane Trevor knows too well, one learns to distrust appearances.

5. Compliance would be a fine thing

Jane Trevor is a compliance officer for a major American brand of sports shoes who agreed to talk about her work only off the record. She said that it was too difficult to go on the record, or to give me access to any of the hundreds of factories for which she is responsible to her corporate employer. It would require permission from her head office, which took a long time to get and was often refused. 'It takes a lot to get them into their comfort zone with the press,' she said.

The profession of compliance officer and that institution known as the NGO, the non-governmental organization, now play a key role in some Chinese factories, and in western perceptions of them. According to Stephen Frost, a Hong Kong academic who works on labour conditions in Asia, their new importance owes a lot to a moment in 1996, when Phil Knight, the chief executive of Nike, was asked about sweatshop conditions in Nike's sports-shoe factories in Korea and China, and replied, 'That's not my responsibility.'

'It was the worst mistake he ever made,' Stephen Frost said. 'It took them a year to realize what a mistake they had made. It was a red rag to a bull. The [anti-globalization] movement took it up and it spread to all the sports shoes, then to the toys and garments.' The anti-globalization movement had found the weak spot of the big brands: not only had they moved their factories to places where labour was cheap and workers' protection was poor, but they had failed to take any responsibility for the conditions that enabled their profits. Their image was at stake. Reebok and Nike were trying to sell an idea of health and well-being; now their names were associated with misery. Nike had paid $45 million to a basketball player, Michael Jordan, to promote their sports shoes, while the workers who actually made the sports shoes might make .000001 per cent of that sum in a year.

Changing the perception would mean changing the facts, but that wasn't easy. The brands no longer owned their own factories, and couldn't directly supervise conditions inside them. Also, the brands continued to try to drive down costs. Since the brands were demanding measures they were reluctant to pay for, the factory owners became adept at avoiding the more costly requirements. The brands hastily set up human rights' departments. The compliance industry was born. Today there are teams of inspectors who audit factories before and during the negotiation and execution of contracts, laying down rules on working conditions, overtime and health and safety. Stephen Frost estimates that as an industry compliance turns over millions of dollars a year. It absorbs the time and energy of NGOs as well as of in-house compliance officers and the specialist consultancies that have sprung up to address the big brands' need for legitimacy. But after nearly ten years of struggling with compliance, Jane Trevor believes that it does not work. 'I've had enough of going into factories, fighting—every day of my life being a battle,' she said. 'The industry is only ten years old but people just burn out. How many times can you go in fighting?'

The compliance inspector tries to ensure that the factory is not going to embarrass the brand by ensuring that the factory is sticking to an agreement that would typically cover the length of the working day, the amount of compulsory overtime, wage rates, safety and health requirements, and fire regulations. But compliance inspection is a cat and mouse game. In China, as everyone in the business told me, 'counter compliance' has become a sophisticated art. Companies keep two sets of payrolls—one for inspection, another that records the real hours the workers put in and the real wages they are paid. Inspectors like Jane Trevor spend their days in the factory, photocopying documents to cross-check with production volumes, then hang around outside after dark to see if the workshop lights stay on beyond the admitted hours.

Trevor said that there was 'massive falsification' of factory documents and that people like her had to cope with too many factories, each with a high turnover of workers. 'Everything was so bad in the beginning. There was no minimum wage, the conditions were unsafe. At that time we all felt a huge satisfaction. But making the next step is really hard. Everything is so much more cut-throat and carnivorous now. The brands are squeezing the last bit out of the factories. Consumers are paying no more for sports shirts than they were ten years ago. You can make a change in your tiny world but you are surrounded by appalling factories and unless you can change on a macro level, it's no good. In Pinggu, outside Shanghai, factories regularly keep half the workers' wages back until the end of the year. In Xinjiang we have a Korean factory that's paying less than the minimum wage but he won't change because it will upset the others.'

Compliance is an expensive process that is aimed at protecting the brands from activists. But the fact is, that for all the pressure the brands say they exert, workers today in the Pearl River Delta are earning less in real terms than they were a decade ago, according to Chinese State Council figures.

One evening in Canton I had dinner with Jane Trevor and a few of her colleagues. Five of us gathered in a Hunanese restaurant beneath an unsmiling picture of Mao, Hunan's most famous son. There was Jane, a serious American woman in her forties with a background in mainstream human rights, two mainland Chinese women called Eileen and Jennie and a colleague of theirs from Taiwan who worked for a Taiwanese manufacturer. They were in their late twenties and early thirties. Jennie was a tough and sceptical woman who had arrived in an expensive car. Jane said she had been a ferocious and effective compliance inspector.

'She was so tough we sometimes had to tell her to ease up,' Jane said. 'I remember her calling me from a factory and saying that she had given them fifteen minutes to bring her the real books or she was leaving.' If she left and gave them a bad report, the factory might lose the contract. Now Jennie had left the compliance business to become a price negotiator working directly for a brand, a job in which she was equally effective but which had transformed her from gamekeeper to poacher: prices not wages were what concerned her now. The conversation turned to a factory that Jennie dealt with in her new job, a place that Jane and Eileen said was notorious for its abuses. Jennie was bent over a bowl of food. She looked at her former colleagues from under her brows. 'Find me a better one,' she said, and shrugged.

I asked the others what kept them going against such heavy odds. 'The money,' Jennie interjected.

'Not the money,' Eileen said. 'The Chinese believe that good deeds help you in your next life.'

There was a feeling, finally put into words by Eileen, that Jennie had sold out. 'I haven't sold out,' she said, still chewing over her bowl. 'I am still on the side of the workers. They still call me with their problems and I try to help. Most of their problems are personal.'

'Maybe,' Jane said. 'But some personal problems are part of the economic system that they are in—separation from their families, long working hours.'

Jennie shrugged again. 'I still say, if you want me to pull out of a factory, show me a better one.'

Consumer pressure has meant that the factories which supply the big brands are probably now the best in China. But there are other kinds of buyers. Jane said, 'The brands may fall short of perfection, but the retailers are much worse. They buy through trading houses and trading agents, layer upon layer of middlemen. They have no idea what goes on upstream.'

Disney, she told me, has 3,000 suppliers. Wal-Mart, who in 2003 bought 15 billion dollars' worth of goods in China, or twenty per cent of China's entire exports to the United States, has nearly 5,000 direct suppliers who themselves have an estimated 30,000 upstream manufacturers. It uses its vast buying power to drive down prices at the factory gate. 'You can't pay the minimum wage and observe health and safety and still produce goods at Wal-Mart prices,' she said. 'It's completely impossible. If I am in a factory where my company accounts for twenty per cent of the output, I can make them change. But if I am in a factory with Wal-Mart, forget it.'

Wal-Mart employs one hundred auditors and inspects at least some of its suppliers. We know this because of a document known as a 'cheat-sheet' which in 2004 found its way to an NGO from a worker at a Wal-Mart supplier, the Heyi factory in Dongguan, in Guangdong Province. The factory had prepared the document in advance of an inspection that was scheduled to take place in February 2004. It showed that workers would be paid fifty yuan each if they memorized the answers to questions that the inspectors were likely to ask them. The correct answer, for instance, to the question 'How long is the working week?' was 'Five days'. The correct number of days worked in a month was twenty-two; overtime was not forced and was paid at the correct rate; they were not obliged to give the factory a deposit when they started work there; wages were paid on time; there were enough toilet facilities in the dormitory and the dormitories themselves were spacious and clean. There were fire drills, and they were not made to pay for their own ID cards or uniforms. If all of this were true, what need would there have been for the workers to memorize the answers?

That is one reason that Jane, an employee of a large American multinational, has reached an unexpected conclusion. 'It's ridiculous for us to be trying to do this private investigation work. The only people who can really monitor compliance are the workers. They are there all the time. They know what's going on.'

I asked if she was proposing to reinvent the trade union.

She laughed. 'Well, I wouldn't say it on the record, but yes.'

6. Punishments

One day in Hong Kong I went to watch a man working at what has become his life's mission: to promote free trade unions in China. Han Dongfang was the only prominent Tiananmen Square protestor in 1989 who was a worker rather than a student. He was arrested after the massacre and suffered a particularly harsh imprisonment. Eventually released on health grounds in 1992—he had contracted severe tuberculosis—he was flown to the US to have most of a lung removed. When he recovered, he settled in Hong Kong, where in 1994 he set up the China Labour Bulletin and in 1997 began to broadcast into China on labour problems for the American-funded Radio Free Asia.

I found him sitting in a small studio, a handsome man with shoulder-length hair, hunched over the telephone, a directory of Sichuan area codes and a microphone on the desk in front of him. 'There's a nice strike in Sichuan that I'm just following up,' he said. He spends his days dialling into China, following up news of disputes, coaxing local officials and nervous workers to talk to him, patiently mapping the symptoms of China's turbulent industrial unrest. He will advise workers on China's rarely applied labour laws and tell them how to find a lawyer to fight a claim in court. Sometimes he reaches the factory managers or the local representatives of a tame, officially recognized trade union and he talks to them calmly in a voice soft with the rounded cadences of his Beijing accent. He announces that he is from the China Labour Bureau, a title imposing enough to sound official. He does not mention, unless asked, that he is calling from Hong Kong. As I listened, he got through to the trade union branch of the Sichuan factory that was in dispute. The man asked where he was calling from and Han Dongfang told him.

'Hong Kong? That's abroad, isn't it?' he said suspiciously.

Han Dongfang laughed. 'No. It came back to the fatherland in 1997,' he said. The man still didn't want to talk, but Han persisted with the conversation, and thirty minutes later he had recorded enough to broadcast a full report on the strike.

Most of the workers he spoke to, he said, had no idea what their legal rights were or how to organize to fight for them. The official and the only legal trade union—the All China Federation of Trades Unions—is at best ineffective and at worst acts as an enforcer for the government. 'They had fifty years in which to destroy all capacity to organize, and all civic society,' Han said. 'Which is why things become violent very quickly. People are hugely frustrated and angry and there's no outlet.'

The factories used by the big brands may be among the better factories in the Pearl River Delta, but that does not mean they are trouble-free. In March last year, a big Taiwanese shoe company called Stella experienced trouble in several of its factories. Stella employs around 35,000 people on five sites around Dongguan, turning out high quality shoes for most of the large international brands, including Nike, Reebok and Timberland. One compliance inspector told me that the brands were not too insistent on compliance in the

Stella factories because relatively few manufacturers could produce the same quality of shoe and the wages paid to the workforce was at least no worse than in many other factories. Still, the Stella factories were plagued with disputes throughout the spring. The food was bad, the days too long, and the pay mediocre. It emerged later that one worker was putting in a sixty hour week for only 450 yuan (£32) a month, of which 400 yuan went to pay for his accommodation. On the nights of April 21 and 22 there was unrest in the Stella factory in Xinxiong. Some workers were arrested but were later released. But on the night of April 23, serious trouble broke out when the management decided to move overtime from the weekend to midweek. Weekend overtime was paid at a higher rate, so for the workers it meant a pay cut. April 23 was payday and at the end of a long shift the workers found their wages short.

According to Liu Kaiming of the Institute of Contemporary Observation in Shenzhen, a rare Chinese NGO that works to alleviate abuse of migrant workers, it was the women workers who provoked what happened next. 'They were shouting and jeering at the men, saying, "Are you a man or not? What are you going to do about this?" They humiliated the men so that the men felt they had to act.' At midnight, the workers marched back from their dormitories to the factory and rampaged through its offices, smashing what they could. The riot lasted two hours. In the morning, the police were waiting at the factory gates. Ten workers were arrested and a further thirty were fired. Others were offered 500 yuan to tell the management the names of the ringleaders.

One of those arrested was a young woman—Chen Suo—who had been discovered to be under the legal working age of sixteen. What was her story? I arranged to meet someone who could tell me, a young man who worked in a workshop near Dongguan. I waited for him at a hotel which had several Mercedes in the car park and a menu where the dishes cost the equivalent of a month's wages in the surrounding factories. When he appeared we found a cheaper place to talk.

His name, he told me, was Yu Xin and he was twenty-four. He was engaged to be married to Chen Suo's older sister and when the trouble started her family had clubbed together to send him here to try to help her. Chen Suo's family came from southern Shaanxi Province, about a thousand miles from Dongguan, from a village locked away in the mountains, he said, a poor place, hard to get into or out of. 'I doubt if the family earns 500 yuan between all of them,' he said. 'There are four children and two parents to feed.' The previous year, a recruiter had come to their village and for a payment of 1,000 yuan promised an introduction to a factory. Chen Suo was fifteen and still at school and though the recruiter, a woman, said Chen Suo was too young to get a job, she also suggested the problem could be fixed with a fake identity card. The family paid for an identity card and the introduction, and in June 2003 Chen Suo set off for Guangdong.

The family back home heard from her only occasionally. She complained in her letters that the working hours were very long and the wages very low. When Yu Xin got engaged on May 1 to Chen's sister, he tried to telephone Chen to tell her the news, but nobody in her dormitory seemed to know where she was. Ten days later, someone phoned the family in Shaanxi and told them she had been arrested.

'Her mother cried for three days,' he said. 'I was working in Xi'an and they called me home. I came here with my future father-in-law. We went to the factory but the security guard wouldn't let us in. We tried the police but they just told us to wait till she came up in court. We found out she was in Number 2 Jail in Da Lan and we tried to send money to her but she never got it.'

On August 28 Chen Suo and the other nine workers went on trial in the Dongguan Municipal People's Court. The trial lasted sixty-six minutes. When I met him, Yu Xin was waiting for the verdict. 'We hired a lawyer who says they should all sue the factory for holding back their wages and having them arrested,' he said. 'I think it's the factory's fault for paying them late and treating them badly. It has cost the family 30,000 yuan and it's caused a problem over her future. Who will want to marry her after a disgrace like this?'

But why had she disgraced herself, if disgrace is the right word? What had prompted her? Nobody at the factory where the riot occurred would talk, but eventually, at a newer Stella factory a few miles away, a middle-ranking supervisor agreed to talk if I didn't use his name. I picked him up outside the factory gate, in a landscape so broken and unrelentingly industrial that finding somewhere private to sit was impossible. So we sat in my car as he described the factory routine. 'You have to march when you go on and off shift. We have to do morning exercise and you have to have your shirt tucked in.

You have to wear leather shoes and you have to leave your bed in the dormitory with the quilt folded square and the pillow inside the quilt. It is like being in the army.' The managers, he said, behaved like sergeant majors. They shouted abuse and enforced a harsh discipline. The night of the riot, he said, the workers were tired, angry and hungry. They had gone back to the dormitory, but later that night they had broken down the fence and got into the canteen, where they smashed up the tables and chairs and broken the windows, before moving on to a workshop and some offices. The workers who had been arrested, he told me, had been picked randomly to serve as an example. They could be sentenced to between three and seven years in prison. 'It was wrong, what happened,' he said. 'But the rage came because of the attitude of the management.'

The signs were that the big brands were embarrassed by the events at the Stella factory. They persuaded Stella to write to the court, asking for leniency, and added their names to the letter. But the most memorable remarks on the Stella case were made not by Nike or Reebok or Timberland, but by the workers' defence lawyer, Gao Zhisheng. The prosecution, he pointed out, had produced no evidence that the accused were responsible for any specific acts of violence or criminal damage or that they had played any leadership role in an incident that even the factory acknowledged had been spontaneous.

'The most prominent feature of the trial has been the court's complete lack of interest either in the facts or in issues of law', he said in his speech to the Dongguan court. The defendants, he admitted, had taken part in 'inappropriate action' but they had already paid dearly for it with the loss of their jobs and the stigma of having been arrested. The cause of the riot was 'the fact that our society today permits and encourages the most naked forms of social injustice, together with an unrestrained level of gross and inhuman exploitation of the workers that has reached truly reactionary proportions.' The factory workers worked a six-day week, four of those days eleven hours long, for a wage that, he said, 'cannot even support normal life.'

Gao continued, 'The inequity of workers within our current system of labour relations is absolute. The channels for resolution of labour conflicts of all kinds in our society are either totally blocked or non-existent; and judicial protections for the rights and interests of the labourer are functionally absent... This is just like the [pre-1949] situation of cold-blooded and ruthless exploitation of the workers by the capitalists...the very same situation that caused the workers then to rise up in revolutionary rebellion! What distinguishes the present situation, however, is that in those days the Communist Party stood alongside the workers in their fight against capitalist exploitation, whereas today the Communist Party is fighting shoulder-to-shoulder with the cold-blooded capitalists in their struggle against the workers!'

It was a brave speech but it seemed to have little effect. In late October last year, five workers were convicted and sentenced: Chen Suo, now sixteen, received a two-year suspended sentence. Four men were sent to jail for up to three and a half years. In November another five Stella workers received similar jail sentences. Unusually, though, the affair did not end there. An article sympathetic to the workers had been published in October in *China News Weekly*; and the China Labour Bulletin and other international NGOs took up the case. How much more pressure the big brands exerted nobody will say, but on December 31 an appeal hearing dropped the sentences—though the convictions till stood—and the workers were quietly freed.

7. The new industrial superpower

Last year in the Pearl River Delta there were reports of labour shortages, caused by the need for workers in other parts of China as its new industrialization creeps across the map, up the Yangtse River and even into the northwest province of Xinjiang. If peasants can find factory jobs closer to home—jobs that will allow them the hope of maintaining a family life—they will obviously do so rather than migrate to the south. The first generations of migrant workers who came to the Pearl River Delta were perhaps more innocent and accepting of their exploitation, and while their successors still want to escape rural poverty, they are growing more choosy about where and in what conditions they will work.

In the new generations of workers, the desire to return home seems less marked. I spoke to young women who were leading single lives separate from their families and who had no immediate plans to go back to the village. The city of Shenzhen, which in twenty years has gone from an industrial park to a sleek managerial city, represents a rupture with the past, populated as it is with young people leading independent urban lives. Three hundred million migrant workers have passed through the Pearl River Delta in the past twenty years and 30 million currently work there. For most of them, their factory lives are brief: after five years, factory owners are reluctant to employ someone who is judged, by then, to be worn out. Their remittances have helped to raise their distant villages out of poverty, but many have paid a terrible price for their willingness to labour. There are some sights in China I shall always remember: the young women from a battery factory, poisoned by cadmium, who pushed forward their thin haired, yellow faced little children for me to look at (they had passed on the contamination, unwittingly, to the next generation); the men who gasped for breath as they contemplated an early death from silicosis; the workers hideously mutilated by a factory fire for which they received no compensation. For the last two decades men and women like them have provided the labour that has given us cheap goods (on the shelves of Wal-Mart and elsewhere) and put fortunes into the pockets of local officials and factory owners.

Some people predict that China will eventually overtake the US as the world's biggest economy. Such a day is still a long way off, but the portents are there. China is now the world's biggest consumer of steel, copper and cement, and the second-biggest consumer of oil. Last year, according to *The Economist*, China attracted $57 billion in direct foreign investment and consumed forty per cent of all the world's coal and thirty per cent of the world's steel. Its oil demand has doubled in the past decade and last year it became the world's second largest car market, after the United States. Guangdong, the province where this economic revolution began, has big plans of its own for the future. The Guangdong Party secretary now wants to create an integrated free trade area that would reach almost to the Indian border and contain a third of the Chinese population—more than 400 million people, as many as now live in the countries of the European Union.

There is no sign of the rush to China slowing. China continues to grow, but at a human and environmental cost that is probably unsustainable. China's growth is already costing more in investment to achieve than it did a decade ago and the environmental cost is devastatingly high. And instead of ushering in political change and an evolution to democracy, China's economic growth has allowed the Communist Party to buy itself some more years of absolute power. China's capitalism is developing in an environment beset by rampant corruption and law-breaking, in a state that remains obsessively secretive.

Thirty years ago, when I first visited Chinese factories, they were inefficient and chaotic, immunized from the market by the peculiar rules of a state-controlled economy. Now China's new factories function under pressure to achieve ever greater production with ever narrower margins. Their products stack up on our shelves, cheaper every year, until we can accommodate no more of them. Their workers are discarded as soon as they are sick, or tired, or too old—at thirty—to present a viable economic proposition. The old lessons of the Marxist canon that I was sent to the factories to learn—the solidarity of the workers, the possibility of unalienated labour, the dignity of labour—have long since been discarded by the same state that once declared them its central conviction.

Outside the old railway station in Guangzhou, the capital of Guangdong Province, there is an open space. To call it a plaza or even a square would be to dignify it with a sense of urban mission. In fact it is more like a transit camp, a no-man's-land, bordered on one side by an urban motorway and heavily patrolled by aggressive police hunting for transgression of all kinds. Encamped on its greasy tarmac and concrete are groups of new arrivals from the remote countryside—badly dressed, shaggy-haired, red-cheeked peasants, more fodder for the factories of the Delta. Around them swirls a steady stream of touts—sharp-voiced young men and women selling cheap hotel rooms, taxis and, they say, factory jobs. If the lives of these peasants unfold in the same way as those of the millions who have gone before, most will serve their time in the factories that make our socks and gloves, our trainers and television sets. They have five to ten years to earn some money before going home. Some will make it and feel grateful for the opportunity, some will fall ill, and others will die. As I boarded the train at Shenzhen for the last time and left the industrial drama of the Delta behind, I wondered whether these peasants would be the generation of Chinese workers who, having built the new Chinese economic miracle, would begin to demand their place in it. □

GRANTA

A JOB ON THE LINE

Desmond Barry

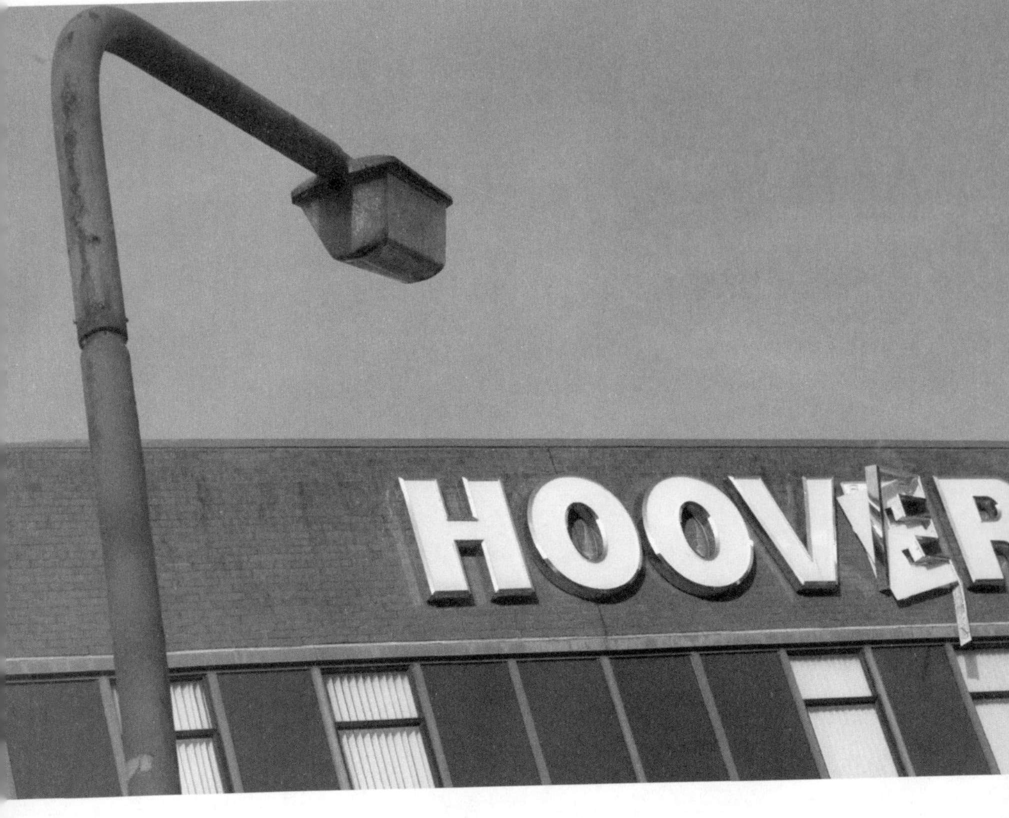
HOOVER

A Job on the Line

My father worked for twenty-eight years in the Hoover washing machine factory in Merthyr Tydfil. In South Wales at that time, when most labour was hard, physical, badly paid and often dangerous, people said it was a good job.

Hoover had been enticed to the town in 1948 by government subsidies and tax incentives, as a new source of employment for men being laid off by the coal mines and steelworks. Unlike a lot of men who grew up in South Wales in the 1930s and 1940s, my father, David Barry, had never been a miner or a steelworker and he never wanted to be. As a very young man he'd been a farm labourer. That occupation and a lack of sight in one eye had exempted him from serving in the forces in the Second World War. It was something that he was sensitive about. All of my mother's brothers had served in the air force, or the army. One of them had been in the thick of the fighting at Monte Cassino. My uncles all considered it unmanly not to have gone to war. Their sentiment lingered, I know, though it was never brought up in conversation or argument and never used against my father when he became part of my mother's family. It was a subject I found difficult to ask him about; like every other kid then, I wanted to know what my father had done in the war.

After the war, my father transferred his agricultural and woodsman's know-how to a new job as a gardener in the town's Parks Department. He was a trim man, about five foot six, clean-shaven, with thick, reddish-brown hair, kept in place by Brylcreem. When I was a child, his face was always ruddy. Every night he would come home in his dungarees to my grandmother's house and sit down in front of the fire and lean over the fender to smoke a Woodbine. I remember my father reading two books by that fire: *Uncle Tom's Cabin*, which brought him to tears; and *Alice in Wonderland*, which he read to me night after night until it was finished. He never read anything else to me that I remember. Mostly, me and my elder brother, Mike, watched the cowboys with him on television: *Wagon Train* and *Rawhide* and *Wyatt Earp*. We had all moved into my grandmother's house when I was about three—after my mother and father decided they couldn't stand living in Gellideg, one of the first housing estates built in the early 1950s and meant as an improvement to the Victorian terraces that lined the valley.

Plymouth House was set on its own little knoll just above the row

DIEGO VIDART

houses of Hankey Terrace. It had once belonged to the Hills-Plymouth ironworks. I don't know how it came into my grandmother's hands. The garden was huge and full of vegetables that my father planted: potatoes, carrots, cabbages, lettuce, beans climbing up bamboo canes, with two gooseberry bushes and a rabbit hutch. It was surrounded by tall pines and was just below a grassy hill, which hid the Hoover factory from view. The living-room wall was dominated by a big picture of Christ baring his Sacred Heart. My widowed grandmother was the stern but benevolent matriarch of the family. Every Sunday, and every holy day of obligation, we all went to mass in the big neo-Gothic Catholic church at the top end of town, and came back for breakfast at the house, which had banisters you could slide down and an attic full of secrets. On some Sundays, I could ride around the lanes beside it on a borrowed horse that my father led by a rope bridle. In Cyfarthfa Park, on walks with my mother, we'd often come across my father and his workmate, Ernie Oates, as they planted flowerbeds or dropped a dead tree with a bowsaw in the woods. I saw him expertly swing a scythe to topple the long grasses on a verge close to Cyfarthfa Castle. I watched him digging in hundreds of trees—saplings—on reclaimed and seeded slag heaps, and those trees are now magnificent forty-five-year-old silver birches. In his spare time, he took care of the gardens of the church. Those grounds were always immaculate. Sometimes he let me help him cut the grass with a pair of hand shears. The only problem with being a gardener was that my father earned less than my mother did as a bookkeeper for Leslie's, a local department store. And when my mother became pregnant again, there were soon going to be three of us children to feed, clothe, educate and to turn out 'respectable'.

In 1961, my father decided he had no alternative but to apply for a job in Hoover's. The factory was expanding to make the new Keymatic washing machine and paying its workers nearly eight times what my father was making as a gardener. He started work on the new assembly line: two weeks of day shift, followed by two weeks of nights, with two weeks off in the summer. His official title was 'semi-skilled assembler'. A close-to-completed washing machine would swing down to a stop in front of him, and he'd push his buttons and pull on his levers and press the final panels into place.

The factory, with its magnificent art-deco entrance, had been built next to the River Taff, and the window opposite my father's workstation looked out across the river to the forestry commission plantation on the Abercanaid Mountain. He'd left that outdoor world behind. Now he watched the seasons change—or the moon move across the night sky—on the other side of the glass.

With the increase in wages, we could now afford to buy a house of our own just off Merthyr High Street. We moved in when I was six. It was tiny compared to my grandmother's. It had no garden and the toilet lay across the flagstoned backyard. Upstairs, my parents had one bedroom and their three children the other; I shared a double bed with my older brother, Mike, while Kevin, the baby, slept in his cot by the front window. From the Hoover employee's shop we bought a washing machine, a vacuum cleaner, and a steam iron; and we got a new three-piece suite on hire purchase. For a while, my father went to work on the factory bus but soon he bought a car—an old maroon Ford Anglia—and took us on outings in it during his fortnight's holidays.

But the constant disturbance to my father's sleep cycle wore him down. For the two weeks of the day shift, he was morose. My brothers and I, and my mother, too, saw less of him than we had when he'd been working in the park. He'd get home from work around the same time as I got home from school, unless he could get overtime, which he always worked if there was any to be had. Workers weren't considered cooperative if they turned it down and were marked for the sack. For a while in the 1960s, overtime was guaranteed.

The two weeks of night shift turned our cramped house into a place of dark and terrible quiet. No one dared speak above a whisper while he was in bed during the day. He'd get up in a foul mood that got worse as the time to clock-in drew closer. His face became darker and greyer. The light caught the copper stubble on his cheeks. He hardly spoke at all. My mother talked a lot, often about her work, and that maddened him, and this lack of communication was desperately frustrating for her. In the evening, when my father was doing overtime, she would knit pullovers for all of us and eat boiled sweets in front of the little box of a television, with its volume down low because the baby was sleeping. Sometimes I heard my mother crying in the night and I never knew what for.

Life began to hold terrors for me. Early one evening, I was playing with my toy soldiers at the bottom of the stairs, making the noise of gunfire and having my soldiers shout orders to each other. My father was on days, working overtime. 'Stop making such a bloody noise,' my mother said. I went on playing. My mother said, 'Haven't I told you? You just wait till your father comes home. He'll give you a damn good hiding.' I remember the next few fearful hours, and how when my father eventually came home from his overtime at Hoover, my mother told him that I had wilfully defied her and told him to beat me. His hard hand stung my legs, my behind, my hands, my arms. He stank of oil. I couldn't understand why my mother had said what she had said, and I couldn't believe that my father did what he did. I was sickened by the injustice of it. I was now living with two completely hostile strangers.

The atmosphere in the house was thick with my father's depression. It wasn't, I think, that he was unaware of what his work was doing to him, just that he saw no way out of it for the rest of his life. And he was terrified of mental illness. There was a history of it in our family. His Auntie Ann had been diagnosed with clinical depression. She'd had electric-shock treatment. It had hollowed her eyes and slurred her speech. I was with him when she told him that if she hadn't been a Catholic with a fear of Hell, she would certainly have killed herself. The idea scared me.

In 1965, we moved to a new three-bedroom council house with a garden and a lot of green in front of it. My father still did his two weeks of days and two weeks of nights but he had learned to cope: this was now normal life, a human being can get used to almost anything. Then the factory managers came up with a plan to change to a three-shift system: one week days, one week afternoons, one week nights. 'At least it's only one week of night shift,' my father said, but it was yet another disturbance to his sleep pattern. Sleep disruption, as torturers in prison camps know, produces disorientation and then compliance. At Hoover, productivity increased.

I stayed out of the house more. I was on track to go to university but some of my older friends were already working in the factory on the assembly line. I wanted to know what they thought of this man who at home was often either depressed or angry.

'Do you ever see my father down there?' I asked a friend, Roger.
Roger said that he was 'amazing'. He said, 'All of us are going crazy. There's boys phoning in bomb scares and setting off fire alarms. Or they're smoking dope and sleeping in the toilets. Anything to break the monotony. He just stands there, does his job, walks out...impressive, like.'

I learned more from Roger about my father's work at Hoover than I ever learned from him. I knew that he would never behave as Roger and his friends did; sometimes I think it would have been better for him, and for his family, if he had. But he was a religious man. He had a strong sense of right and wrong. He was also a Labour and trade union man. He did everything by the rules. If he was going to live by the rules, I wasn't. At seventeen, I published an underground newspaper called *Norman* that attacked a wide range of targets, including Merthyr town council and the presence of British troops in Northern Ireland. *Norman* was banned in my grammar school the same day it went on sale. I came home one Friday night and my mother said, 'Where have you been?'

'Selling the paper in the pub,' I said.

'You'll end up in jail, you will. You'll disgrace the family.'

She wanted to see a copy. I gave one to her and then went up to my room with its pictures of Angela Davis, Che Guevara and Jimi Hendrix on the walls. Somehow, my mother thought that one of the articles in *Norman* attacked the Catholic Church. She came into my room in a rage of retribution, hands flailing, and told me to get out of the house. I was sick of family life in this town that paid its homage to Hoover's. All this desperate struggle to be 'respectable' and for what? The anger at home; a job you hated all your life; the destruction of your family. That night I slept at my grandmother's house. My elder brother was already living there permanently. I decided to leave for London and stay with my friends who had already gone off to college. I went to say goodbye to my father.

'What about university?' he said.

'I'll go if you sign the grant forms,' I said.

'Come back and stay here,' he said. 'It's only for a few months. I'll sort it out with your mother.'

Somehow, he did. It was a rare and precious moment of his being able to show his love for me. And so I went to university in London and did my degree and—eventually, after spells on the dole—got work teaching English in Rome. From time to time, I went back to visit Merthyr but I always had one eye on the next train out of town. One Sunday, about noon, while my mother was making the roast dinner, I went for a pint with my father in the Gurnos Tavern. This was in the late 1970s, before Thatcher, during the years of industrial unrest that preceded her election victory. We were talking about an imminent strike on the railways.

'Your mother reckons the communists are behind it,' he said. 'But it's not communists. You got to stand by the union. You got to know what kind of people ordinary workers are up against.'

My father and I hadn't talked about anything other than football or the weather for years. He knew my politics. He wanted to connect with me in some way.

'A while ago, right? We had this time-and-motion bloke come around,' he said. Time-and-motion men are despised in the valleys, but my father had a guileless look on his face.

'In front of the machine where I work,' he said, 'there was this big window… Looking out over the mountain. This bloke decided that if they changed the windows for frosted glass, we'd spend less time staring out at the grass and trees, right? It would probably increase productivity. So they put the frosted glass in. And they were right. Productivity did go up.'

I remember how my father shifted in his seat, a bit nervous, and then looked straight at me.

'So what they did next, right? They decided that if productivity went up when they put the frosted glass in, it would go up even more if they bricked the windows up completely. Now I've got a blank wall to look at, haven't I?' 'That's the kind of people we're dealing with,' he said.

I couldn't tell him just to get out of the factory. He needed his pension. But I badly wanted to hurt the time-and-motion man. I would have happily left him bleeding in some Merthyr back alley at the time. Perhaps this desire to damage someone was a pose on my part, but it gave me the illusion of power over a situation in which I, and my father, had none.

My father had a heart attack at the age of sixty-two. He survived it, but he never went back to work on the assembly line. Eight years later, in June, 1993, he died of a second heart attack. I was living in New York then, and flew back for his funeral. The last time I saw him alive was a few months before, when we'd drunk a bottle of red wine as we watched a Welsh international rugby match on television. 'Red wine,' he'd said, 'good for the heart'.

Five thousand workers stood on the Hoover assembly lines at Merthyr in the 1960s. There are only 380 workers there now. Last month I drove up from Cardiff to see it—up the dual carriageway that now cuts across the Aberdare Mountain above the River Taff, and past the grim cemetery at Aberfan which marks the lower end of Merthyr borough and holds the remains of the children who died when an old coal tip slipped down on their school in 1966.

I got out of my car and walked around the green cricket pitch where, in the summer, my brother Kevin coaches the sons of factory workers, council clerks and maybe a drug dealer or two. I went through the underpass below Pentrebach railway station, water seeping from the bridge's stones and dripping from the stalactites on its roof, and emerged at a narrow footbridge across the Taff. There, a hundred yards away, was the Hoover factory: twisted pipes, rusted chimneys and water tanks, disused gantries beside the abandoned loading docks. Another footbridge, this one enclosed, spans the river from the original factory to the extensions of it—three big red-brick buildings—which were built quickly in the 1960s to cope with the new demand for washing machines. All three buildings are empty now and the windows of the bridge are cracked or boarded up. On this side of the river, the 'e' in HOOVER is shattered and askew and bright graffiti has been sprayed across the walls.

A great deal of economic and social damage has been done to Merthyr since my father began to work at Hoover's in 1961: so many mines and factories closed, so many people sacked, a whole way of living overturned. But for every dole boy, scam artist, car thief, and drug dealer I know of, there are maybe twenty people with their own taxis, driving their own catering vans or making music and films; or so I told myself that day standing next to the River Taff.

It was a cold, clear day in November, with the sun lighting up the plantations of pine trees and the nearly leafless birches that my father had planted on the slag heaps so long ago. Closer by, blue plastic bags had got entangled with the willows on the river bank, but I could see a heron standing in the river in front of them. There was never a heron this far up the Taff when I was a kid. My father, had he been near his factory window, had there still been a factory window, would surely have stopped work on his washing machines to watch it. □

GRANTA

THE MAKING OF PARTS

Alec Soth

Text by Matt Weiland

DIVISION
STAMPINGS
SUPERSTAMPER

The Making of Parts

In the American Midwest of the 1970s and 1980s, 'factory in ruins' was a stock phrase with all the force and familiarity of 'farm crisis' and 'long cold winter'. At least 2.5 million manufacturing jobs in the industrial heartland of the US were lost in just the period 1979 to 1983. The remains of the places where all that work was done littered the Midwest around the time Walter Mondale, a Minnesotan, popularized the term 'rust belt' in his failed presidential campaign of 1984. There was a sense, then, that even the rust might disappear before long.

A generation later, factories are still there and factory work remains a basic fact of life for many Midwesterners. Almost 4 million people work in manufacturing in the Midwest, nearly 400,000 in Minnesota alone. Division Stampings, in Rogers, employs about sixty of them. Rogers lies in the far north-west corner of Hennepin County, at the edge of the vast metro area of which Minneapolis is the centre. More than a million people live in the county, one of the more Democratic in the US; nearly sixty per cent of its voters chose John Kerry in the 2004 presidential election. But Rogers is a solidly Republican town: its voters went nearly 2:1 for George W. Bush. In other ways, too, Rogers is more like rural towns further west: an old railroad runs through it (once part of the Great Northern Railway, now renamed the Burlington Northern, built to connect Minneapolis to the Pacific and so bring Minnesota spring wheat flour to Asian markets); a wide interstate highway runs past it; and its local courts are full of tweakers—teenage users of crystal meth, the scourge of rural America.

Division Stampings makes metal parts—abstract things that tend to have cryptic names ('brake flanges', 'flywheel shrouds', 'wear and swivel pads') and that are difficult to recognize out of context, but that are vital to the workings of everyday products: cars, refrigerators, toasters, lamps, power tools. Metal stamping may seem banal but it is a huge industry, with its own trade publications (*The Fabricator*, *The Stamping Journal*) and websites anxious to explain the industry's mysterious ways to people who have never been near a lathe or press ('Look at a simple desk stapler—it forms parts in the same way that a metal press does!'). Something of the industry's importance can be gleaned from the fact that the head of a large metal-stamping firm in Missouri was recently named chairman of President Bush's national Manufacturing Council.

Matt Weiland

Division was founded in 1968 by Robert Groenke in a garage in Eden Prairie, a half hour's drive south of Rogers. When Groenke retired a few years ago, his son Dan took over; Dan's sister is the accountant. Most of the work Division does is short-run, meaning it makes products in smaller quantities and uses fewer automated tools than long-run factories do. Often the dies themselves cost more than the sum of the parts they produce. Many long-run stamping factories have moved to Mexico or China, but there's not much need for (or potential profit in) short-run factories such as Division to go, at least not yet. It is a busy factory, with clients all over the US. Its biggest customer is a hospital-bed manufacturer in Michigan.

When Alec Soth went to Division last autumn to photograph the workers there, what struck him first was the noise. 'It was very, very loud. Too loud to talk to the person sitting next to you, and listening to music on headphones isn't permitted. Given the loud banging machines, the hard fluorescent lighting, all the concrete and metal, I wondered where the worker's mind drifted during the day.'

Soth asked the workers he met what they thought about while they work, and some of their answers—written by the workers themselves—appear among the photographs. They tend to emphasize their lives outside the factory ('my first kid will be born real soon') or reflect on the happenstance of their lives within it ('if they want to keep me'). But it's too easy to assume their boredom or cynicism; they also express pride in the parts they make, even if it sometimes comes mixed with bemusement or incomprehension at what these parts are eventually used for. □

BLISS
C-150
1501

It wasn't me

When I'm stamping I think about what I'm going to do after work. If the job I am working on is going well, sometimes I can blank out what I'm thinking about and get into a good fast rhythym.

SR/90

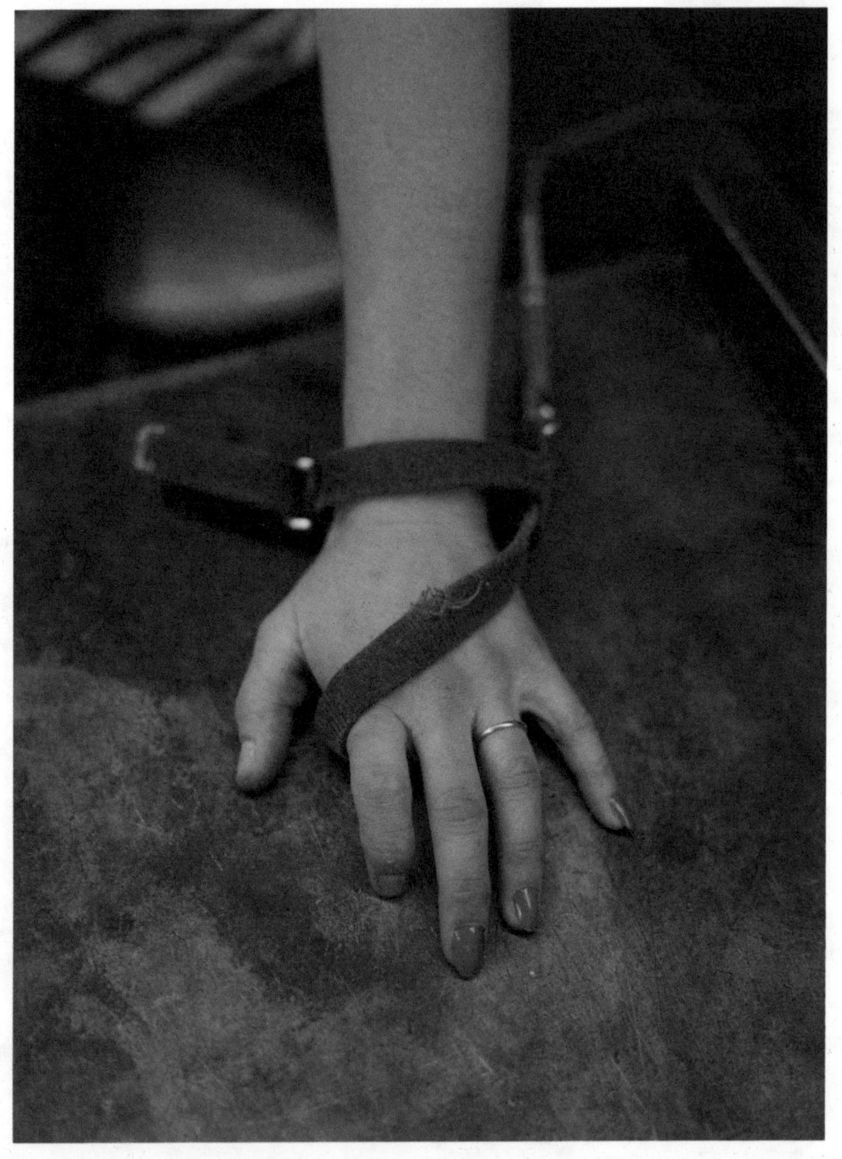

When I'm punching I wonder just What some of these parts I'm making are for ~~and it makes me happy knowing that people need the~~ I don't ~~think~~ have much of a life so I consentrate mostly on my Job.

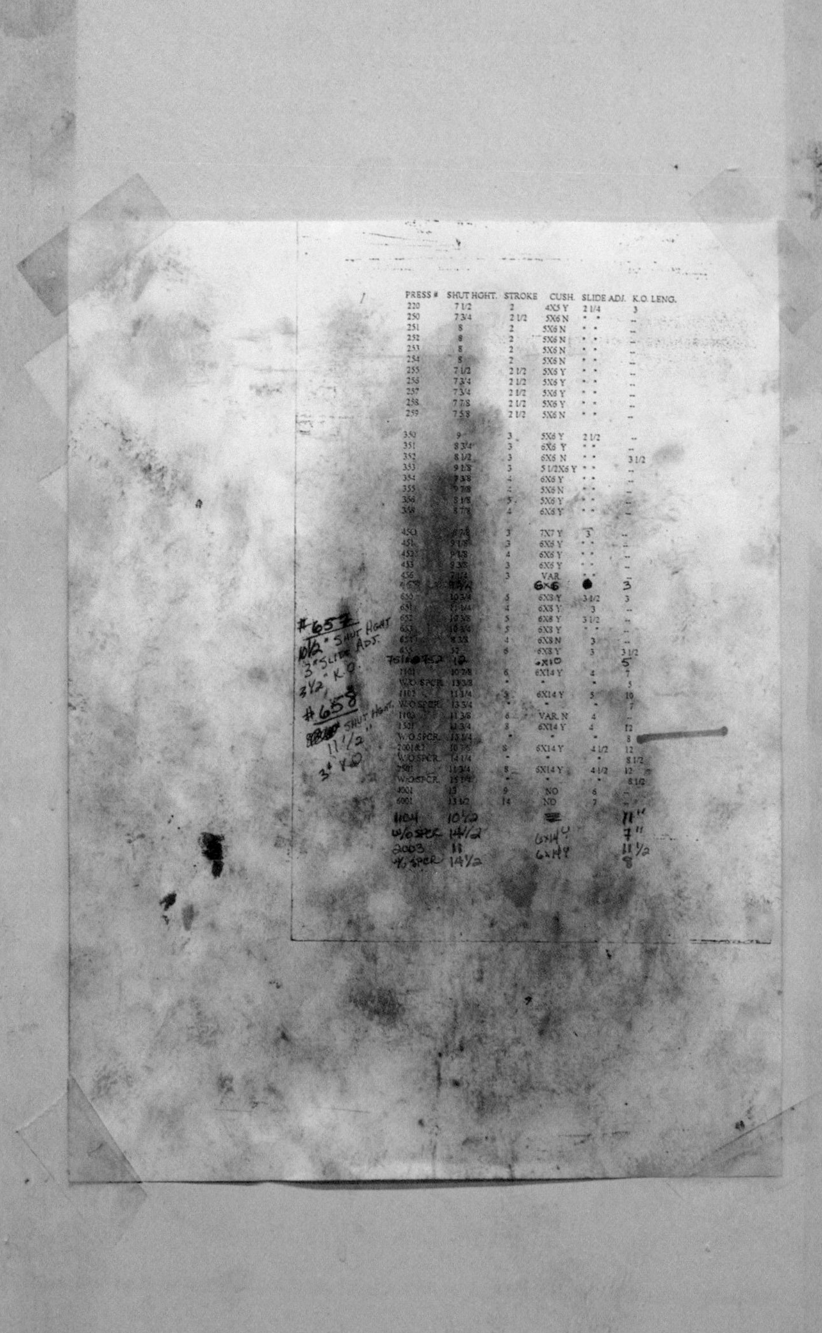

PRESS #	SHUT HGHT.	STROKE	CUSH.	SLIDE ADJ.	K.O. LENG.
220	7 1/2	2	4X5 Y	2 1/4	3
250	7 3/4	2 1/2	5X6 N	• •	--
251	8	2	5X6 N	• •	--
252	8	2	5X6 N	• •	--
253	8	2	5X6 N	• •	--
254	8	2	5X6 N	• •	--
255	7 1/2	2 1/2	5X6 Y	• •	--
256	7 3/4	2 1/2	5X6 Y	• •	--
257	7 3/4	2 1/2	5X6 Y	• •	--
258	7 7/8	2 1/2	5X6 Y	• •	--
259	7 5/8	2 1/2	5X6 N	• •	--
350	9	3	5X6 Y	2 1/2	--
351	8 3/4	3	6X6 Y	• •	--
352	8 1/2	3	6X6 N	• •	3 1/2
353	9 1/8	3	5 1/2X6 Y	• •	--
354	7 3/8	4	6X6 Y	• •	--
355	9 7/8	[illegible]	5X6 N	• •	--
356	8 1/8	5	5X6 Y	• •	--
358	8 7/8	4	6X6 Y	• •	--
450	9 7/8	3	7X7 Y	3	--
451	9 1/8	3	6X6 Y	• •	--
452	9 5/8	4	6X6 Y	• •	--
453	9 3/8	3	6X6 Y	• •	--
456	7 1/2	3	VAR.	• •	--
[illegible]	[illegible]		6X6	•	3
650	10 3/4	6	6X8 Y	3 1/2	3
651	[illegible]	4	6X8 Y	3	--
652	10 3/8	5	6X8 Y	3 1/2	--
653	10 3/4	5	6X8 Y	• •	--
654	8 3/8	4	6X8 N	3	--
655	12	6	6X8 Y	3	3 1/2
751 [illegible] 752	12		6X10		5
1101	10 7/8	6	6X14 Y	4	7
W.O. SPCR.	13 3/8	•	•	•	5
1102	11 3/4	[illegible]	6X14 Y	5	10
W.O. SPCR.	13 3/4	•	•	•	7
1103	11 3/8	6	VAR. N	4	--
1501	11 3/4	8	6X14 Y	4	12
W.O. SPCR.	13 1/4	•	•	•	8
2001&2	10 7/8	8	6X14 Y	4 1/2	12
W.O. SPCR.	14 1/4	•	•	•	8 1/2
2501	11 3/4	8	6X14 Y	4 1/2	12
W.O. SPCR.	15 1/4	•	•	•	8 1/2
4001	13	9	NO	6	--
6001	13 1/2	14	NO	7	--
1104	10 1/2				11"
W/O SPCR	14 1/2		6X14 Y		7"
2003	11		6X14 Y		11 1/2
W/O SPCR	14 1/2				8

#657
10 1/2" SHUT HGHT
3" SLIDE ADJ.
3 1/2" K.O.
#658
SHUT HGHT.
11 1/2"
3" K.O.

When I am stamping :-
I make sure that I do not bring
my personal or home issues to work.
And I also make sure that I leave
my work issues as I take off my
jacket, work hart, shirt and boots.

1001 WAYS
TO ENERGIZE
Self-Directed Teams
Continuous Improvement
BOB NELSON

Dave

L. F. #55

When I'm stamping I think about my life on how much my life is going to change when My first kid will be born real soon.

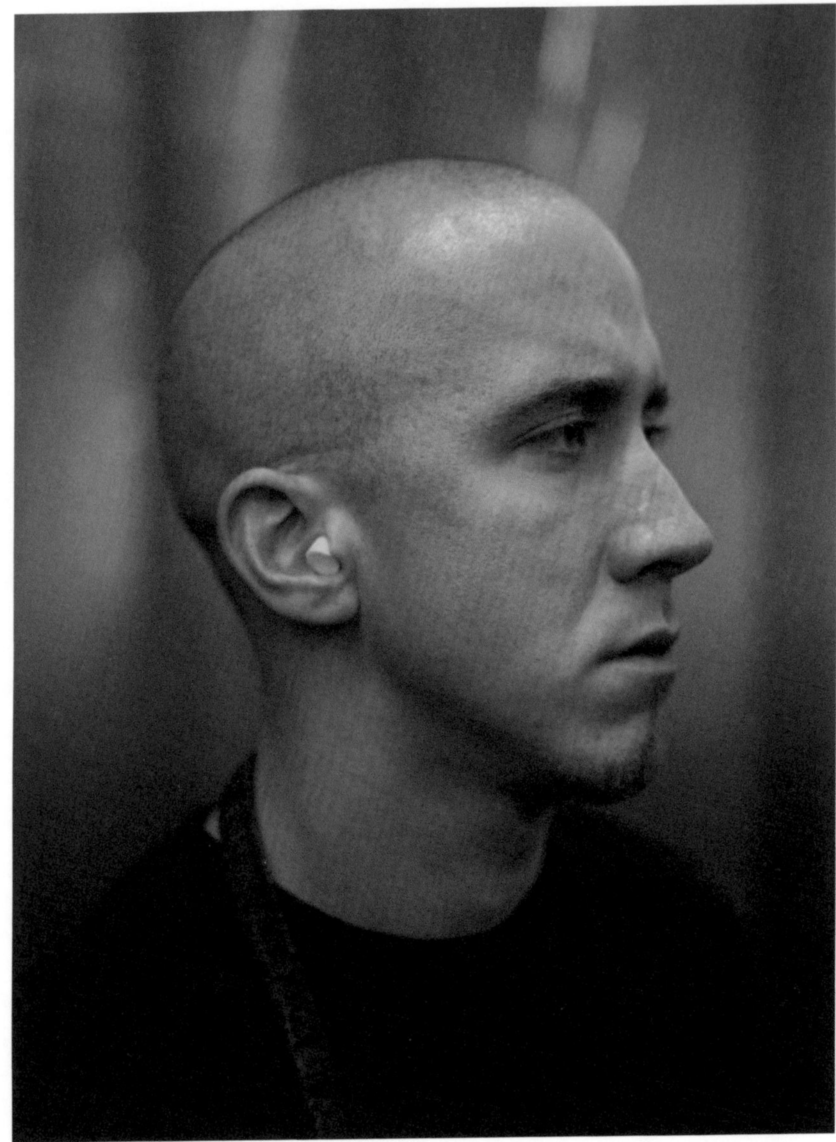

ELKAY
WITH FLEXI-GUARD

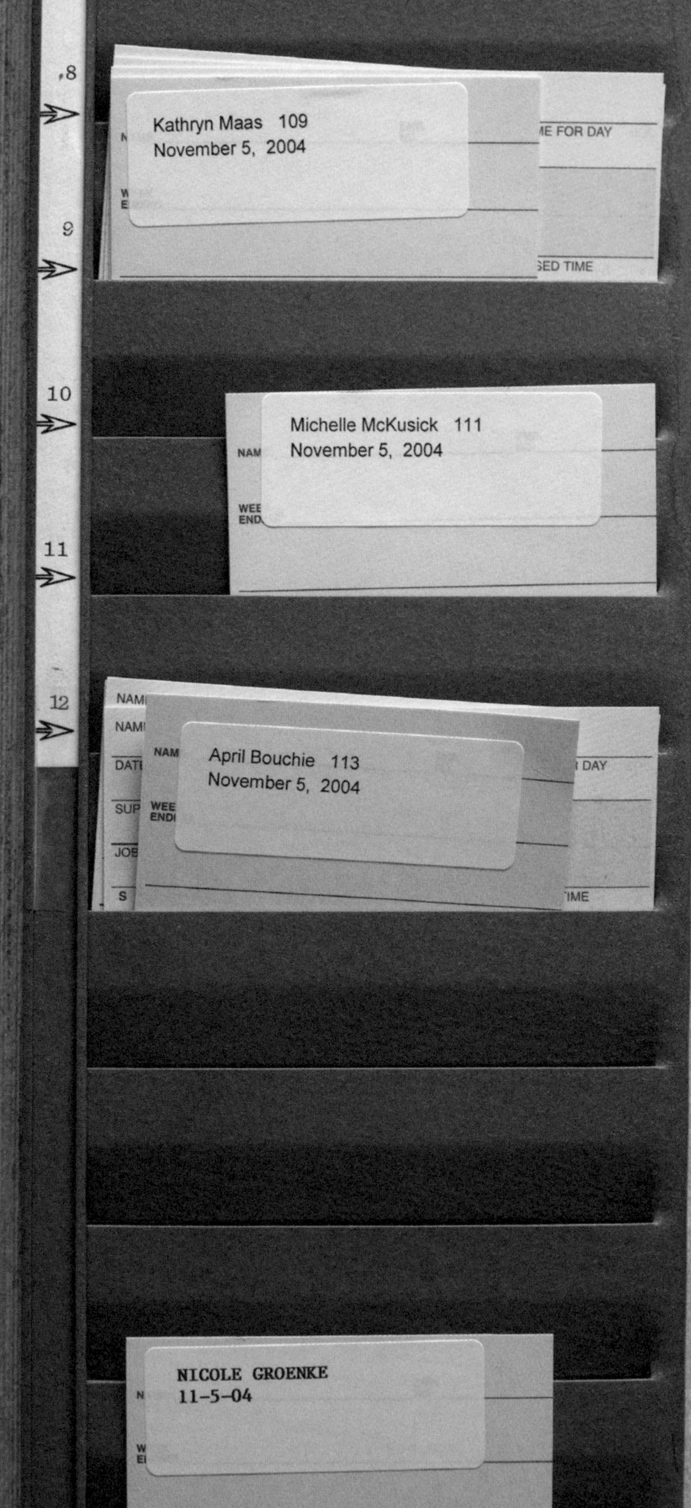
8
9
10
11
12
Kathryn Maas 109
November 5, 2004
ME FOR DAY
SED TIME
Michelle McKusick 111
November 5, 2004
NAM
WEE
END
NAM
NAM
NAM
DATE
SUP
JOB
S
WEE
ENDI
April Bouchie 113
November 5, 2004
DAY
TIME
NICOLE GROENKE
11-5-04

I think about my Job and my boy and the people I work with and my position in this company – if they want to keep me.

©TDK T-160
maxell
maxell
maxell

LYON

GRANTA

CHOCOLATE EMPIRES

Andrew Martin

BARRY LEWIS/NETWORK PHOTOGRAPHERS

My grandfather kept chocolates on his sideboard, in what ought to have been his fruit bowl. He would offer them to us, in a casual, cursory sort of way, and I was never sure how grateful to be. After all, the bags they came in were stamped with the words REJECT, WASTE OF MIS-SHAPES. They came from Rowntree's chocolate factory, where he'd worked as a fitter. Growing up in York, about one in five of the adults I knew worked at what had originally been called the Cocoa Works, including my stepmother, my auntie Dot, my uncle Peter, and many of my dad's friends, including a man called Bob Dixon, an electrician at Rowntree's, who once vouchsafed to me the strangely memorable information that Smarties were made with technology adapted from button making. All of these people possessed a card enabling them to claim free chocolates. Like the children allowed into Willy Wonka's chocolate factory, they were granted free chocolates for ever.

As a ten year old, I was torn between jealousy of them and the feeling that the waste or reject chocolates did not have the lustre of the marketable, thoroughbred chocolates. They were scarred and dusty-looking, and eating a bagful of, say, rejected Dairy Box was a frustrating experience. You'd bite into the first one, and it might be mint cracknel. You'd then eat the second one, and that would be mint cracknel too, as would the third, but the fourth one could well turn out to be coffee crème, at which point a whole new, exciting horizon seemed to open up. But when you bit into the fifth one, you'd be back to mint cracknel.

Sometimes, my grandfather would give us reject Kit Kats, and these tended to be spongy, which was down to the fact that he would hang on to his reject supplies for a long time, and seldom returned to the factory to replenish them. From my ten-year-old perspective, he was fascinatingly resistant to the appeal of chocolate, and yet he had spent forty years making the stuff, living and breathing it, because not only did he work at Rowntree's, he also lived in the shadow of York's second chocolate factory, Terry's. York's chocolate smell, which for other people came and went according to wind direction, was for him a continuum.

Also perplexing was the fact that my grandfather, a lifelong churchgoing Conservative, never seemed to display any of the technical ability you'd expect of a fitter. As long as I knew him there were a couple of broken bikes in his backyard, and his toolkit, which he kept in the coalshed, looked like something out of a museum. I would inspect it regularly, exasperated that no tool had been disturbed since the last time. It all came down to a riddle-and-answer that had long been lodged in my brain: 'Q: When is a factory not a factory? A: When it's a chocolate factory.'

My grandfather was not a typical factory worker because Rowntree's was not a typical factory, and nor was Terry's. Leetham's Flour Mill in York, where he had worked before Rowntree's—now that was a typical factory, an example of that cruel imbalance produced by heavy industry: a very large factory surrounded by very small houses. Another characteristic of factory-ness was the fact that bodged functionality had ended up looking like nightmarish fantasy: what appeared to be doors had been placed high up in the walls, for instance, so that if you'd opened one and stepped through unawares you'd have plunged to your death.

In his ninety-sixth year, my grandfather's always sparse conversation dwindled to a tight loop. He would describe over and over how, as a fifteen year old, before the Great War, he was required to get out of bed at five a.m., drink a tin mug of lukewarm cocoa placed in the oven the previous evening by his mother (although he didn't eat chocolate, he never lost the Edwardian habit of drinking cocoa), then walk the four miles from his home village of Bishopthorpe to the flour mill, usually—as he told it—through falling snow.

My grandfather rarely asked me any questions, so it was disturbing that he would turn to me during these accounts and demand: 'Can you imagine it? Can you?' He knew that I couldn't. As far as he was concerned I spent my life 'clerking down south', which, to my snobbish frustration, was the nearest he ever came to acknowledging that I was attending Oxford University. Sometimes I expected him to break off from his one, repeated tale of the flour mill by putting his head in his hands, and moaning, like Kurtz in *Heart of Darkness*, 'The horror! The horror!'

Forty years at Rowntree's, by contrast, seemed to have left no scar.

The first Rowntree factory was in the middle of York, alongside the River Ouse. It made cocoa—Rowntree's Elect—and every evening, a carter called Mr Laycock took all the day's produce to the railway station. The factory was run by Joseph Rowntree, son of another Joseph Rowntree, who had started in business as a general grocer in 1822.

In 1893 the Rowntree business moved to a larger factory, the one that survives to this day, on Haxby Road, York. This was thirty-three acres in extent, and consisted of several clean-looking red brick buildings, seven storeys high and surrounded by trees. It took me five minutes to cycle past its full extent. I think I always took it for granted that one day I would see inside, as a sort of settling of accounts with my native city. I remember that one year, the *Yorkshire Evening Press* published a guide to the various parts of the complex, and I noted with amazement that every confection—Matchmakers, Polos, Aeros, Smarties—had a small skyscraper to itself. I also noted that two-finger and four-finger Kit Kats each had their own buildings, and I wondered: would an employee graduate from the former to the latter over years of hard work? Or did promotion lie in the other direction, towards the more demanding miniaturism of the two-finger brand?

Whereas the Rowntree workforce had numbered only 200 in the old premises, it was 4,000 by 1906. But the factory was not like some great black maw waiting to claim the citizens of York. The notion of leisure was incorporated within it. Just inside the main gate was a library for staff, and directly over the road was the Joseph Rowntree Theatre, built for the entertainment of the employees. During lunchtimes, cowboy films would be shown in instalments. The theatre was also used by the city's amateur drama groups, some of which I belonged to.

The other chocolate factory, Terry's, seems to levitate above the district of South Bank where my grandfather lived, and where I was born—sometimes it seems to *be* the horizon. It was built in 1924, a sort of neo-Georgian castle, with a clock tower that lends it a restful, cathedral-like air. At night, the huge, white clock face—on which are spelt the words TERRY and YORK—is like a substitute moon. There are extensive gardens, in which the chocolate workers would walk during the lunch hour, dressed all in white, the ladies with white turbans on their heads, and their curlers in underneath.

In 1977, my final year at my secondary modern school, I plucked up the courage to ask the prettiest girl in the year what she would be doing after leaving. She moved her hair out of her eyes, and mimed the placing of chocolates in boxes. She was smiling as she did it. To work at an unskilled job in a chocolate factory—'Choccie Bashing'—was regarded as a semi-comic rather than a terrible fate. For many young women, the factories were the normal staging post between leaving school and first baby, and the art of tying the white turban was passed on from mother to daughter.

There is something salubrious about chocolate production, after all. It's an amiable, Toy Town kind of business, and helped make York seem like a northern city without the usual grit. The city also had the railway (only Crewe and Carlisle were more important here), but that too was benign: an open-air concern, generating an almost indecent loyalty among its workers. The two industries, taken together with the somehow embarrassingly pretty medieval and Georgian architecture of the city, the ameliorative flatness and fogginess of the surrounding Vale, made York a less brutal place than Sheffield, Leeds, or the nearby pit towns. If, on a Saturday night, you went along to Ziggy's Nightclub in Micklegate, the bouncers would anxiously ask: 'You're not from Wakey, are you lads?' Wakefield was a mining town, therefore hard, whereas we Yorkies were just so many chocolate soldiers.

The Rowntrees, along with Britain's other chocolate dynasties, the Frys and the Cadburys, were Quakers. Having been excluded by legislation from the universities, and by belief from the army or navy, they brought to manufacturing an excess of moral energy.

Joseph Rowntree II seemed to devote more time to giving money away than to making it. He believed in temperance, fair trading, workers' welfare, the League of Nations. His factory at York, along with the Cadbury's factory at Bournville, represented the high watermark of applied liberalism. The man was relentlessly enlightened: a female welfare worker was installed at the factory in 1891; sick and provident funds were established in 1902; a doctor's surgery was set up in 1904, a savings scheme in 1905, a pension scheme in 1906.

In 1904 he established the Joseph Rowntree Charitable Trust, the Joseph Rowntree Social Trust, and the Joseph Rowntree Village Trust which created for his employees the model village of New Earswick, the counterpart of the other chocolate community, Bournville, built by the Cadburys in Birmingham. My bicycle always seemed to fly along very merrily in New Earswick, a place so quaint and friendly that individual shops were pointed out on signposts reading BUTCHER, GREENGROCER, NEWSAGENT. All the houses were supplied with planted gardens, and as a ruse to get neighbours talking and swapping produce, no two adjacent gardens were planted with the same fruit tree. There was no pub.

Joseph Rowntree's second son, Benjamin Seebohm Rowntree, was so apparently heedless of commerce that early in his career he took two years out of the factory to write *Poverty: A Study of Town Life*, which was published in 1901, and coined the term 'poverty line'. The lives of hundreds of working-class York citizens were dissected to find out what made them tick, or not tick. The book is full of figures, charts and tables—the *Encyclopaedia Britannica* refers to its 'numerate austerities'—and at one point Rowntree neurotically adds up not only the number of pubs in York, but also the number of entrances to those pubs, his theory being that a pub with two entrances was almost twice as bad as a pub with one.

Under Seebohm, the actual chocolate was largely the province of George Harris, who was the confectionary genius, the Willy Wonka of Rowntree's. He introduced Aero and Kit Kat (both in 1935), and Dairy Box (in 1936). These products were great successes, and a small flicker of ostentation may have flared by the 1950s, when Peter Rowntree, Seebohm's son, was seen to be driving a car with the registration plate PR 1.

But the philanthropy continued, and I was a beneficiary in many ways. As a juvenile amateur actor with the York Settlement Players I performed several times at the 'Jo-Ro Theatre' as it was known. It was on too big a scale for amateur drama, and I recall playing to the great black void of the empty balcony. I played football in the Homestead Park, originally the grounds of the Rowntree family mansion, and in Rowntree Park, by the river, which was opened in 1921 to commemorate those factory workers killed in the First World War and, so it was said, to check any expansion of Terry's original factory, which was nearby. Indeed Rowntree Park was impertinently built on the riverside street that had already been named Terry Avenue.

I swotted for my exams in the Central Library, which the Rowntrees had funded; when I was Herod's Messenger in the York Mystery Plays in 1976, many of the rehearsals were at the Friends'

Meeting House in Castlegate, famous for its Rowntree associations. I knew people who attended Bootham and the Mount, Rowntree-funded Quaker schools both.

York was lucky in the Terrys, too, although they were not Quakers, but employers of the Tory Paternalist strain. Their factory of 1924 (their second in the city) was, like Rowntree's, a garden factory. There was a fish pond, a bowling green, a tennis court, a football pitch.

If they did not go in for good works as such, then Terry's lent an opulence to York. Half a mile down the road from the factory is Middlethorpe Hall, a Georgian mansion once owned by Francis Terry, grandson of the first Joseph, and chairman of the company for thirty-five years in the early twentieth century. My father used to fix a small supplementary seat on to the crossbar of his bike, and take me there to see the stone eagle on the roof.

The firm kept a cake and confectionary shop in St Helen's Square. The word TERRY'S was embossed in the stone. Behind the shop was the Celebration Restaurant, wainscoted and candlelit. I never dined there, but it always looked as if a wedding was going on, with cakes, cake stands, flowers, ladies in hats walking in and out. It closed in 1985, and the ladies in hats decamped to its smaller heir, the Terry's Tea Room in the Dean Court Hotel, opposite the Minster.

On the walls of the tea room are Terry's factory memorabilia and literature:

> Four centuries ago, Cortes sent home to Spain the first chocolate and cacao beans as part of the spoils from his conquest of Mexico. In the New World this chocolate Theobroma—the food of the Gods—was believed to be a supreme gift of divine origin, and certain kinds, reserved for the Emperor Montezuma himself, were served only in golden vessels in honour of the giver.

Hence Terry's All Gold chocolate assortment, invented in 1931. This was the major Terry's line, along with the Chocolate Orange, which was developed in 1932 as a result of some lateral thinking arising from a struggle to create a Chocolate Apple. To eat an entire Chocolate Orange in one go was the benchmark of decadence in the York of my boyhood.

Peter Terry, the last family member to hold a senior position in the firm, was deputy managing director of Terry's until his retirement in 1987. He lives in a large house north of York, which is Edwardian, but approximates in moneyed glamour the mansion bearing the stone eagle. By coincidence, it was built by Fred Rowntree, a member of the rival chocolate dynasty who had branched out into architecture, and its first occupant, from 1909, was Oscar Rowntree, a director of the firm. In the grounds are some cottages that were once used as convalescent home for Rowntree factory workers.

Meeting Peter Terry was a big moment for me: here was the man whose name was written on the moon. Now in his mid-eighties, he is elegant, charming, amusing, a Yorkshire Gentleman of the old school, which means, for a start, that he was educated outside the county: Marlborough, then Pembroke College, Cambridge. He always regarded chocolate-making as a unique sort of enterprise. 'The factory was so *clean*. To have a big dirty furnace somewhere...it wouldn't do at all. And I felt it was appropriate that York should have light industry because York is such a beautiful place.'

When I called on him, Peter Terry had just left a luncheon party given by his wife. 'Actually,' he confided, 'I have just been eating a chocolate.' 'What kind?' I challenged. 'Terry's All Gold,' he replied, triumphantly. He had been doing something else that would have been anathema to a Rowntree: drinking a glass of wine. But he knew and liked the Rowntrees and has never seen himself as being in competition with them. 'They would use the cocoa beans from West Africa, which had a purpley colour before roasting. We preferred beans from the West Indies or Malaysia, which were light brown, and had a finer taste.' Terry's selling point was luxury. Their chocolate was of a high quality, and was more expensive than Rowntree's. 'All Gold,' Peter Terry recalled, 'was five shillings a pound, whereas Black Magic was two shillings eleven. But then you shouldn't expect a Rolls Royce to cost the same as a Morris Minor.'

I told Peter Terry that I had applied to see around the Terry's factory, and had been refused, at which, in his gentlemanly way, he expressed pained surprise.

The Rowntree and Terry factories still stand, pumping out that soft, dark smell that seems to take you right to the mysterious heart of chocolate. The Swiss flag now flies alongside the Union Jack on the roofs of the Rowntree factory; since 1988 it has been owned by Nestlé, the largest food producer in the world. Terry's has been owned since 1993 by Kraft, the second largest. Kraft has announced that the York factory will close some time in 2005, which is not a popular decision in the city. The Chocolate Orange and All Gold can be produced more cheaply in Sweden and Eastern Europe, and the future of the factory building, which is not listed, is uncertain. There was no question of my being admitted to the factory. It was a 'sealed environment', and visitors brought a risk of contamination. My subsidiary questions ('What is the size of the factory?' 'What else is made there apart from the Chocolate Orange and All Gold?') went unanswered.

Nestlé has been boycotted by campaigners who contend that it promotes its baby milk formula too aggressively in the Third World. This might explain why the Rowntree factory is not the hospitable place it once was, with its regular tours for York citizens. I was advised that, if the factory were to admit me, then there'd soon be other writers massing at the gates, a response that seemed to contain an echo of the Willy Wonka notion of a chocolate factory as something hallowed, infinitely mysterious. If only I'd been able to say to the press office: 'I gave your factory the best years of my life.' Unfortunately, 'A lot of people I *know* gave your factory the best years of their life,' doesn't have the same force.

It began to occur to me that, in never having worked for Rowntree's or Terry's, and never having benefitted from one of those civic-minded tours, I was in a minority among my fellow citizens. I felt frustrated by this. Like the young aspirants in *Charlie and the Chocolate Factory*, I wanted to see inside a chocolate factory.

I was given my chance by the fact that Cadbury's Dairy Milk is a hundred years old in 2005. A PR person who'd heard I was writing about chocolate called to point this out, and to offer me a tour of the Cadbury's factory in the Birmingham suburb of Bournville.

I stepped off the train at Bournville station feeling like an exile: it was disturbing to be in among that soft chocolate aroma in some place other than York. I could see the factory from the platform. It looked like the Rowntree's factory: a series of tree-ringed red brick blocks arranged at perplexing intervals like the pieces on a chess board in mid-game. The words BOURNVILLE and CADBURY'S boomed out in giant black letters from two of the blocks.

All around the factory was the chocolate suburb of Bournville, built by George Cadbury from 1893. On its fringes were ordinary red-brick terraces, but fancy plasterwork above doorways denoted the benevolent hand of the chocolatier. And at its heart Bournville was pure New Earswick, pure Garden City: the arts-and-crafts style, the fruit gardens behind the houses, the carefully variegated shops standing in a row, the Friends Meeting House and the lack of a pub.

Everyone who comes from York has heard of Bournville, and they think of it as the second chocolate colony. In fact, of course, it's the first. Cadbury's garden factory predates the Rowntree's factory by twenty years, and Bournville came before New Earswick. You could say that the Cadburys were like the Rowntrees, only more so. In 1866, Richard and George Cadbury adopted the Van Houten cocoa press, which removed cocoa butter from the cocoa bean. The production of drinking chocolate had been complicated by the presence of cocoa butter (additives had been required to screen the fattiness), and the use of the press to make cocoa essence created the cocoa drinking boom.

The Cadburys also prised open the eating-chocolate market by perfecting the formula for making creamy chocolate—Dairy Milk—in 1905. Before then, most mass-produced eating chocolate had been dark chocolate. But people wanted milk in their chocolate. Milk is more expensive than cocoa beans, and symbolized luxury and healthiness, hence the early Cadbury boast: 'A glass and a half in every pound and a half'.

The Cadburys were Quakers, like the Rowntrees. Doubly so if you consider that, from 1921, they absorbed the other great Quaker chocolate dynasty, the Frys of Bristol. It seems wrong to ask whether the Rowntrees or the Cadburys were the more altruistic, the more untypical of factory owners. It goes against that whole business about not looking a gift horse in the mouth. The Cadburys were perhaps more worldly, better at combining philanthropy and profitability.

Cadbury's ceased to be a Quaker firm in the strict sense in 1962, when the company went public. In 1969 the merger occurred that created Cadbury Schweppes, but this company still boasts of 'doing the right thing' (a favourite company phrase) in its factories around the world, of which Bournville is the biggest. It is also the best surviving example of Victorian paternalism. Women in the factory who marry are still presented with a carnation and a Bible or Qu'ran as appropriate, a tradition that began in the early 1880s when George Cadbury gave the flower in his buttonhole to a factory girl on hearing that she was about to be married.

I met my company guide at the factory gates, opposite an arts-and-crafts cottage called Number One Lodge. A sign reading STAFF SHOP pointed towards a pathway lined with Victorian street lamps. The path wound through a garden and towards a door behind which lay the holy grail of all children: mountains of free chocolate.

My guide and I put on our white coats and white hairnets in the wood-panelled room that had once been the office of Richard Cadbury, who built the firm up to its Victorian eminence with his brother, George. Richard's portrait hung on the wall. It was, apparently, very hard to persuade any Cadbury to sit for a portrait. This was on account of their modesty, and once persuaded they would not sit down for the painter—they thought that gave an impression of laxity. The room was cluttered with Christmas parcels, which my guide casually explained were to be distributed to poor children in Africa.

We then walked towards one of the factory blocks, pushed our way through some double doors on which a notice read OUR WORK IS NEVER SO IMPORTANT THAT WE CANNOT TAKE THE TIME TO DO IT SAFELY, and a woman pushing a trolley on which rested a polythene sack full of chocolate debris shouted: 'Mind your backs!'

I was in a chocolate factory at last.

A chocolate factory consists of large rooms with walls of whitewashed brick, a few machines, a few people—looking lonely among the machines—and a lot of white pipes. To understand the factory you must understand the route of the chocolate through the pipes. It will rise at will up through a ceiling, emerge through a floor, cross from one factory block to another. To keep it moving, the chocolate factory is kept at the melting temperature of chocolate: blood temperature. The whole place, in fact, reminded me of a Christmas Day at home: slightly cloying warmth, bright lights, chocolate smell. Another characteristic was its asexuality: there were as many women as men supervising the machines, and the hairnets tended to emasculate the men.

Cadbury's cocoa beans mainly come from Ghana. They are initially processed at another factory, at Chirk in North Wales which roasts and crushes teh beans and removes the cocoa butter to produce what's known as either chocolate mass or chocolate liquor. This is Theobroma, food of the gods in the New World. It tastes awful, like a mistake. The heaviness of it is extraordinary, and your tongue quests after sweetness as intently—and futilely—as an alcoholic might search for a pub in Bournville or New Earswick.

Chocolate is made by the addition of sugar (always), milk (in the case of milk chocolate) and the restoration of a certain proportion of the cocoa butter, and all of this takes place at the Bournville factory. I was taken first to a conveyor belt carrying 'chocolate crumb', which is 'almost chocolate'. Sugar had been added, but the cocoa butter had not yet been put back. It tasted gritty, like a very old Cadbury Flake. The crumb flowed into a pipe that went through the floorboards to a room where the cocoa butter would be restored in the right proportion. The resulting mixture—which could truly be called chocolate—would then be milled to make it smooth, but not completely because chocolate must have a certain graininess to taste right.

We now stopped next to a pipe that pointed down towards a giant electrical sieve. As we watched, a single lump of chocolate popped on to the sieve, obligingly making a perfect circle. A chocolate drop, in fact. The full flow would resume shortly, I was assured.

We walked on, towards a rotating drum three feet wide. Inside it was Dairy Milk chocolate being mixed with bits of biscuit, for the Dairy Milk-with-Shortbread-Biscuit line, one of several variants on the basic theme. From this drum, the chocolate and biscuit bits were dropped into chocolate-bar-sized chocolate moulds. We walked on, climbed some stairs, and saw these same chocolate bars at a later stage, rising from the floor on a conveyor belt, each chunk displaying the Cadbury's signature, which is Richard Cadbury's signature.

The bars were next funnelled single file towards a weight sensor adjacent to an air hose. Any bar not forty-nine grams exactly in weight was blown off the conveyor with a contemptuous snort. The survivors were then enveloped in the plastic wrapping which recently replaced the old foil-and-paper-sleeve combination. This process of wrapping—a matter of hypnotically converging paper rollers—happens faster than the eye can take in.

We drifted on, into another room. Many machines; two people. 'I think they're getting ready to do some Whole Nut,' my guide speculated, 'maybe after lunch.' As we passed a large window, my guide pointed out a fountain in the grounds. Workers could sit beside this in summer; beyond it was 'the rec', the sports ground, which included a palatial pavilion and a football pitch turfed with grass from Wembley Stadium. We walked through the library, where the recent House of Commons Health Committee Report on obesity was displayed. The obesity question has cast a large shadow over chocolate production. In response to the report, Cadbury's and other chocolate manufacturers made a pledge: they would make labels clearer, strive to reduce sugar, salt and fat levels, amend the size of their bigger bars and—the homeliest, or possibly most futile, measure—divide them into greater numbers of chunks, to encourage sharing.

We walked into a recreational part of the factory that had the air of a nursery: brightly lit rooms, colourful paintings on the walls. There was a doctor's surgery here, and the Cadbury's dentist—a paradoxical notion, I thought. The sign of the surgery was painted in the colours of the Cadbury's Dairy Milk bar.

We came to the science and technology department, and the tasting room. Roald Dahl tasted chocolate for Cadbury's as a schoolboy, and this planted the seed for *Charlie and the Chocolate Factory*. Today, the job is mainly done by Cadbury's employees who've passed a test to establish the sensitivity of their taste buds. The employee enters a room adjacent to a laboratory. He sits down at a long table with partitions either side, as if making or receiving a prison visit. In front of him is a serving hatch. He pulls a string to say that he's ready, and a light is lit on the other side of the hatch, where a lab technician places the chocolate to be tested on a tray along with a glass of water. The technician opens the hatch, passes the chocolate through, and closes the hatch. The only sense at work must be taste. The taster must have no contact with the giver of the chocolate, and any brand marking on the chocolate (it may be a rival's, an established Cadbury's line, or a proposed new line) is scrubbed off. The taster tastes at his hatch underneath a red light, to disguise the hue of the chocolate. He fills out a form, answering certain specific questions: 'Is chocolate A sweeter than chocolate B?'; or he might be asked to detect flavours unwanted in chocolate: musty, smoky, yeasty, bready. As I peered inside, I saw a taster eating chocolate, head in hands. I was allowed only the briefest glimpse, such was the level of concentration involved.

It seems likely that the most dynamic Quakers of two generations went into chocolate production in the hope of weaning the working classes off alcohol. 'They were all dead keen against drink,' Peter Terry told me, by way of summing up the Rowntrees, 'and they'd begun by having these sort of cafes that sold drinking chocolate. They wanted people to go there rather than to pubs.'

It seems such a touchingly naive notion: that chocolate, with the tiny kick it gives from its moderate amounts of phenylethylamine and caffeine, could ever have been thought a match for alcohol. Yes, many people adore chocolate; some become addicted to it. (The secret of its seductive power, apparently, is its melting point: once on the tongue it deliquesces pleasingly.) But for most of us, its appeal is pretty fickle. The number one marketing fact when it comes to chocolate is that seventy per cent of purchases are not envisaged more than thirty seconds beforehand.

The project was all the more unworldly for having been conducted in my native city, which, as Seebohm Rowntree sadly noted in *Poverty*, was over-endowed with pubs: one licensed house for every 230 people in 1901. The book provides a pull-out 'drink map of York' over which, I suppose, the reader was meant to shake his head, although I wonder how many used it as a guide to boozing in York. In his later book, *English Life and Leisure: a Social Study* (1951), the largest chunk of which is devoted to the problems of alcohol, Seebohm Rowntree made the case for 'cafes of a new type... comfortable but unpretentious', and serving non-alcoholic drinks.

While the Rowntrees could only suggest a non-alcoholic way of life to the general public, they could go some way towards creating one for their workforce, hence the Bible-reading groups, the churches, the garden village, the fruit trees, the library, the theatre.

The last time I performed in their theatre—the Jo Ro, opposite the factory—I played Abdullah, a street urchin in Tennessee Williams strange, static play, *Camino Real*. I was thirteen years old. As Abdullah, I was photographed by the *Yorkshire Evening Press*, and the accompanying caption came very near to praising my brief performance. I would read this caption over and over in the hope that unequivocal praise for my acting talent might somehow emerge from it.

After each performance, having carefully retained some eyeliner,

I wandered out of the theatre in a daze of self-congratulation and walked through the garden that fronted it towards the bus stop standing directly before the mighty factory. I would gaze up at the brilliantly lit windows and imagine all the products being made inside: Kit Kat ('Have a break'), Aero ('Lovabubble'), Rolo ('Get together, with Rolo'), Smarties ('Cor, what-a-lot-I-got'). The factory seemed intent on a fantasy, pursued with admirable consistency yet not quite manly, and in this I—a bookish and daydreaming adolescent—felt a certain affinity with the chocolate emperors. □

GRANTA

PLASTICS

Luc Sante

NINA ZANDER 1919/HERMITAGE MUSEUM. ST PETERSBURG, 2004

I was fated to work in a factory. I was born in a Belgian textile-factory town, and my ancestors had worked in the mills for at least two or three centuries before I came along. Almost all of them were employed by Simonis, once the most prominent of many local makers of worsted cloth, now the world's leading manufacturer of billiard-table baize. It is very nearly the last survivor of a once-crowded industrial hub. My father managed to avoid working in the textile plants, but he couldn't help being employed by ancillary businesses; there wasn't anything else. When I was born he had been working for about five years in an iron foundry that made equipment for the plants. When the industry collapsed a few years later the foundry, like so many other local businesses, fell with it. We emigrated to the United States, where the initial promise of new and fulfilling employment soon gave way to uncertainty, then near-despair. Eventually my father was hired by yet another factory, which manufactured pipes and rods from a hard, resilient, slippery synthetic that for household applications is trademarked Teflon. He worked there until his retirement at the age of sixty-five. Immediately thereafter he began displaying symptoms of Parkinson's disease, unprovably but almost certainly the result of twenty-seven years' daily exposure to ambient powdered fluorocarbons. Dementia followed a decade later. His death at eighty came as a consequence of his refusing food and drink for a week, a mode of death known in nursing-home jargon as 'Alzheimer's suicide'.

My father did not want me to follow in his footsteps. He never pushed me in any particular direction, but he let me know from an early age that mental labour was far preferable to the physical sort, and he often regretted his lack of formal education—he had quit school at fourteen, as was then the norm, to contribute to the family purse. I didn't disagree; I had vague artistic leanings, and I knew from a few visits to his factory that I would never want to work in such a place. When at sixteen I got an after-school job it was at a five-and-dime, a Woolworth's clone, where I worked as a stock-boy. My duties consisted of unloading boxes, stocking shelves, vacuuming and buffing floors, and, every night, transferring the trash from the loading-dock area to the large wheeled-bin outside.

Reporting for duty one afternoon, after I had worked there for about a year, I was met at the door by the manager and the assistant manager. I had clashed with them many times before. Junior-college graduates, probably not over thirty, they were a skilled Mutt-and-Jeff torture team. Jenkins, the manager, was tidy, distant, thin-lipped, and narrow-shouldered; his assistant, called Mr Z, might have passed for a good-natured slob to anyone but his underlings. 'Come with us,' said Jenkins, briskly turning on his heel, while Mr Z favoured me with one of his shit-eating grins. They brought me outside to the bin, from which Mr Z retrieved two large cardboard boxes. He scooped out some crumpled newspaper from each, triumphantly revealing a layer of small boxes labelled TIMEX. 'We won't call the police as long as you leave now,' said Jenkins. I was too flabbergasted to reply. What was going on? I knew it couldn't have been an accident, since there were two such boxes, and yet I doubted my colleagues would have known any more than I did how to fence a gross of cheap watches. Were Jenkins and Mr Z covering up some plot of their own? Was that why they refrained from calling the cops? I remain baffled to this day.

Fortunately my parents were away, so I was spared having to explain, having my father arrange a meeting with Jenkins and Mr Z, possibly even having him believe them rather than me. But I needed a job, and fast. I was in my last year of high school, and even though I had been awarded a scholarship to college, the costs of room and board stretched my parents' finances to the limit. Spending money would be entirely my responsibility, as it was already. Friends told me about a plastics factory in a nearby New Jersey town where anybody could get a job. 'Just tell them you're eighteen'—that was the minimum legal age for factory work. I needed no further urging. The reason anyone at all could get a job there was because the turnover was constant, and the reasons for the constant turnover were themselves an inducement to me. The place was strictly for hard cases, and I very much wanted to qualify as a hard case. The pay was low, the conditions were brutal, the work was relentless and the workforce was possibly dangerous—a few months earlier a friend of a friend had been stabbed in the leg during an argument with the foreman, a recently released convict.

It was doubly fortunate that my parents were away, since my father would have insisted on visiting the place beforehand—if indeed he'd even have considered allowing me to work there—and none of the stories were exaggerated. It was a small factory, with just four machines, three of them deafeningly packed into a space the size of a two-car garage and the one behemoth allotted its own separate shed. Nobody worked there if they could get a better job elsewhere. The employees—twelve machine operators over three shifts, plus one foreman per shift—were ex-cons, former mental patients, drunks, acid casualties, illegal immigrants and the illegally underage. The company was run by a father-and-son team: ancient, silent, diminutive father and huge, loud, hairy son. I filled out some perfunctory paperwork in which I claimed to be eighteen; they promised to pay me two dollars per hour and sent me off to my machine.

I was on the number three machine, by the north wall. Had I been able to see through the tiny, smeared window over my head and to the left, I could have gazed upon the Passaic River. Number three was medium-sized and middle-aged, a good beginner's machine. Tiny number one, in the middle, looked like a nineteenth-century relic. It was operated by Esmeralda, from Honduras, who was relieved at midnight by her daughter. Number two, on the south wall, was larger and newer, but unpredictable. Working her that day was a man in a watch cap who quit a week later. In the shed, on number four, was Frank, a man of around sixty who came every day with red jug wine decanted into a juice bottle that fooled no one. He was so clearly a person of substance that rumours of a former life on Wall Street did not seem implausible, although he was known to wander off or fall asleep next to his machine. It was said that one night, when only Frank had shown up for the night shift, he had ambled down the road and nodded off in an abandoned car. His machine, running highly volatile silicon, exploded, sending the hopper magnets clear through the roof.

The routine at first looked impossible. On the average job the cycles ran four times a minute. Each cycle required me to open the machine door, remove the extruded item, strip it of its excess (its tree), put the tree into the grinder, and pack the item in a box, all in the space of fifteen seconds. There were many variations: cycles ran faster or slower; the tree was easier or harder to remove. The items ranged in size from four-foot-square Parsons tables down to toothpicks, which came a hundred to the tree and were sliced off with a razor into a forty-gallon drum (at the end of a week, three daily shifts had barely managed to fill a quarter of the drum). Some kinds of plastics were forgiving, but most required that the door be opened as soon as the light went on and closed the instant the product was removed. Otherwise the plastic would 'freeze'—would clog the mould, requiring you and the foreman to lengthily chip away at the gunk with screwdrivers and ice picks, and if the freeze lasted too long your pay would be docked.

Anxiety attended every part of the manufacturing process, nearly all of it focused on the foreman. The foreman had to supply plastic granules to the machines' hoppers, empty the container of the grinder, haul away the boxes of product, supply boxes to be filled, and relieve workers when they needed to go to the toilet and during their legally mandated but unpaid half-hour lunch breaks. If the foreman failed to fulfill any of these requirements with regard to you, you had no recourse. If you had no boxes, for example, you could not leave your machine to procure some from the storeroom, but would have to find creative ways of stacking finished pieces on your tray-sized table or somewhere in your available few bits of space without clogging the aisle or blocking access to the machine door.

Foremen came in two flavours: choleric and slack. The former, frequently ex-convicts, tended to act as if they owned the factory, and would harass workers for such things as not maintaining the quota. How anyone could work faster than anyone else was a mystery to me, since the tempo was entirely dictated by the machine and its protocols as determined by the type of plastic and the size of the mould. Slack foremen were the norm, however. They were slack because they were stoned, and they would disappear for long intervals during which they presumably either read comic books or threw stones into the river, there being few other distractions available on the desolate stretch of road that was home to the factory as well as an auto-body shop and a pair of shuttered cinder block edifices. As annoying as the choleric foremen could be, the slack foremen were a menace, requiring one to attempt improbable feats, such as climbing up the side of the machine to dump the contents of the overflowing grinder box into the hopper, while simultaneously opening the mould door with one foot.

The products manufactured by the plant were the sort of junk that isn't much made in America any more. It is left to China, Mexico, and a few Third World countries to supply the globe with playing-card boxes, audio-cassette boxes, toy boats, toy sand-shovels, ice-cube trays, novelty picture-frames, dildos (rumoured but unseen by me), and hundreds of unidentifiable widget components. The owners could not have grossed more than a fraction of a cent per unit of any of these. Accordingly they had to run the place with the lowest overhead the law would permit—if indeed the law played much of a role in their calculations. The two dollars an hour they lavished upon me was the minimum wage of the time; the result was something like seventy-five dollars after taxes for a full week's labour. I seldom reached even that amount, since I was always being docked, either for freeze episodes that were seldom my fault or for coming in late, since the factory was in a town seven miles from mine and I had to hitch-hike to work immediately after school. The punch-clock at the door was set to record only fifteen-minute intervals, so that a minute's delay would result in a loss of fifty cents. I never asked how much the illegal aliens were paid.

After a day or two I had absorbed the machine's rhythm. As I fell asleep every night in my bed I could feel each muscle group involved in the cycle going through its paces in sequence, again and again.

My job, once I had achieved a rhythmic trance in which I could do my work without thinking about it, was excruciatingly boring. The place was too loud for a radio and the machines were too far apart for even shouted conversation. For a while I entertained myself by singing—I could bellow and no one would hear—and by reciting poetry, although I quickly exhausted my repertoire. I wanted to read, but reading was circumscribed by the rhythm of the cycle. I arranged my space for maximum efficiency, moving the boxes to the other side of the grinder so that I could pack product with one hand while discarding excess with the other. Having pared my movements down to the strict minimum I had enough time between one cycle and the next to read about half a sentence. I tried crime novels, for example, but kept losing my place. Finally I had a stroke of inspiration. Only one author would do: Céline. His works beginning with *Death on the Instalment Plan* were all spat out in brief, angry bursts separated by ellipses. The solution was perfect. Not only did I have exactly the time required to read one such particule between every two cycles of the machine, but their emotional content might have been designed for the circumstances.

The job was both real and not. The relentless monotony of

repeating a chain of actions four times a minute over seven and a half hours—1,800 times a day—was certainly real enough, as were the broiling heat, the poisonous and unmoving air, the bad light, the punishing din, the ridiculous pay, the unpredictably varied annoyance of the commute. On the other hand, I had an end date and a ticket out. In September I would be going to college. I would not be facing an unchanging diet of that sort of despair for years, perhaps for the rest of my life, the way many of my colleagues did, and the way various of my relatives had. It was something I merely had to withstand for about six months. One night, around that same time, I was arrested, along with half a dozen of my friends. We were driving home from a party in an overcrowded car when we were stopped. A dirty hash-pipe was found under a seat. We were drunk, and thought that the fingerprinting and the mugshot session were hilarious. 'You laugh now, but just wait until you try to get a good job or apply to college,' the cop said. I laughed even harder—I had been accepted the week before. (The case was eventually dismissed on the grounds of illegal search and seizure.) The job had that same sort of unreality.

I was about to be sprung from my class status. My father worked in a factory, my parents owned a tiny house and a secondhand car, they were socially awkward and didn't speak very good English; I didn't really know what a rise in status would entail. I had no desire to work in finance or to join any clubs. All I knew was that I would be avoiding the sort of life to which my parents had been sentenced. Nevertheless, I referred to myself as working class, and was even more insistent about it in college, when I met kids from fancy backgrounds. This was partly in emulation of my proudly Socialist father, partly because I was an outsider in so many ways that I had no choice but to be defiant about it, and partly because it was 1972. Revolution, the great panacea of a few years earlier, had definitively been scratched, but hopes had not yet crumbled.

Neither had a certain romantic notion of the working class. The United States was famously supposed to be classless, of course, but then almost everybody knew better. In 1972 the working class (along with a few other more or less murky categories, such as 'street people' and 'our brothers and sisters in prison') was still being floated among middle-class would-be revolutionaries as an edifying model for imitation and as a permanent source of guilt. It was a bit complicated, because 'hard-hats', unassailably working class, had beaten up antiwar protesters on the streets of New York City and been hailed as pillars of the Silent Majority by Richard Nixon and Spiro Agnew. But there remained the lingering aura of the Wobblies, of the miners' strikes and auto-workers' strikes of the 1930s, as well as a cascade of images from the Paris Commune and the October Revolution and the Long March. We imagined basking in the radiance of that aura when we wore our blue chambray shirts and listened to the MC5, not suspecting that within a decade or two so much of American industry would be exported or terminated. Then the remnants of the working class would either be handed neckties and told they were middle class, or forced into fast-food uniforms and told they didn't exist.

In 1972, then, I was a member by blood of the working class who was pretending to be a member of the working class, rather like an African-American in blackface. My job was maddening, and I was constantly exhausted from the combination of a full day of high school with an eight-hour shift of work and usually a few hours' partying afterward, and I stoked my rage by reading Céline, but I was impressed with myself. I needed the money and didn't have other prospects, let alone entrée to glamorous sinecures the way some of my friends did, but the job was in part a role I was playing. I was being a badass and a hard case, converting into defiance the fact that my parents were poorer than almost anyone else's parents in our comfortable New Jersey suburb. Working at the factory the night of the senior prom, I enjoyed a strange feeling of triumph, as if I were deliberately boycotting such bourgeois shenanigans, rather than conceding that I was so sure of not getting a date—in part because I didn't have a car—that I didn't even try.

I took pride in my ability to endure. Indeed, in those six months at least four or five of my school friends signed on, but only two of them lasted out the first week, and neither of them managed more than a couple of months. In enduring the job I was imitating my father, who always boasted that he had spent only one week of his life on the dole, no mean feat in 1950s Belgium. I never entirely plumbed the reasons for his preferring labour, no matter how stultifying or demeaning or ill-paid, to collecting benefits, but it seemed to involve a combination of worker solidarity—not accepting handouts when others were toiling—with a version of the drive that causes people to run marathons even as they know they have no chance of placing. Every night as I made my way to beer or bed I was under the impression that I had accomplished something, although all that I had accomplished, besides earning something less than fifteen dollars, was to have withstood eight hours of being converted into a machine part. And that, for reasons both familial and cultural, was something I thought of as ennobling and rather macho. After all, while most of my friends and classmates came from more prosperous families, I had no real idea what it was that their fathers did in their offices, wearing their suits. Labour was all that I had been exposed to, and I equated it with adult masculinity.

Nevertheless I was bored out of my mind. Reading was crucial. When occasionally I was assigned a task with a cycle so tight that I was unable to carve out an interval for reading, I suffered terribly. Reading allowed me to mentally leave the premises, while letting my empty body do the work. Otherwise the job was like solitary confinement in eight-hour instalments, something I understood when my friend Garry came to work having just ingested 500 mikes of Orange Sunshine. He felt nothing, he reported afterwards, 'Everything was grey.' The inhuman pace and atmosphere could apparently overwhelm even LSD. As it happened, the two longest-serving employees, Frank and a fearsome character called One-Legged John, were both drunks who tippled on the job. When I left in August, hardly anyone was still there from when I began in March. The job might best have been borne by someone who had survived solitary confinement—someone with the ability to, say, mentally re-enact long journeys or make chess moves on an imaginary board.

Otherwise the only recourse for the imagination, and a feeble one at that, was the making of 'homers'. This was a word I would not learn until years later, when I read Miklós Haraszti's *A Worker in a Worker's State* (1977); it refers to strictly personal items that are turned out at work using the equipment provided. Haraszti and his colleagues in 1960s Hungary, operating lathes and milling machines, made for their own purposes

> key-holders, bases for flower-pots, ashtrays, pencil boxes, rulers and set squares...counters in stainless steel to teach simple arithmetic to children...pendants made from broken milling teeth,

> wheels for roulette-type games, dice, magnetized soap-holders, television aerials...locks and bolts, coat-holders...knives, daggers, knuckle-dusters...

The Hungarian machinists were on piece-rate, meaning that they voluntarily lost money in order to work on their crafts. At the plastics factory, where we were paid a set wage but were not in control of our time, we had rather more limited resources. All that we could make were useless items from scrap. For example, using as a base an unidentified transparent cylinder that might have been part of a pill box, you could pile up widening rings of bullet-shaped tree elements, also in clear plastic, sticking them on when they were still hot from the mould, ending up with a conical whatsit you could pretend recalled a crystal chandelier. It occupied the mind, gave you something to take home and perhaps present to a slightly embarrassed loved one, and offered a tiny score against the bosses, whom you were depriving of a few pennies' worth of raw material.

My high school was the low-slung 1950s suburban type rather than the inner-city red-brick fortress model; still, like all American high schools, it resembled a factory. Immediately to the right as you came in was the office of the guidance counsellors, which prominently featured a rack of yellow-covered booklets issued by the state of New Jersey, offering instruction to prospective air-conditioning mechanics, beauticians, cashiers and correction officers in how to achieve their career goals. On the single occasion I can recall visiting that office, I noticed to my astonishment that one of these was entitled *Injection Moulding Machine Operator or Tender*. I was immediately impressed by the realism of the cover photograph, which clearly showed a catchment device under the door of the machine that had been fashioned from a ragged piece of cardboard, exactly in the style prevalent at my factory. After offering a brief history of plastic, the booklet went on, for ten pages, to worry the distinction between an 'operator' and a 'tender', cite the physical requirements for the work ('Operators must have the use of both hands and arms... They should have the temperament to perform repetitive work...'), discuss employment opportunities ('positions will become available as some workers retire, advance through promotions, or leave for personal reasons'), and speculate on the future of the industry ('the future of plastics manufacturing is very bright'). I tried to imagine a student, shopping around for a way to live after being released from school, picking the booklet out of all the ones on offer and deciding that this was the job for him. Nothing in the booklet was false, even in its implications, but it made as little sense as if an equivalent booklet had been entitled *Prison Inmate*.

And yet someone had to make toy sand-shovels for the world. What, in a just society, could ever induce someone to do that sort of work? Should all youths be conscripted to work in factories for a year? Should plastics-factory labour be reserved for the punishment of white-collar criminals? Finally I decided that salaries should be determined by a factor that averaged the arduousness, tediousness, futility and imbecility of a job. The richest people in the world then would be coal miners. Injection-moulding machine operators or tenders would fly to work in their own planes, and competition for such work would be stiff. Having had the experience, I would be quite content to be poor. □

GRANTA

IN THE MILK FACTORY

Joe Sacco

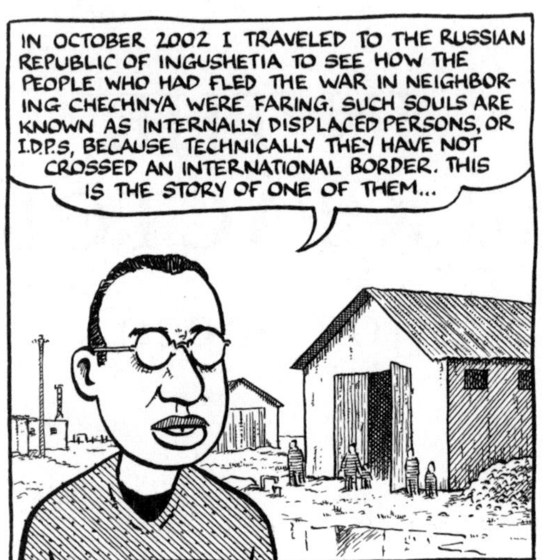
IN OCTOBER 2002 I TRAVELED TO THE RUSSIAN REPUBLIC OF INGUSHETIA TO SEE HOW THE PEOPLE WHO HAD FLED THE WAR IN NEIGHBORING CHECHNYA WERE FARING. SUCH SOULS ARE KNOWN AS INTERNALLY DISPLACED PERSONS, OR I.D.P.S, BECAUSE TECHNICALLY THEY HAVE NOT CROSSED AN INTERNATIONAL BORDER. THIS IS THE STORY OF ONE OF THEM...

IN THE MILK FACTORY
Zamani lives in a cowshed at the abandoned Nasir-Kort milk factory.
She isn't well.
She barely leaves her stuffy particle-board room, which is a bit more than six feet square and just over six feet high.
IF THE CHILDREN SUPPORT ME, I CAN GO OUT.
BUT USUALLY I GO JUST ON THE OTHER SIDE OF THE PARTITION.
On the other side of the partition is an unlit corridor that divides rows of similar box rooms made by I.D.P.'s from the same particle board or mud bricks.
Referring to the Russians, Zamani says...
SOME-TIMES THEY CUT THE ELEC-TRICITY.
SOME-TIMES THEY CUT THE GAS.
IF THEY CUT THE GAS, WE HAVE NOTHING ELSE TO HEAT THE ROOM.
FOR-TUNATELY, WE HAVE CANDLES.
Zamani has lived here for two months. Her husband died of natural causes in Chechnya. Zamani refused to flee to Ingushetia before the mourning period ended...
and then–
"–a rocket hit our house and my daughter was killed, and I was wounded in the head by shrapnel.
"Actually, my daughter wasn't killed immediately.
"Her spine was broken.
J. SACCO 10.04

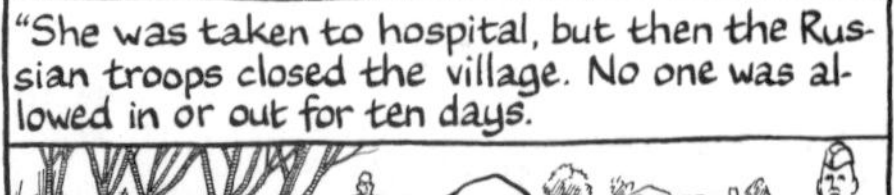
"She was taken to hospital, but then the Russian troops closed the village. No one was allowed in or out for ten days.

"On the 11th day I was able to visit her.
"I told the doctor I'd come again the next day, but after I left the hospital she died."

Her other daughter, Samani, traveled from her home in Nagrovsky, elsewhere in the Russian Federation, to bring Zamani here. Samani then collected her children and moved in with her mother.
Wait!
You left your home in Nagrovsky for a cow-shed?
I'M USED TO DIFFICULTIES, AND INCONVENIENCES DO NOT SCARE ME.

MY HUSBAND REMAINED BECAUSE HERE HE WOULDN'T BE ABLE TO FIND A JOB.
AND HE DIDN'T WANT TO GET INVOLVED IN ALL THIS WAR STUFF.
She says she's happier here among her own people where her children can be raised with Chechen values.

"I don't like the behavior of the young boys and girls in Russia. They smoke, they drink, they could kiss, and this doesn't coincide with Chechen traditions and culture."
J. SACCO 10-04

But there was something else...
SINCE THE WAR BEGAN THE ATTITUDE OF THE RUSSIANS HAS CHANGED GREATLY TOWARD THE CHECHENS.
THE ATTITUDE HAS BECOME MORE AGGRESSIVE TOWARD THE SCHOOL CHILDREN.
OF COURSE THERE WERE GOOD PEOPLE THERE, TOO, BUT THE BAD ONES PREVAILED.
o now amani ves here ith her nother and four children.
They have two mattresses between them.
I BROUGHT NOTHING FROM HOME.
EVERYTHING WAS DESTROYED, BURNED.
IT WAS A BIG ROCKET.
BUT DID YOU AT LEAST BRING OUT A COAT?
I DIDN'T BRING A COAT.
I DON'T HAVE CLOTHES HERE.
ONLY WHAT PEOPLE GAVE ME... PEOPLE ALWAYS HELP EACH OTHER.
So what's the most important possession you own now?
I HAVE THIS STOVE, BUT IT DOESN'T BELONG TO ME. SOMEONE LENT IT.
But what about income, Zamani? Don't you have a pension?
I'M GETTING A PENSION, BUT I'M AFRAID TO TAKE IT.
Can't your daughter go to Chechnya to collect it for you?
I DON'T LET HER.
I'M SCARED FOR HER.
IF SOMETHING HAPPENS TO HER, WHAT WILL I DO WITH THE CHILDREN?
J. SACCO 10-04

* STALIN EXILED THE CHECHENS EN MASSE TO KAZAKHSTAN AND ELSEWHERE IN THE SOVIET UNION, WHERE TENS OF THOUSANDS DIED OF COLD AND HUNGER. THE CHECHENS WERE NOT ALLOWED TO RETURN HOME UNTIL 1957.

Zamani takes a plastic bag from the wall.
It's not there.
MY GRAND-CHILDREN HAVE HID-DEN IT AGAIN.
But why do you hide it?
BE-CAUSE WHEN SHE SEES IT, SHE CRIES.
Zamani sends her granddaughter to fetch the photo.
A minute later, here it is.
Just a photo.
A mother standing with her two daugh-ters.
SACCO 10.04
We leave Zamani with her daughters and make our way out of the cowshed.

GRANTA

FANCY LAMPS

Neil Steinberg

From the street, the factory housing the Frederick Cooper Lamp Company is not as ugly as most. The building was originally a ladies undergarment plant, built around 1900; it has a courtyard and windows, luxuries that would later be dispensed with in most factories. The four-storey brick building, with a square tower double that height, is a reminder that a factory was once the centrepiece of a neighbourhood, second only to the local church. The tower, like a steeple, catches the eye; it advertises the product with a sign informing the 260,000 cars that pass every day along the Kennedy Expressway leading out of Chicago that Cooper produces LAMPS OF ELEGANCE.

'Elegance' can be taken as an euphemism for 'costliness' and Cooper lamps are indeed expensive. The lamps are made of brass and copper, maple and marble, bronze and china, silverplate and gold leaf. No one has any idea how many different styles they make and the number keeps changing. The cheapest costs $200, and from there prices soar into the thousands for crystal chandeliers.

None of the luxury of Cooper's product extends to the factory itself. The entrance is through a single flight of narrow stairs leading to a small, not particularly clean, reception area. This was last decorated, from the look of it, in the early 1970s: pea green carpeting, and fake wood-panelled walls. A few well-tended plants, a carved eagle and some handmade sparkly butterflies on the bulletin board save the room from dreariness.

The public face of Cooper Lamp is more attractive: Suzanne Lauren, an energetic woman whose dangly bracelets bear an uncanny resemblance to decorative elements of certain Cooper lamps. She has worked at Cooper for twenty-three years and is now the vice president of design. She is accompanied by her dog, Cooper, a German shepherd that has the run of the front office, a room as cluttered as the reception area is bare. One wall is given over to manila folders; the desks are piled high with catalogues and promotional materials; lamps in various stages of assembly crouch in the corner as if they have wandered off the factory floor.

A lamp is divided into four parts. First is the shade—a screen of paper or cloth that softens the harshness of a bare bulb. Second is the electrical socket that receives the light bulb. Third, holding the socket aloft, is the base which is often decorative. Anything can be used for a lamp base—bowling balls, football helmets, toy trains—

KURT ESLICK

but given Cooper's high-end market, the bases tend to be brass urns, china vases as well as an eclectic range of objects that seem designed to appeal to wealthy widows: brass elephants, bronze bulldogs, Chinese horses, verdigris dancing frogs, copper Nepalese horns, metal palm trees. Floor lamps tend to be more uniform because of their larger size, their bases simple brass poles or turned wooden posts.

Under the base is the part that most non-lamp people never consider: the mounting. This is a little circle of wood or stone or, in less expensive lamps, plastic, that acts as a buffer between base and table top. The mounting is like a pedestal for a statue. Without it, a lamp looks unfinished, like an urn with a lampshade on top.

In practice a lamp has many more pieces than just these four main components; each part consists of many more parts. A mounting might be three circles of wood, each a bit smaller than the one below. A base might be an urn that is assembled out of a dozen various rings and handles and curving sections. An electrical socket includes a cord threaded through a metal channel and a plug and a harp (the loop of brass that holds the shade). A shade can be a complex confection of cloth, metal, cardboard, or even a decorative fringe consisting of one hundred inch-long threads, each one holding a colourful glass bead.

This multitude of parts—wooden feet, stone discs, copper tubes, glass beads, porcelain dogs, brass finials, tin pineapples—dictates the set-up of the 240,000 square foot Cooper factory. Most of the plant is given over to rows of shelves and bins and tables to hold the thousands of dusty parts. The pieces are stored where they are made since the Cooper plant consists of a series of shops. This makes the factory unusual in this age. The typical modern factory either *makes* something—forging steel rods, moulding rubber tires, dipping chrome plating; or it *assembles* something—putting together bicycles. But Cooper does both, out of necessity.

'All the small businesses in the Chicago area stopped—wood carving, plating, metal forming and casting,' says Frederick Gershanov, who owns Cooper Lamp with his older brother Peter. 'So all those operations we took into our company.'

Cooper has an enormous woodshop where rough planks of maple are turned into lamp bases. While there are numerous electric tools—planers and sanders and band saws and radial saws—there are also plenty of hand tools, some with wooden handles: chisels and augers and mallets. A plywood board displays cutting-wheel bits at the ready. They are objects of surprising beauty, resembling little steel suns and crosses and starfish.

Bedpost-shaped lamp bases are common and the lathe work for such bases is done here. The really time-consuming part is not turning the wood but setting the cutting knives on the lathe to produce a particular pattern of curves and bulges and ripples. So, rather than keep changing the settings on the lathe bits, the knives are kept in place and locked into the machines when needed. Dozens of the pointy, yard-long assemblages are stored leaning upright on a rack, in a kind of library; an example of the post each set of lathes produces is placed in front of the knives that produce it.

This is a very old fashioned way of doing things—no bar codes, no computerized imaging of the lamp bases, just the objects themselves guiding workers to the lathe set-ups they need. This is typical of the overall Cooper system; a person new to Cooper would have no way of locating a particular bolt of leopard-print cloth for a particular lampshade. There is no general system tracking where things are, other than the memories of the workers, several of whom have been here for almost forty years.

The average vista that presents itself, as you walk through Cooper Lamp, is completely inert—lifeless rows of parts, on shelves, or in large, square, heavily scarred wooden bins on iron wheels. 'I saw one at an antique store, selling for a thousand dollars,' Lauren says.

The factory is surprisingly quiet and dim; lights are kept low to save money. Occasionally you will hear the whine of a saw, or the low murmur of Mexican or Polish or Korean music a certain worker is listening to on an ethnic radio station. Cooper has 150 employees. Workers are usually by themselves when you encounter them: you typically meet an older person, sitting on a stool at a workbench, in a small pool of light, bringing a hand tool to bear upon one of the dozen or so lamps spread out before them, all in a uniform degree of partial completeness. There are no conveyor belts, no quotas. Nobody seems in a hurry.

'You can't use anything sharp because it will scour the pieces,' Richard Beitler explains. He is standing at a table and using steel wool to burnish fifteen swan-handled urns, each of which has been assembled from seventeen different pieces. 'You rub on it, rub on it, it's glossy and you want it matte, you change the direction from a buffing motion to a rubbing sideways in the opposite direction. See how it flattens the colour out? How it dulls it?'

He wears cotton gloves—once white, now deep black except for the cuffs. He is working his way through a batch of a hundred of these urns. He says that buffing each urn should take about twenty minutes if you do it properly.

'That's if you're God,' he says. 'I can do it in fifteen.'

Beitler has worked here for ten years, and says you can tell at once when a lamp has been rubbed by hand. Machined lamps, Beitler says, are 'very uniform, very glossy. When you do a hand finish, it looks like its been sitting around. It has a warmth to it, a nice texture, tone, patina. The bronze hand finish looks great. You can't do it on a machine. It has a very nice antique look. It's very beautiful.'

Cooper Lamp should not be here. Cooper should have vanished in the great death of American manufacturing that gathered steam in the last half of the twentieth century and has accelerated in recent years. The United States has lost almost twenty per cent of its manufacturing jobs just since 2000. This was the year that Cooper's biggest local competitor, Stiffel Lamps, collapsed under debt, selling off its assets—which included a headquarters building that dated back to 1871—and tossing hundreds of people out of work. Cooper Lamp should have been torn down to make way for the expensive town houses going up all over Chicago's North Side. These are occupied by professionals who then begin to complain about the noises and smells of whatever industry remains around them. The Stiffel factory, which once turned out 250,000 brass lamps a year, now holds loft condominiums.

The choice seems to be either perish, like Stiffel, or move overseas where labour costs are a fraction of what they are in the United States. Anyone vaguely familiar with Chicago business can reel off a list of the departed. Just last summer, the red wagons of Radio Flyer, made in Chicago for ninety years, relocated to China. Brach's Candy, produced in an enormous West Side plant, moved down to Mexico to dodge high American sugar tariffs. A thousand workers lost their jobs.

Stiffel's collapse was blamed on the company's failure to flee to China. Cooper survives by one of several strategies that—at least so far—have thwarted the competitive advantage of manufacturers in the Far East. The saving fact is this: really expensive lamps are a niche market, with a tiny demand compared to the overwhelming global hunger for cheap lamps. When the Chinese build lamp factories, they want to make lamps that can be sold by the hundreds of thousands, for $20 apiece at Wal-Mart, not lamps that cost $500, of which Saks Fifth Avenue can maybe sell a hundred over the course of a year.

'We offer a very high quality product,' says Lauren. 'Our shades are hand sewn, using unique fabrics. We use unique materials. We put things together in a unique fashion and as a result we have a very good name among the designers and decorators, and the stores. We sell to very high-end stores, some of the best department stores: Macy's, Marshall Field's, Bloomingdale's, Neiman Marcus, Horchow.'

Laboriously constructed, high-end goods are one way for American companies to survive, at the moment. Another is to embrace technologies that trump the benefits of cheap labour. A Chinese worker might earn $6,000 a year. But a Kawasaki industrial welding robot doesn't earn any salary at all.

Set amidst black hillsides of slag, the Ford Assembly Plant, on the South Side of Chicago, is a shapeless, windowless expanse of white concrete buildings and bay doors. The pipes and steel metalwork which cover the building give way to brick at the entrance which is flanked by the models of new cars currently being put together inside. Though Fords have been made on this spot since 1924—the plant originally made Model Ts—the factory has been completely rebuilt thirteen times. A few traces of the original structure remain—a brick wall, part of a roof, and an entranceway.

A large blue sign set on an easel greets visitors. Today it declares 003 DAYS WITHOUT A LOST TIME ACCIDENT, which is rather like someone bragging that he has not taken a drink since lunch.

Visitors are ushered into a bright, clean conference room containing a horseshoe laminate table and no fewer than eighteen managers, representing the various aspects of the huge 2.8 million square foot plant. There is a Quality Control Manager and a Material Planning and Logistics Manager, a Human Resources

Manager, an Off-Shift Manager and even one whose title is Lean Operations Manager. They are enthusiastic, their language peppered with code phrases and production mantras. The engineers, in particular, speak in a language that the layman can barely grasp.

'Right now we're going through surface transfer for '08,' says head engineer Ken Couey. 'We're always driving toward the CAD nominal—this fixture is an exactly moulded fixture of the CAD nominal data.' CAD stands for 'computer-aided drawing'. Couey is talking about the idealized computer image of a perfect car that is the blueprint the actual automobiles are constructed from. An automobile consists of roughly 10,000 individual parts—tyres, bolts, axles, panels, cams, knobs, pistons, seals, hinges, shafts, wires, gauges. By the time they arrive at Ford Assembly, some have already been put together leaving only 2,400 components: an instrument panel, for instance, which is the entire dashboard of a car, arrives in one piece, gauges and buttons and all, ready to be installed.

The Ford plant is like an aeroplane hangar—high ceilings criss-crossed with white steel trusses. It is never particularly loud, and occasionally a bank of exquisite, new-car smell wafts delightfully by. The entire factory radiates control and order—clean, well lit, floors freshly painted. Everything is methodical, even to the smallest detail: the fire extinguishers at the clearly marked fire stations are not only sealed in protective plastic bags, but those bags are emblazoned, FORD FIRE EXTINGUISHER.

The easiest way to understand the intricate process that gathers these thousands of parts and binds them up into a car (at the rate of a new finished automobile every 64.8 minutes) is to break the process down into two central tasks.

The first task is the actual assemblage. Henry Ford is famous for creating the assembly line, an innovation he pioneered in the years before the First World War, but the line today has nothing so crude as a conveyor belt. Rather, it is a complicated, snaking track of individual, computer-monitored racks that hold the growing cars and move them through the factory. Like Cooper, Ford Assembly can seem oddly empty at times, with no workers in sight, only lines of unpainted cars, their sides shiny naked metal, inching slowly along. At times the line even doubles back and arches above itself. The cars then hang on harnesses instead of rolling, as if on parade across the ceiling.

The workers, when you can see them, are small figures standing in the heart of the machinery. There are 2,000 workers at Ford Assembly. They are divided into task teams of between five to ten people, depending on what they are doing. They dress casually and chat among themselves, handling electric wrenches that hang on tubes from the ceiling, or lifting door sections using robot-assisted suction devices. They are members of the United Auto Workers Local 551, but they work harmoniously alongside non-union labour—four hundred Kawasaki industrial robots, used primarily for welding. Each six-foot-high robot moves back and forth on a rubberized track resembling half a tank tread.

There is an almost poetic grace to the various swoops and gestures of the robots. A half finished section of car slides in, and a frame moves in and locks it in place. Then four robots, one at each corner, roll forwards and start to weld, throwing out sprays of sparks—molten metal—each time the pinchers close with 1,200 pounds of pressure, to make the weld. Ford, which likes to keep track of such things, says there are 2,700 welds in an average car.

To visualize how the robots move, take your hand and make a variety of gestures—a fist, a flattened palm, a peace symbol—as quickly as you can while twisting and turning your wrist abruptly. In that way, the robots rush and pause, rush and pause, with something of the grace of a hand, something of the clumsiness of a dinosaur, and perhaps a little dinosaurian menace, particularly since they do their work behind cages, as if they might break free. The cages are to keep workers from walking too close to the scope of the robots, which could crush them just as effectively as movie robots, although without the malice.

After each task is done, while the freshly welded car section moves away and a new one takes its place, the robots draw back and settle into a kind of repose, their welding beaks tucked under their bodies, as if resting after their exertions. What is actually happening is that since impurities build up on the circular copper welding contacts, the robots are cleaned automatically after every welding.

The robots are not blind, but use lasers to look at what they're doing. The pieces they are assembling are not all the same—there is, for instance, a half millimetre variance in the metal door panels, and those half millimetres can add up, so the robots need to adjust. At one station, car roofs are being lowered into body assemblies and welded. The robots first position the roof for the best fit, so that it is as perfectly centred as it can be, then burn it into place.

Sometimes different types of car go through the line at the same time. The body of the new Ford Five Hundred can slide into place, be attended to by the welding robots, and then be followed by a Freestyle—a different sized body that requires its own unique pattern of welds. The Ford engineers are immensely proud of this. Until very recently, an assembly line would have to shut down for weeks or months to re-tool for a new line of cars. This is a revolution. Like the stockpiled lathe set-ups at Cooper, the changing production line at Ford is a reminder that one way factories stay in business is by minimizing the time they spend preparing to make things.

In the process of welding a roof, the only time humans intervene is to remove the roof section from the rack of incoming parts and place it into a frame where the robot can pick it up. The arrival of that roof section—a square piece of metal set on a rack—demonstrates the second great task at Ford assembly: getting the right part to the right place at the right time.

This is more difficult than it sounds; the delivery of parts is almost as complex a challenge as the construction of the cars themselves. A chance discovery in the dusty stock pilings at Cooper can lead, fairly quickly, to the designing of a new product: a bin of old, wooden perfume-bottle stoppers can inspire the creation of a lamp with a bamboo-like base made of stacks of those stoppers. Nothing can be haphazard at Ford. Parts arrive continually. They have to, since Ford tries to have only enough inventory to keep the plant operating for three hours.

The three-hour turnaround is an incredible feat. It means, when the morning shift arrives for work, the parts they'll be installing after lunch are just arriving at the plant, and those they'll need by quitting time are still on the trucks, heading to the plant. Ford does this because it costs money to hold inventory, and reducing the time a part is in Ford's possession to the barest minimum serves to narrow the gap between when a part is paid for, and when it goes out into the world and earns its keep as a car, helping draw to Ford the $7,000 average profit it makes on every vehicle it sells.

The consequences of such a quick turnaround time is increased risk: if one of those 2,500 parts is missing, production stops—cars are assembled in a fixed order, from the frame up, and a single absent or defective component can bring the $1 billion plant to a halt. Most of the factory floor space is taken up not with the production line, but with one vast loading dock, with forklift trucks hurrying, say, racks of bumpers to where they are needed. Floors are painted with yellow lane markers, and there are stop signs and street lights. Pallets are high with colour-coded bins—bright purples and greens and reds—and computers keep track of where every part is at all times, even as they journey to the plant.

The parts don't have far to travel. It would be impossible to keep to the three-hour inventory rule, if they did. Sixty per cent of the parts are made in what Ford calls 'the Chicago Manufacturing Campus', a dozen suppliers, employing another 1,400 people, encamped around the assembly plant—companies with far-less famous names such as Facil LLC, Flex-N-Gate, Plastech Engineered Products Inc., and Summit Polymers. Ford estimates that, by having the suppliers right there, half a mile from the assembly plant, they save fifty dollars in shipping costs on each new car built.

Even the transit of the arriving parts from the loading bays to the assembly line was given careful study. 'We used Euclidian drawings to show exactly how far it takes to get material from one area to the next,' said Couey.

The average car-buyer never contemplates the challenge of getting properly machined front left-side doors to the Ford assembly line, just as few lamp buyers think about the hidden achievement of Cooper Lamp which isn't the burnishing and working of the materials that go into their products but the less romantic challenge of getting the finished lamps to their destinations. 'One of those things you never think about is how important the packing is,' said Lauren. 'If it can't get there in good shape…'

If a lamp isn't packed properly—and sometimes even if it is—it will break en route, and the customer will send it back. Floor lamps are particularly problematic, because they are long and less robust and customers have a tendency to half unpack them and then tug, hard, throwing them permanently out of alignment. Every floor lamp leaves Cooper with a bright, yellow sticker on the box reading, DO

NOT PULL ON ANY PART OF THIS LAMP TO REMOVE IT FROM BOX. It doesn't always help.

Just as welding robots have revolutionized car assembly, technology has come to the aid of packing lamps. Thirty-nine years ago, when head packer Ruby joined Cooper, the lamps were packed in excelsior, a material which she describes as something that 'looked a little like hay but it wasn't hay'. Then came Styrofoam popcorn, a substance that no one remembers fondly, due to its genius for spilling and getting everywhere. '*Everywhere*,' says Lauren. 'We tried *everything*. Oh boy did we hate those—I don't know who hated those more, us or our customers.'

Now the packing material is contained within rolls of grey plastic bags that are filled with a beige polyurethane liquid—actually two liquids, shot from a pair of fifty-five-gallon drums, that, upon interacting with each other, undergo a chemical reaction and begin rising, like warm bread. Once filled, a bag is tossed inside its box, then a lamp is set on top of the bag as it slowly puffs upwards, and another bag is filled and set upon that. The foaming bags fit themselves perfectly to the contours of the lamp, protecting it from the rigours of shipping to—in this case—the Akane Lighting Company in Kawaguchi City, Japan.

There is one baroque, horror movie aspect to the rising foam packaging. Its uncontrolled growth would normally split apart the cardboard carton. To prevent this from happening, each freshly filled and sealed box is briefly slid into its own custom-made plywood vice—they look like little coffins—which keeps the cardboard carton intact in the thirty or so seconds it takes for the expanding to stop.

The Ford and Cooper plants are identical in one respect—both pause production for ten minutes, twice a day, at nine a.m. and at two p.m., although at Ford these respites are called 'daily shutdowns for relief for our employees' and at Cooper they are referred to with less ceremony as 'breaks'.

This is a reminder that, for all the focus on the things that factories make, a factory is also a place where people live. A factory worker spends almost as much time at his or her station as in bed. For all the impact that each individual new lamp or new car may have on its owner's life, the effect is dwarfed by the impact that the making of thousands of new lamps or the making of new cars has on a person.

Both factories stress the empowerment of their workers and the ability of their employees to exert control over their work and their lives. This is easier to see at Cooper Lamp than at the Ford factory. Cooper workers make their work areas into their own personal environments, posting pictures of grandchildren and home towns, stringing their work benches with Christmas lights or cheesecake calendars. Lauren introduces them one by one, talking about their various strengths, the innovations they suggested, the tools they helped develop—sometimes something as simple as a section of hacksaw blade that happens to be perfect for pushing the edge of a cloth lampshade neatly beneath its trim.

At Ford, the workers are kept ten or twenty yards away from visitors, and there is scant evidence of any kind of individuality. At Ford, culture comes from the top down just as the car components do. Some rules are for safety—no exposed jewellery allowed. Some are for cleanliness—no chewing gum. Others instill a sense of esprit d'corps and productivity. A series of triangular signs exhorts SAFETY and QUALITY and DELIVERY and similar lofty sentiments.

The workers at the Ford Assembly Plant are divided into 'Kaizen groups'—Kaizen being the overarching Japanese production philosophy which stresses teamwork, quality, cost-cutting and improvement. Detroit was caught napping by the Japanese car revolution of the 1980s, which left American products seeming woefully expensive and shoddy by comparison. American carmakers such as Ford leaped to adopt Japanese quality-control standards. 'Kaizen' is just one of the Japanese terms incongruously banded about in an afternoon at an auto plant on the South Side of Chicago.

For instance, there is a cord running the length of the assembly line, referred to by workers as the 'andon cord'. Any worker can pull it and stop the line, and the problem will be displayed on large display boards ringing the assembly line.

'Andon' is Japanese for 'paper lantern', and originated in the Toyota Production System, where workers are encouraged to take a personal role in making sure that mistakes either don't happen or are immediately corrected, a philosophy one Ford executive put as: 'Don't create it, don't take it and don't pass it along.'

With all deference to Ford and Japanese quality assurance, that is what Cooper employees—members of Professional, Technical, Office, Warehouse and Mail Order Employees Union, Local 743—have always done. Another challenge of lamp construction is to get it balanced so it can stand up straight. Picture a lamp that is constructed of wooden spools on a metal core—if the spools are not stacked with perfect precision, the core will be crooked and the lampshade will never hang properly. People spending $500 for a lamp return them and get their money back if the shade doesn't hang properly. So many things can go wrong in the found objects—the Cambodian silver cups and Thai dragons—used for lamp bases. The pre-drilled centre poles can be off and their bottoms might not be entirely flat, and the Cooper workers spend a lot of time laboriously correcting these flaws.

Cooper is proud of the initiative of its individual workers. When I ask Suzanne Lauren how Cooper Lamp keeps a step ahead of the Chinese, she doesn't talk about the niche of luxury lamps; like the Ford engineers, she speaks of innovation, and offers up their latest model of cord-free, low-light lamps being introduced under the 'Lightini' brand. 'We had a very good customer come in whose wife had just bought a series of antique bookcases, and spent the entire weekend on-line trying to find lamps because she didn't want to drill holes for lamp cords in them,' Lauren explains. 'So that's how this started.'

The lamps—small with fist-sized granite bases and brass shades—are powered by three C batteries and can run continuously for about a month, before needing to have the batteries replaced. 'We're working on a rechargeable one, that's in the pipeline as we speak,' she said.

Replacing batteries, or even recharging a lamp once a month seems a bother but Lauren points out that the true market for these lamps is not rich ladies with expensive bookshelves, but restaurants, where the new lamps would replace candles. Replacing a candle every night is a far greater inconvenience than changing a battery once a month. Cooper is just about to start attending the big restaurant shows, promoting the lamp not only for its convenience, but for its ability to save businesses money. Restaurants can significantly cut their insurance rates by replacing candles with the low light lamps, a fact of which most of them are unaware, Lauren said, 'until we tell them.'

Cooper Lamps was founded by Leo Gershanov, the father of the current owner. He was born in Russia, was drafted into the Tsar's army and captured by the Hungarians during the First World War. He jumped off a train in Slovakia, and worked his way, first to England and then the United States, where he started all sorts of businesses. He was selling eggnog when he saw in the *Chicago Sun* an advertisement to buy the studios of Frederick Cooper. Cooper had been an artist and sculptor whose work, popular in the 1920s, was often incorporated into lamps. When Gershanov responded to the ad, he met another man also interested in the studios, Benjamin Markle, and rather than bid against each other, they bought the studio together and went into business.

It was a good time to start making decorative lamps.

Frederick Gershanov explained that after the Second World War there was a huge demand for lamps. The copper needed for the electrical cords and sockets had been in very short supply. 'So there was a huge pent-up demand, because of the new housing, and they turned some of the statuary they were making into lamps.' What we think of as garish, late 1940s lamps—your basic hula girl statuette lamp—are the result of desperate lamp makers turning whatever decorative objects they could find into lamps.

In recent years, however, it is all Cooper can do to stay afloat. The loss of American manufacturing jobs is not merely a story of cheap foreign wages. Soaring real estate prices are part of the problem, too. One by one, the children of the founders of vast suburban furniture stores realized that they could make more money selling the land under their stores than they made selling furniture.

'High-end stores that were our best customers, these high-end stores had lots of land in the suburbs, or in the downtown area,' Gershanov said. 'Their founders retired or their kids said, "Hey, I can sell this land and make as much money as working seven days a week."'

Fewer fancy furniture stores mean fewer fancy lamps.

'There are just a certain number of tables in furniture stores that can take lamps,' said Lauren. 'Competitive is an understatement.'

The greatest harm low price imports cause to a place such as Cooper Lamp is not the fact that they encourage people to buy cheap lamps. It's that, as the years go by, cheap lamps are the only lamps they know, and the whole idea of a well-made lamp begins to seem lamp, designed by Raymond Waites) and might have decided to pay the freight costs, never stops to look at it because they've already bought their lamps at Target.

'Everybody's got lamps now,' said Gershanov. 'Drug stores sell lamps. So it's a very difficult environment.'

We have come to accept low quality goods, if they're cheap enough, as standard, and this drives up the price of high quality goods even further. There was time when a humble office worker would visit a tailor and buy a suit; now handmade suits are a luxury of the wealthy. The average person can't conceive of paying $500 for a lamp in any circumstances. Even Cooper has found that there aren't enough well-to-do people to justify trying to sell its most labour-intensive products, such as lamps with intricate inlaid wood designs. 'We used to do beautiful, beautiful, beautiful marquetry, but unfortunately there's no market for it,' said Lauren. 'It's gone. Very minimal demand.'

Once a product requiring a highly specialized skill is phased out, it is almost impossible to bring it back, even if the demand for it were to resurface. Professions vanish. Cooper won't be able to sell inlaid lamps again because they won't be able to find anyone with the skills to make them. To the owners of Cooper Lamp, it can seem, on bad days, that no matter how hard they work, it is only a question of time before their factory goes the way of Dad's Root Beer across the street: yet another manufacturing shell to be turned into lofts for young professionals.

'There's no market for our goods,' said Gershanov, in a gravelly tone. 'There's no market...' and here his voice trailed off to a whisper, 'for our goods'. □

On February 9 2005, just as this issue of Granta *went to press, the Frederick Cooper Lamp Company announced it was to close on June 30. There are reports that a buyer has already been found for the building and intends to convert the factory into lofts. Fred Gershanov told the* Chicago Sun-Times*: 'I hope it gets the best possible use. It's a beautiful building.'*

GRANTA

LISTER'S MILL

Liz Jobey

TIMSMITHPHOTOS.COM

Lister's Manningham Mills

Lister's Mill

The third week of November last year brought the first cold snap of the season. Across the North of England people woke to a white frost, followed by bright sunshine and clear blue skies. In Bradford, in north-west Yorkshire, where the overnight temperatures had dropped to minus five, Mario Buitrago, a Colombian man who was sleeping out on the street, found his sleeping bag covered in a layer of ice. Inside it he was wearing several layers of warm clothing and his head rested on a smart backpack which looked as if it might contain a vacuum flask and a couple of days' worth of food. Mr Buitrago was not homeless—he lives, in fact, in Hayes, in Middlesex—nor was he unemployed. In the spirit of those steadfast ladies who camp out in Knightsbridge to be sure of a bargain on the first day of Harrods' sale, he was determined to be first in the queue to buy something expected to be in short supply: in this case, an apartment in a newly converted Victorian textile mill, formerly called Manningham Mills, at the heart of the Bradford district of the same name. What Mr Buitrago was sleeping outside had once been the greatest textile mill in Yorkshire and the largest silk mill in the world, which at its peak employed 11,000 people. Its new developers have renamed it 'Lister Mills', after Samuel Cunliffe Lister, the textile magnate who built it.

Whether these historical details had interested Mario Buitrago, I don't know. When I first heard of him, I assumed that, like a whole generation of young homebuyers in Britain, he was attracted by the idea of 'loft-style' living, that combination of old industrial exterior and sparkling modern interior, open-plan, that has swept through almost every city in Europe and North America that once made things and now no longer does. It began when artists and bohemians started to take over the abandoned warehouses of downtown Manhattan forty years ago and is now the popular regenerative solution for inner city planners and a profitable enterprise for property developers: so popular and profitable, in fact, that construction companies have become adept at building new 'loft-style' buildings that ape the architecture of the old. To anyone over a certain age, who grew up in the era when a three-bedroom semi with a garage and garden represented an ideal home (and a factory was a factory), this can come as a surprise. But ideas of the ideal have changed. What does living in a loft offer its inhabitants? Perhaps it gives the illusion, if not the reality, that the owner is a dynamic, creative, modern and urban individual with an intellectual and aesthetic appreciation of the past.

When I was growing up in South Yorkshire in the 1960s, driving north towards the Yorkshire Dales took you up and down a series of steep river valleys, into mill towns such as Halifax and Keighley, Bingley and Shipley, where the mills were still working and you could read the names of the firms written vertically on the chimneys. This was wool country—it made woollen goods for the world—with factories that owed their riverside position to the facts that the earliest of them had once been driven by water-power and that abundant water was still integral to their processes even when steam engines replaced the wheels that drew their energy from the river. Driving the same route now, most of the mills have disappeared, either demolished or turned into warehouses or garages or furniture marts—or, like the enormous Dean Clough in Halifax, the former home of Crossley's carpets, into a mixture of offices, shops and apartments.

But Bradford is different. In Bradford there are still mills that stand empty. The city has defied many plans for its regeneration and its centre is a dispiriting mess: the familiar evidence of modernity gone wrong—a newish but scruffy shopping 'precinct', new roads driven through the old centre, pedestrian underpasses and walkways, a conglomeration set down as if to prove the words of J. B. Priestley, who was born there, that Bradford was 'a good place for discouragement'. One of its problems is size. In the nineteenth century Bradford was the British capital of wool spinning and weaving—Worstedopolis was one of its Victorian nicknames—with a trading exchange that set the world price for wool. It had hundreds of mills employing many thousands of workers, a one-industry town whose population had jumped from 13,000 in 1801 to more than 100,000 by 1851. Even in the second half of the twentieth century it still turned out great quantities of clothes, fabrics and carpets. And then the trade shrank, slowly and sneakily; and then it abruptly stopped. By the 1990s, a working mill in Bradford was a rare sight. Non-working mills, on the other hand, were plentiful. Their weaving sheds and chimneys still stood there, as if their uselessness was only temporary (as it had been in the depressed 1930s), but the textile trade had quit Bradford for good.

Lister's mill, which stands on a hill above the city, is the trade's greatest and most visible memorial. As Manningham Mills, it once covered twenty-seven acres in two manufacturing divisions: the north mill was a series of unspectacular single-storey sheds with north lights, the south mill altogether different. *The Times* once described it as being 'as breathtaking as Versailles' and now, as the first part of the mill to be renovated, the south façade is indeed breathtaking in its perfect symmetry. It stretches for almost a quarter of a mile and, when the sun is out, its yellowy-brown stone glows golden in the light. Built in an Italianate style, long rows of high rectangular windows mark each of its five storeys, decorated only by neat stone arches along the topmost row and a band of decorative stonework above them. At the north-west corner stands the pièce de résistance: the chimney, the tallest chimney in Bradford, rising 255 feet as it tapers upwards to two elaborate cornices, which project outwards to the final perimeter twenty-four-feet square. The Bradford legend is that Samuel Cunliffe Lister carried a bottle of champagne up there when the chimney was finished in 1873 and christened it 'Lister's Pride'. Bradford people also say that 'you could drive a horse and cart around the top', though they admit that such an event is unlikely.

This chimney on the hill is Bradford's most famous landmark and can be seen for miles around. It and the south mill below survive because in the early 1970s, when the mill was still working, the government listed it as a building of architectural and historic interest (category Grade II*) which meant it couldn't easily be knocked down. The question became: what to do with it? Bradford did not then think of its industrial past as something that might be celebrated or aestheticized; it was too close for that, the day before yesterday, and the social and economic problems that textile manufacturing's near disappearance brought in its wake were all too evident. Bradford saw its goal as modernity: it needed to find new reasons and new ways for a city of nearly half a million people to exist and to flourish. Old mill chimneys were an obstacle to the image, and Lister's rarely appeared on Bradford's abundant supply of promotional leaflets. It was almost as though the city were ashamed of what it had so recently been. And yet, with Lister's, there was very little to be ashamed of.

This is how the Versailles of Bradford came to be. Samuel Cunliffe Lister was born in 1815, the fourth son of Ellis Cunliffe Lister, one of Bradford's first Whig MPs, who already owned spinning mills in the area. Samuel had been expected by family tradition to go into the church, but instead, while still in his teens, he became a commercial traveller for his father's firm, selling shawls in America. In 1841 he took charge of one of his father's mills near the family home in Manningham Park. He was an inventor as well as a businessman. By the end of his life he had taken out 150 patents—'more than any man in England' according to his hagiography—including a refinement of the wool-combing machine which had been devised by Edmund Cartwright (famously, the inventor of the power loom). Combing was the last of the wool processes to be mechanized. When Lister patented his machine in 1845, there were 10,000 hand-combers in Bradford. Less than a decade later, hand combing had more or less vanished.

Manningham, like most of Bradford's mills, was given over to producing worsted, the fine, soft yarn that took its name from the Norfolk village that once wove it. Then in 1857, on a visit to a London textile warehouse, Lister noticed piles of unpromising looking material which he was told was silk waste. He bought the lot for a halfpenny a pound, had it brought to Manningham, and spent several years and £360,000 devising a sequence of processes which turned the waste into fine silk thread. In 1867 he bought the patent to a Spanish velvet-loom process and worked in partnership with a Spanish weaver, José Reixach, to perfect it. In 1870, the original Manningham mill burned to the ground, taking Lister's experimental models with it, but he had retained the drawings for the velvet loom. In less than three years he had replaced the old mill with the present building, fitted out with looms for silk, velvet and plush fabrics, and said to be the largest factory in the world. The profits from it made Lister a multimillionaire and a local philanthropist (though in this respect he was not in the same league as his rival, Sir Titus Salt, who built an entire model village for his workers around his textile mills at nearby Saltaire). Lister sold the family house, Manningham Park, cheaply to Bradford Council on the understanding that it be turned into a public park (it was, and his statue still stands in a corner of it). Later he funded the building of a public art gallery on the site of his old family house and named it Cartwright Hall, after the man whose invention had done so much to make him, and many others, wealthy. In 1892 he was given a peerage and took the title Lord Masham. In 1904, opening Cartwright Hall, he said something prescient that was taken as a joke. As the reporter in the local journal has it: '"I have a very strong impression...that the East will overcome the West in the coming years, and that instead of our clothing the East, they will want to clothe us." (laughter).' The idea was an absurdity in Edwardian England. A month later the Prince and Princess of Wales, later to be King George V and Queen Mary, opened a trade exhibition in Lister Park and afterwards visited Manningham Mills. In 1910 a thousand yards of Lister's velvet was ordered to decorate Westminster Abbey at George V's coronation.

As for his workers, he was by most accounts respected by them, though he was far from a soft touch. In 1890, after new tariffs were introduced by the United States, the velvet workers at Lister's were told to expect a cut in their wages of up to twenty-five per cent. The velvet workers did not have a trade union. They called for support from the Weavers Association, but Lister and his directors refused to budge and on December 17 a strike began at Manningham which lasted for nineteen weeks. At first only the velvet workers came out, but by March the dyers and spinners had joined them and almost 5,000 workers were on strike. There were violent confrontations between strikers and the police, but the strike was defeated and the production of velvet resumed. This had a large, lasting and unexpected consequence, because, by drawing attention to the lack of union organization inside the Yorkshire textile industry, it helped cause the formation of a political party to represent the interests of the working classes. The Independent Labour Party, later the Labour Party, was founded in 1893 and one of its first branches was in Bradford.

Lister seems to have retained, or at least regained, some of the affection of his workforce by the time of his death in 1906 aged ninety-one. His mill workers took an unpaid day's holiday and thousands travelled to his funeral which was held at Addingham Church, about thirty miles south of his country estate, Swinton Castle, near Masham in Wensleydale. The *Bradford Observer*'s correspondent gave a fine description of the arrangements. Church bells tolled all day in Bradford, and the flags on public buildings were at half mast. Special trains were laid on from Bradford to bring those who could afford the fare, but many workers walked from Bradford to Addingham, about fifteen miles over the moors in cold February weather, and back again.

Of course, Lister had been right about competition from the East. Foreign manufacturers undercut British prices, and as fashion fabrics diversified, Bradford's large, inflexible old mills found it hard to keep up. But Lister's survived the interwar depression by developing new yarns and new kinds of cloth. It expanded the production of hand knitting wools, and developed all kinds of mohair and velvet plush and moquette, which brought in orders from bus, tram and train companies who wanted these cloths for their passengers' seats. The boom in cinemas brought in more orders for seat coverings, this time in crushed velvet. The Second World War kept the mills running at full capacity. Then, in the 1950s, Lister's began to lose out to smaller and more enterprising mills such as Aked's, a local firm which had been taken over by two London businessmen, Eugene Kornberg and John Segal, who were successfully weaving a mixture of worsted and man-made fibres, particularly Terylene. In the next two decades Terylene/worsted would become the staple suiting cloth of high street stores, and pure wool worsted would, like silk and velvet, become a luxury cloth. Kornberg and Segal took over Lister's, but by the mid-1970s it was clear that its grand days were over. The workforce shrunk to fewer than two thousand. The mill stuttered on, amid various schemes to turn its southern portion into flats, small-business premises, and a northern outpost of the Victoria & Albert Museum (the idea was that it should house the London museum's South Asian textile collection). The schemes came to nothing and Lister's continued to lose money. In 1997 the receivers were brought in.

The mill now stood empty and increasingly derelict: the lead from the roof, the copper from the boilerhouse, and hundreds of thousands of square feet of York stone flooring all disappeared. In 2000, Tom Bloxham, a property developer, met one of the receivers at a party. He asked Bloxham if he wanted to buy a mill building: 850,000 square feet. Bloxham made him an offer, said to be about £450,000. The receiver accepted. And so Lister's passed into the ownership of a company called Urban Splash, which Tom Bloxham had founded with an architect partner in Liverpool seven years earlier and which specialized with increasing success in taking old and decrepit industrial buildings, mainly in the North of England, and turning them into sought-after workspaces and lofts. Urban Splash quickly developed a plan for Manningham: the site would be decontaminated of its industrial poisons, and large chunks of its most derelict buildings demolished; a public square would be laid out; the five floors of the south mill would be converted into apartments (the top floor duplexes will have glass pods on the roof) with commercial spaces on the ground floor. The cost is estimated at £110 million, £6.3 million of which will come from public funds, and the development will take ten years to complete.

This is Lister Mills and the first phase of it was launched on that bitter November morning last year, after months of promotion and newspaper advertising which showed Lister's glorious façade and its chimney rising into a bright blue sky: 'One hundred and thirty-one outstanding one- and two-bedroom apartments and duplex penthouses in the most iconic building in Bradford...' At night a beam of light shot out upwards from the chimney into the dark, emulating the light-show that had been put on at the Tate Modern, (itself converted from a disused Thames-side power station) when it was opened by the Queen in 2000. It seemed probable that Manningham had not seen such a fuss since Lister, Lord Masham, had shown the Prince and Princess of Wales around his factory one hundred years before.

I got to Lister's that same morning soon after the doors had opened and joined a queue that stretched round the block. I had gone along out of curiosity, because I'd seen the adverts and because, like many people who grew up in Yorkshire, I knew of Lister's wool and Lister's velvet as products that our parents and grandparents talked about as being the best in the world. While I waited there was plenty of time to inspect the other people in the queue. Who would want to live here? On this evidence, plenty of couples: young and middle-aged or elderly white couples, young Asian couples. There weren't as many single white males—the people who were once called yuppies—as I'd expected. Instead, what the developers called 'empty nesters', men and women whose children had left home and who fancied quitting the family semi or avoiding the retirement bungalow with its 'manageable garden'. But I also knew that 'living in' and 'buying' are two separate ideas when it comes to houses now, and that this could explain the presence of some prosperous-looking men in smart leather car coats, who probably had enough money to gamble on the area 'coming up', in the meantime renting out their purchase until they could make a good profit at resale.

Members of the Urban Splash sales team stood at the entrance, all of them in the kind of black suits worn by the staff of boutique hotels and nightclubs. One of them handed me a ticket and asked, 'Are you buying today, or just looking?' I said I was just looking, wasn't everybody? Oh no, she said, people had already bought. The ticket was to specify my place in the queue when I had decided which flat I wanted to buy. I'd arrived about forty minutes after the opening time. I was number 233.

Inside, computer screens on the walls were continually updated with information about which flats had been sold, and which others had just been 'released' for sale. I couldn't understand why they couldn't all be 'released' together. Reluctantly, after being interrogated by me and a few others, one of the Urban Splash staff explained that the company reserved the right to increase the price of properties later in the day, so they were available in groups: if the early ones sold well, the prices of the later ones could be increased.

We went to see the show flat and it was exactly as I had expected—unforgivingly modern: solid wood floors, fitted cupboards, exterior walls of plain stone and brick, two bedrooms. It had already gone for £250,000, kitchen appliances included, a snip by London standards. No other flat at Lister's yet existed. If we wanted to buy one, we did so from the evidence of a piece of paper—'off-plan'—because none would be ready for another eighteen months. As someone for whom purchasing a house had been one of life's largest and most protracted decisions, I hadn't understood how swift and simple such a transaction could be. The sales procedure was explained. If I wanted to reserve a flat, I could help myself to free coffee or drinks at the bar and wait in the seating area to talk to a salesperson. Once I had found my flat I could reserve it for a period of four weeks in exchange for a non-refundable deposit of £1,000. Then if I wanted to go ahead, I would exchange contracts and put down ten per cent of the asking price. Sometime in the next year or so, I would pay off the balance and move in.

The smallest flat in Lister Mills, one bedroom with a kitchen/living room, costs £95,000. In the streets outside, you can still get a three-bedroom terrace house for £60,000. For £285,000, the cost of a Lister duplex apartment, you could buy a detached house in one of the surrounding villages with a decent-sized garden. But price per square foot isn't the point. What Lister Mills offers is a 'signature' building, full of local history, with domestic interiors that suggest, though a glance outside would tell you that you are undeniably living in Bradford, that you might be living in Leeds (fifteen minutes away by train: trendy, fast-growing, successfully 'post-industrial'), or London, or Barcelona, or Manhattan; that you have signed up to the international idea of modern urban living. Bill Maynard, one of the directors of Urban Splash, put it like this when he was describing the early history of his company: 'We're all travellers. If you see the stuff in New York and Barcelona, it's not rocket science to apply it to the UK.'

But can it be applied to Bradford, and in particular to Manningham? Urban Splash believes so—and the evidence of the queues to look at the Lister flats suggest it might be right—but the fact is that to buy a home in Manningham is to chose to live in one of the most deprived and troubled urban districts of Britain: a place where the consequences of the collapse of the textile trade can still be felt. In the 1960s, when many mills invested in new weaving technology and began three-shift work patterns, there was a sudden demand for labour, met mainly by encouraging migrant workers from Pakistan. The rundown Victorian terraces of Manningham offered cheap housing, as white families quit for newer homes on the city's outskirts. By the 1980s Manningham had become a substantially South Asian place—in its schools, where white children were a small minority, in its shops and curry houses, and in its religious beliefs, where fifteen mosques replaced five Anglican churches (one still survives, with two Roman Catholic churches and one or two nonconformist chapels). But as Manningham grew in its difference from the rest of Bradford, the mills that remained began to close. Opportunities for other kinds of work were sparse, particularly for men who had spent their working life in the mills and were traditional heads of their households. Their children found themselves caught between their family's expectations of a traditional religious culture on the one hand and the attractions of secular consumerism on the other. They also found themselves living in a place that had become a local byword for street crime, drugs and prostitution.

By the end of the 1990s Manningham was officially one of the ten most deprived wards in England. According to the 2001 Crime and Disorder audit for Bradford, the number of households in Manningham living with 'multiple stresses'—unemployment, poor housing, crime—is ninety-nine per cent. Since then, there has been rioting between young Asian men and white right-wing extremists, and the area has suffered from the growth of anti-Muslim feeling which followed the September 11 attacks on the United States. Nearly half of Bradford's black and Asian residents expected to be the victim of a racial attack within the next year. In the same survey, twenty-two per cent of people felt less safe in their neighbourhood compared with two years earlier. Their main fears—in order of priority—were of groups of young people, mugging, and drug users. They were more fearful after dark. The daytime locations where they felt most at risk were 'quiet or isolated areas, parks and playgrounds, the town centre, subways,' and 'Manningham'.

It is hard to see how a few hundred new homes for the relatively well-off could change these facts or perceptions, and I expected local people to be sceptical about the benefits that the redevelopment of Lister's mill would bring; sceptical and perhaps also antagonistic towards the kind of people who might move in. But in this I was wrong. That morning, as I walked back to my car, two Asian girls in black headscarves, going in the same direction up the hill, asked me what I'd thought. Pretty good, I said. I asked them if they thought it was just going to be a load of yuppies moving in who wouldn't mix with their neighbours. But they liked the idea. 'It'll make the place more interesting.'

In the next couple of weeks I went back to Manningham and talked to some of the people who lived and worked around the mills. The streets were peaceful, with a constant trickle of women in saris and overcoats, and men in Punjabi tunics, trousers and small woollen caps, walking up and down the hill. Only the police station, a fortress-like building right opposite the entrance to the mills, surrounded by a high stone wall and strung with banners announcing a local crime-fighting initiative, offered a reminder of Manningham's recurring troubles. (The police station was built in the 1990s, on the site of the reservoir that Lister built to ensure a constant supply of water for his mills.)

Right next door to Manningham Mills is a large supermarket with a halal butcher advertising meat for the cheapest prices in Bradford. There I talked to a young Asian man who was working in the supermarket offices part-time while he studied for an economics degree. He knew all about Urban Splash. They had a good track record, he said. His boss, the owner of the supermarket, had bought one of the flats as an investment. He said they had already discussed what they could offer to people living at Lister's: deliveries, extending the opening hours, that sort of thing. Obviously they didn't sell pork, pork sausages or bacon. 'But if they don't find things they want, then they might look at what alternatives we've got,' he said. 'We've got a few ideas going through.'

About a hundred yards up the road from the mill I came to a parade of little shops, including a new mobile-phone franchise called Fone Zone that was filled with young Asians buying and topping up their mobiles. Its owner was a young Asian girl who'd left school and gone into business with an Asian friend, a man who had worked for two years in London. She said they wanted to provide employment for some of the local young people. She was already planning her next shop, a beauty spa, somewhere Asian girls could go. I asked what her parents thought of her working for herself. She said they were behind her a hundred and ten per cent. She thought the mill redevelopment was going to bring a lot of attention to the area, more people circulating, it would set a new standard. They were still lagging a long way behind Leeds and Manchester, she said. Bradford had got itself stuck in an era.

Zahid Quereshi owns the night security company which currently guards the Urban Splash site at Lister's mill. He worked there when it was a mill, after he came to Bradford from Pakistan in the late 1960s. 'Weaving was one of the best jobs around, then. It was like computers today. We were all mixed together: women, Asians, English. It was a time when everybody just got on with work. People didn't know about benefits or social security. They only knew they had to work. Lister's velvet was famous in the world. You felt proud to work there.' He counted off the reasons for the decline: 'The Common Market. We started importing cheaper fabrics. We couldn't compete. Firms were happy to buy from outside. We used to have very old machines. I came to learn how to make cloth; I picked it up very quickly and I became an instructor. Once they called a meeting and they asked me what I thought, and I said in my opinion it was time to change the machines. We still had machines that were producing ten yards of cloth in a day when there were machines that could produce sixty to seventy yards in a shift. They took that very seriously. And they did change some machines. But the competition was so high. I left after one or two years to go to another mill. I started doing nights. It was better pay.'

And Lister's now? 'Well, it's a good start,' he said. 'Nobody else was going to buy it. They are doing a business directly benefiting the community, bringing more people into the area. The way they've planned it, it will be one of the best things to happen. I hope it works.'

Fifteen or twenty years ago in Britain, that kind of optimism would have been harder to find. The future, in a place like Bradford, was seen as some tattered continuation of the present, which itself was infused by the very recent past. People mourned what Bradford had been, and no doubt many of them still do, but now in Britain we know that there is no going back: no ships, no pits, no cotton, no wool. Something else then, something that will work. I found this optimism even in Bill Edmondson, a man of eighty-eight and one of many former workers at Lister's who had been drawn by the publicity about the mill's redevelopment to go along and have a look. He read about it in the paper and went to the opening day, introducing himself to the staff in their black suits and proving himself to be something of a one-man historical society, with a pin-sharp memory of everything that had gone on during the years he worked there, 1931 to 1953.

He was born in Manningham and started as an office boy at Lister's at the age of fourteen earning ten shillings a week. His father had served as a cotton buyer at Lister's for fifty-six years. His three older sisters started at twelve, working part-time in the mill after school. Now he lives in a retirement bungalow in Wilsden, a little village on the moors to the north of the city, and when I went to visit him he had arranged a pile of bound copies of *Lister's Magazine*, from 1927 to just before the war, on the kitchen table, along with his own photographs and memorabilia. The magazines recorded all the social events of the mill: the weddings and funerals, the visiting dignitaries including several royal visits and one from the Shah of Persia. There were holiday snaps from workers' outings to northern resorts, such as Blackpool and Scarborough, Bridlington and Skegness. There were trophy-giving ceremonies for cricket and football, netball, hockey, boxing and all the other interdepartmental sports tournaments that went on. There were photographs of Bill, who had a good tenor voice and described himself as 'an early Bing Crosby-type of thing', in various theatrical productions with his band, the Hawaiian Serenaders. He showed me photographs of Lister's steam lorries that used to haul the coal up the steep hill from the railway depot in the bottom of the valley to the boiler house at the top. He remembered as a little boy having to run out on Mondays, which was washday, to lift up the clothes line to let the lorries through, otherwise the washing got covered with coal dust. As an office boy, he said, 'The beauty of it was, I did errands all the time, and I used to have to take short cuts through the mill so I went through all the departments, such as "Processes Preparatory"—to weaving, you see. And I used to nosy round, see what was happening. So I got quite a good knowledge, which came in very handy when I went to night school.' After moving to the velvet and tapestry weaving department he was sent to technical college in Bradford to learn how to become a Jacquard card-cutter, that is, to translate the point-patterns produced by the fabric designers into the punched pattern cards that guided the looms.

When war broke out Bill joined the Royal Artillery. He followed up the D-Day landings in Normandy, and then was sent to India. He came home in 1946 and went back to his job in the design department at Manningham. 'Well, we were all different after the war. When I came back I had to go into the office once and the boss said, "We're getting complaints, Bill, that you're trying to go too fast." And I was always, "Get moving, get moving". I used to run down the aisles instead of walking, you see, and people were saying it didn't look right...' So that was one thing. I'd speeded my life up. But it was marvellous really. It was a super place to work.'

I asked Bill if he thought the new development was a strange idea, wanting to live in a mill. When mills were going, after all, the people who worked in them wanted to get out of their shadow and smoke;

the bus home every night to a little house with a garden and trees on the horizon—that was the ideal. Marx invented a term for it: alienation—the product of how the industrial worker under capitalism was supposed to feel about his work. But Bill said, 'Oh no, I'm over the moon about it. In recent years I've been keeping an eye out, ready to write to the papers, as I sometimes do, watching in case they tried to get it knocked down. When this Urban Splash came, I thought it was the best thing that could happen. That way three or four more generations can continue speaking about Manningham Mills.'

How will they speak of it? My small research into the question suggests that some will speak of their flat there as an investment, some as a pension, some as 'my northern base, really handy for the moors', some as their first step into home-ownership. They will look at the motto which in 1873 Samuel Lister had scrolled in stone above the factory's main entrance—FIDEM PARIT INTEGRITAS [Soundness Begets Faith]—and ponder its meaning, in both Latin and English, in an age when money counts most.

This brings us back to Mario Buitrago, who slept outside Lister's on that very cold night. The day before the opening, the staff of Urban Splash found him freezing on their doorstep when they arrived for work at seven in the morning. They invited him in and gave him a cup of tea. It made a wonderful story for the local papers. He spoke little English but was 'all smiles and handshakes', according to the *Yorkshire Post* reporter who interviewed him. He explained that he wasn't waiting to buy a flat for himself. He had been paid to queue on behalf of an anonymous client, thought to be a private investor from London and staying in a Bradford hotel, who was keen to secure a particular flat and willing to pay somebody else to sit out in the cold to do it. □

GRANTA

BUCKETS OF BLOOD

Tessa Hadley

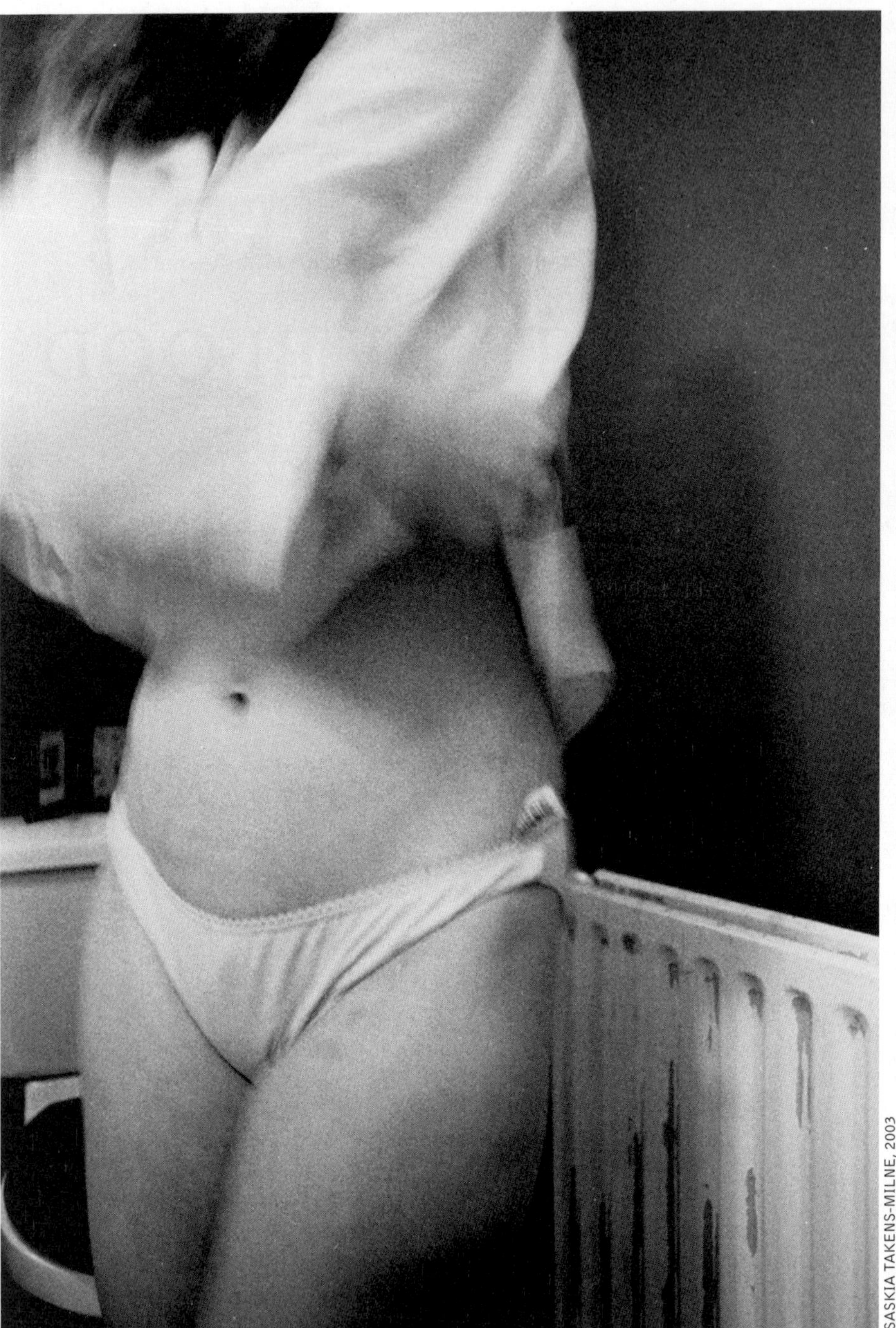

SASKIA TAKENS-MILNE, 2003

Buckets of Blood

The coach journey from Cambridge to Bristol took six hours. Hilary Culvert was wearing a new purple skirt, a drawstring crepe blouse and navy school cardigan, and over them her school mac, because it was the only coat she had. The year was 1972. In the toilets at Oxford bus station where they were allowed to get out she had sprayed on some perfume and unplaited her hair. She worried that she smelled of home. She didn't know quite what home smelled like, as she still lived there and was used to it; but when her sister Sheila had come back from university for Christmas she had complained about it to Hilary.

—You'd think with all these children, Sheila had said, —that at least the place would smell of something freshly nasty. Feet or sweat or babies or something. But it smells like old people. Mothballs and Germolene and damp feather pillows: who still uses mothballs apart from here?

Hilary had been putting Germolene on her spots; this was the family orthodoxy. She put the little tube aside in horror immediately. Sheila had looked so different, even after only one term away. She had always been braver about putting on a public show than Hilary was: now she wore gypsy clothes, scrumpled silky skirts and patchwork tops with flashing pieces of mirror sewn in. Her soft red-brown hair was fluffed out in a mass. She had insisted on washing her hair almost every day, even though this wasn't easy in the vicarage: the old Ascot gas heater only dribbled out hot water, and there were all the younger children taking turns each night for baths. Their father had remonstrated with Sheila amusedly.

—There's no one here to admire you in your glory, he said. —You'll only frighten the local boys. Save your efforts until you return to the fleshpots.

—I'm not doing it for anyone to admire, said Sheila. —I'm doing it for myself.

He was a tall narrow man, features over-sized for the fine bones of his face, eyes elusive behind the thick-lensed glasses; he smiled as if he was squinting into a brash light. His children hadn't been brought up to flaunt doing things for themselves, although the truth was that in a family of nine children a certain stubborn selfishness was essential for survival.

Now Hilary in her half-term week was going to visit Sheila in the fleshpots, or at Bristol University, where she was reading classics. A lady with permed blue-white hair in the seat next to her was knitting baby clothes in lemon-yellow nylon wool which squeaked on her needles; Hilary had to keep her head turned to stare out of the window because she suffered terribly from travel sickness. She wouldn't ever dream of reading on a coach, and even the flickering of the knitting needles could bring it on. The lady had tried to open up a conversation about her grandchildren and probably thought Hilary was rude and unfriendly. And that was true too, that was what the Culverts were like: crucified by their shyness and at the same time contemptuous of the world of ordinary people they couldn't talk to. Outside the window there was nothing to justify her fixed attention. The sky seemed never to have lifted higher all day than a few feet above the ground; rolls of mist hung above the sodden grass like dirty wool. The signs of spring coming suspended in a spasm of unforgiving frozen cold. It should have been a relief to leave the flat lands of East Anglia behind and cross into the hills and valleys of the west, but everywhere today seemed equally colourless. Hilary didn't care. Her anticipation burned up brightly enough by itself. Little flames of it licked up inside her. This was the first time she had been away from home alone. Sheila was ahead of her in their joint project: to get as far away from home as possible, and not to become anything like their mother.

At about the same time that Sheila and Hilary had confided to each other that they didn't any longer believe in God, they had also given up believing that the pattern of domestic life they had been brought up inside was the only possible one, or was even remotely desirable. Somewhere else people lived differently; didn't have to poke their feet into clammy hand-me-down Wellingtons and sandals marked by size inside with felt-pen; didn't have to do their homework in bed with hot-water bottles because the storage heaters in the draughty vicarage gave out such paltry warmth. Other people didn't have to have locked money boxes for keeping safe anything precious, or have to sleep with the keys on string around their necks; sometimes they came home from school to find those locks picked or smashed. (The children didn't tell on one another; that was their morality. But they hurt one another pretty badly, physically, in pursuit of justice. It was an honour code rather than anything resembling Christian empathy or charity.) Other people's mothers didn't stoop their heads down in the broken way that theirs did, hadn't given up on completed sentences or consecutive dialogue, didn't address elliptical, ironical asides to their soup spoons as they ate.

Their mother sometimes looked less like a vicar's wife than a wild woman. She was as tall as their father but if the two of them were ever accidentally seen standing side by side it looked as if she had been in some terrible momentous fight for her life and he hadn't. Her grey-black hair stood out in a stiff ruff around her head; Sheila said she must cut it with the kitchen scissors in the dark. She had some kind of palsy so that her left eye drooped; there were bruise-coloured wrinkled shadows under her eyes and beside her hooked nose. Her huge deflated stomach and bosom were slapped like insults on to a girl's bony frame. She was fearless in the mornings about stalking round the house in her ancient baggy underwear, big pants and maternity bra, chasing the little ones to get them dressed: her older children fled the sight of her. They must have all counted, without confessing it to one another: she was forty-nine, Patricia was four. At least there couldn't be any more pregnancies, so humiliating to their suffering adolescence.

As girls, Sheila and Hilary had to be especially careful to make their escape from home. Their older brother Andrew had got away, to do social policy at York and join the Young Socialists, which he told them was a Trotskyite entrist group. He was never coming back, they were sure of it. He hadn't come back this Christmas. But their sister Sylvia had married an RE teacher at the local secondary modern school who was active in their father's church and in the local youth clubs, and Sylvia already had two babies, and Sheila and Hilary had heard her muttering things to herself. They remembered that she used to be a jolly sprightly girl even if they hadn't liked her much: competitive at beach rounders when they went on day trips to the coast, sentimentally devoted to the doomed stray dogs she tried to smuggle into their bedroom. Now, when they visited her rented flat in Haverhill, her twin-tub washing machine was always pulled out from the wall, filling the kitchen with urine-pungent steam. Sylvia would be standing uncommunicatively, heaving masses of boiling nappies with wooden tongs out of the washer into the spin-tub, while the babies bawled in the battered wooden playpen that had been handed on from the vicarage.

In the coach, aware of her reflection in the window from time to time when the scenery was dun enough behind to make a mirror out of it, Hilary sat up very straight. She and Sheila had practised with one another, remembering never to lapse into the crumpled unawareness that smote their mother if ever for a moment she left off being busy. She was almost always busy. She had driven Hilary in to catch her coach that morning only because she had to go in to Cambridge anyway, to buy replacement school shorts and other uniform from Eaden Lilley for the boys. The boys had larked around in the back seats of the ropy old Bedford van that was their family transport, kicking at each other's shins and dropping to wriggle on their bellies about the floor, so that their mother—who drove badly anyway, with grindings of the gears and sudden brakings—spent the whole journey deploring fruitlessly, and peering to try and locate them in the rear-view mirror. She had taken to wearing dark glasses when she went anywhere outside her home, to cover up the signs of her palsy. She stopped the van on Parker's Piece and had to get out to open the door on Hilary's side because the handle was broken. Hilary had a vivid idea of how her mother must appear to strangers: the sticking-up hair and dark glasses and the worn once-good coat she never had time to button up; her jerky burrowing movements, searching for money or lists in bags or under the van seats; her cut-glass enunciations, without eye contact, of bits of sentences that never became any whole message. When Hilary walked away with her suitcase to take her place in the little huddled crowd of waiting travellers she wouldn't look to see if any of them had been watching.

Bristol bus station was a roaring cavern: everything was greasy and filthy with oil, including the maimed pigeons. Green double-decker city buses reversed out of the bays and rumbled off, important with illumination, into the evening. A whole day's light had come and gone on the journey. Hilary looked excitedly for Sheila while she shuffled down the aisle on the coach. She wasn't worried that she couldn't see her right away. 'Whatever you do don't go off anywhere,' Sheila had instructed her. 'Stay there till I come.'

Someone waited slouching against the metal railing while she queued for her suitcase, then stepped forward to confront her when she had it: a young man, short and soft-bodied, with lank light-brown hair and a half-grown beard, wearing a pinstriped suit jacket over jeans. He also had bare feet, and black eye make-up.

—Are you Hilary?

He spoke with a northern accent.

Hilary felt the disapproving attention of the blue-rinsed knitting lady, focused on his make-up and his feet. She disdained the disapproval, even though in the same instant she judged against the man with Culvert passionate finality. 'What an unappealing little dwarf of a chap,' she thought, in her mother's voice. Of course her thought didn't show. To him she would look only like the sum of what she was outwardly: pale with bad skin, fatally provincial, frightened, with girls' school gushing manners.

—Yes.

—Sheila couldn't be here. She's unwell. You have to come with me.

He swung away without smiling or otherwise acknowledging her; he had only ever looked perfunctorily in her face, as if he were checking basics. She had to follow after him, out through the bus station back entrance into a twilit cobbled street and then up right beside a high grim wall that curved round to join a busier road. The tall buildings of a hospital with their lighted windows rose sobering and impassive against the evening sky, where the murky day in its expiring was suddenly brilliantly deep clear blue, studded already with one or two points of stars. The man walked ahead and Hilary followed, hurrying, struggling with her suitcase, three or four steps behind. The suitcase was an old leather one embossed with her grandfather's initials; he had taken it to ecumenical conferences in the Thirties. Because the clasps were liable to spring open she had fastened an elastic Brownie belt around it.

Unwell! Unwell was the word they had to use to the games mistress at school when they weren't having showers because they had a period. Hilary saved the joke up to amuse Sheila. Then she was flooded with doubt; why had she followed this rude man so obediently? She should have at least questioned him, asked him where Sheila was and what was wrong with her. Sheila had told her to wait, whatever happened, at the bus station. She opened her mouth to protest to him, to demand that he explain to her, and take a turn carrying the case. Then stubbornly she closed it again. She knew what a squeak would come out of it if she tried to attract his attention while she was struggling along like this. And if she put the case down and stopped she was afraid he'd go on without noticing she was no longer behind him, and then she would be truly lost in an unknown city, with nowhere to spend the night, and certainly not enough money to pay for anywhere. She could perhaps have hired a taxi to take her to Sheila's hall of residence, although she wasn't sure what that would cost either. She had never been in a taxi in her life, and would never have the courage to try and signal to one. And what if Sheila wasn't at the hall of residence?

Pridefully she marched on, though her breath was hurting in her chest and her hand without its glove—they were somewhere in her shoulder bag but she couldn't stop to find them—was freezing into a claw on the case handle. Her arm felt as if it was being dragged from her shoulder. It wasn't clothes that made her case heavy, but some books Sheila had asked her to bring. Every forty paces—she began to count—she swapped her case and shoulder bag from hand to hand, and that gave a few moments of relief. She fixed her eyes on the back of the rumpled pinstriped jacket. Once or twice, on the zebra crossings, he looked back to check for her. Luckily his bare feet seemed to slow him down somewhat, probably because he had to keep an eye out for what he might be walking in. There were quite a few people on the streets, even though the shops were closed; sometimes he held back to let a crowd go by, perhaps because he was afraid of someone stepping on his toes. Perversely Hilary started slowing down too whenever this happened. She was damned now if she wanted to catch up with him. Even if he stopped to wait for her, now, she thought that she would stop too and wait, as if the distance between them had become a fixed relationship, an invisible rigid frame of air connecting them and holding them apart in the same grip.

She thought she recognized the streets that they were walking through. When their father had driven Sheila over with her things at the start of the autumn term, Hilary had come with them; she had wanted to be able to picture where Sheila was, when she wasn't at home. This shopping area was on a hill behind the city centre: it had seemed lively and fashionable, with tiny boutiques, cafes, a department store whose long glass windows were stuck with brown-and-yellow paper leaves. She had seen Sheila taking it all in from her front seat in the van, satisfied with her choice, impatient to be left alone to explore. At home they could only get lifts in to Cambridge every so often, and anyway their shopping there was dogged by waiting parents, ready with ironic comments on whatever the girls chose to buy with their money. Dimly in the dusk now, Hilary could see the Victorian gothic university tower where it ought to be, over to her right. Manor Hall residence where Sheila had a room should be somewhere off to the left, up past a little triangle of green grass. The pinstriped jacket struck off left, and Hilary was relieved. They must arrive soon, and she would be able to put her case down, and be rid of her dreadful companion.

The road he took didn't lead up past any triangle of grass but downhill; it was wide, busy with fast through traffic but not with people. They left the shops behind and it seemed all at once to be completely night; the pavement ran alongside a daunting high wall to their left. The steep hills and old high walls of this city were suddenly sinister and not quaint, as if they hid dark prisons and corruptions in their folds. Hilary followed the pinstriped jacket now in a grim, fixed despair. In spite of the cold she was sweating, and her chest was racked. She thought that catastrophe had overtaken her. She had made an appalling mistake when she meekly followed this man out of the bus station, like a trusting child, like an idiot. The only form of dignity left to her was not to falter, not to make a worse fool of herself screaming and running, not to break the form of the rigid relationship in which they moved. She thought he might be taking her somewhere to kill her with a knife. She wouldn't say a word to save her life; she might swing at him with her grandfather's suitcase. Or she imagined drugs, which she didn't know anything about: perhaps drug addicts recruited new associates by bundling strangers into their den and injecting them with heroin. She didn't ever imagine rape or anything of that sort, because she thought that as a preliminary to that outrage there would have to be some trace of interest in her, some minimal sign of a response to her, however disgusted.

The pinstriped jacket crossed the road, darting between the cars. Following, Hilary hardly cared if she was hit. He struck off up a narrow precipitous hill with tall toppling houses facing on to the pavement on either side. Because of the effort of climbing she had her head down and almost walked into him when he stopped outside a front door. He pushed the door and it swung open. The house inside was dark.

—In here, he said, and led the way.

Hilary followed.

In the hall he switched on a light: a bare bulb hung from the ceiling. The place was desolate: ancient wallpaper washed to colourlessness hung down in sheets from the walls. Even in her extremity, though, she could tell that this had been an elegant house once. City lights twinkled through an arched window. The stairs wound round and round a deep stairwell, up into blackness; the handrail was smooth polished wood. Everything smelled of a mineral decay. They climbed up two flights, their footsteps echoing because there was no stair-carpet. He pushed another door.

—She's in there.

Hilary didn't know what she expected to find.

Sheila was sitting with a concentrated face, rocking backwards and forwards on a double bed which was just a mattress on bare floorboards. She was wearing a long black T-shirt, her hair was scraped carelessly back and tied with a scarf. The room was lit by another bare bulb, not a ceiling pendant this time but a lamp-base without a shade, which cast leering upwards shadows. It was warm: an electric radiator painted mustard yellow was plugged in the same socket as the lamp. Hilary felt herself overheating at once, her face turning hot red, after her exertions in the cold outside.

—Thank God you've come, Hills, Sheila said.

She sounded practical rather than emotional. That at least was reassuring.

Pinstripe stepped into the room behind Hilary. He put on a shifty uncomfortable smile, not quite looking straight at Sheila, focusing on the dark tangle of sheets and blankets that Sheila seemed to have kicked to the bottom of the bed.

—D'you want anything? Tea?

Sheila shook her head. —I'm only throwing it up.

—D'you want anything?

Hilary couldn't believe he was actually talking to her. —No, I'm fine, thanks, she said.

—I'll be downstairs, he said. —If you need anything.

They heard the sound of his footsteps retreating. Hilary put down her case: her hand for quite a few minutes wouldn't ease from its frozen curled position. —Shuggs: what's going on?

Sheila groaned: not in answer to the question, but a sound ripped from inside her, a low and embarrassing rumble as if she didn't care what anybody heard. She rocked fiercely.

—I'm miscarrying a pregnancy, she said, when the spasm seemed to have passed. —It's a fine mess. Blood everywhere. Buckets of blood. You'll have to help get rid of everything.

—I can't believe this, Hilary said. She felt she was still somewhere inside the Bluebeard story she had been imagining. For a few pure moments she blazed with anger against Sheila. It wasn't fair, for Sheila to have spoiled her visit with this, her so looked-forward-to chance to get away. Sheila's mission had been clear and certain: to cut herself free of all the muffling dependencies of home and childhood. If she could succumb to anything so predictable as this melodrama—just what their parents would have warned against if only they hadn't been too agonized to find the words—what hope was there?

—What are you doing here? she demanded. —What is this place?

—It's a squat, said Sheila calmly. —Neil's squat. I told them at Manor Hall that I was going away for a few days. They're not to ever know anything about this, obviously.

—You'd be kicked out.

—Uh-oh, said Sheila, attentive to something inside her. Then she lunged from the bed to sit on something like a chamber pot in the crazy shadows on the far side of the room. Hilary tried not to hear anything. —Oh, oh, Sheila groaned, hugging her white legs, pressing her forehead to her knees.

—They wouldn't kick me out, she said after a while. —It's not that.

—And who's Neil?

—That's him, you idiot. You've just walked back from the bus station with him.

Hilary hadn't stirred from where she stood when she first came in, or even made any move to unbutton her mac. She felt as if there was an unpassable waste of experience between her and her sister now, that couldn't be crossed. Sheila had joined the ranks of women submerged and knowing amidst their biology. She realized with a new shock that Sheila must have had sexual intercourse, too, in order to be pregnant.

—I don't want Mum to know, that's why, Sheila said. —I'll simply kill you if you ever tell anyone at home.

—I wouldn't, said Hilary coldly.

—I just can't bear the idea of her thinking that this is the same thing, you know? The same stuff that's happened to her. Because it isn't.

Hilary was silent. After a long while Sheila stood up stiffly from the chamber pot. She stuffed what looked like an old towel between her legs, and moving slowly, bent over as if she was very old, she lay down on the bed again, on her side this time, with her eyes closed.

—You could take it down to the lavatory for me. It's a flight and a half down, door on the right.

Hilary didn't stir.

—Please. Hills. You could cover it with a newspaper or something.

—Did you do this deliberately? Hilary said.

—No. I might have done, but I didn't. I'd only just realized that I was pregnant. I've only missed two periods, I think. I never keep track. Then this just happened.

—Who is the father of it?

Sheila's eyes snapped open incredulously. —Who do you think? she said. —I wouldn't have just sent any old person to get you.

Hilary helped. Several times she carried the chamber pot down one and a half flights of stairs, holding the banister rail, watching her feet carefully in the gloom (there was only the one bulb in the hallway, which Neil had switched on when they first came in). She covered whatever was inside the pot with a piece of newspaper, then tipped it into the lavatory without looking and flushed the chain. Thankfully it had a good strong flush. She stood on the stairs listening to voices downstairs, a long way off as if they came from underground, from a basement room perhaps: Neil's voice and others, male and female, subdued but nonetheless breaking out into laughter sometimes. Behind a door off the landing above the lavatory, Hilary found a filthy bathroom, with a torn plastic curtain at the window, overgrown with black mould. She ran the bath taps for a while, but although the pipes gave out buckings and bellowing noises and hiccoughed gouts of tea-coloured cold water into the grit and dirt in the bottom of the bath, she couldn't get either tap to run hot.

—There's no hot water, Sheila said. —This is a squat: what did you think? Everyone goes into the halls to bathe. We're lucky to have electricity: one of the guys knew how to reconnect it. You could ask Neil for the electric kettle. What do you want hot water for anyway?

—I thought you might like a wash. I thought I could put some things in to soak.

—Don't worry about it. I'll wash in the morning. We can take all this stuff to the launderette later.

Although they had always lived so close together in the forced intimacy of the vicarage, where there was only one lavatory and fractious queues for the bathroom in the mornings, Sheila and Hilary had been prudish in keeping their bodily functions hidden from one another. This was partly in scalded reaction to their mother, who poked curiously in the babies' potties to find swallowed things, and delivered sanitary towels to the girls' room with abandoned openness, as if she didn't know that the boys saw. They had even always, since they stopped being little girls, undressed quickly with their backs turned, or underneath their nightdresses. It was a surprise how small the step seemed, once Hilary had taken it, over into this new bodily intimacy of shared secret trouble and mess. Sheila's pains, she began to understand, had a rhythm to them: first a strong pang, then a pause, then a sensation as if things were coming away inside her. After that she might get ten or fifteen minutes respite. When the pain was at its worst, Hilary rubbed her back, or Sheila gripped her hand and squeezed it, hard and painfully, crushing the bones together.

—Damn, damn, damn, she swore in a sing-song moan while she rocked backwards and forwards; tears squeezed out of her shut eyes and ran down her cheeks.

—Are you sorry? Hilary said, humbled.

—How could I possibly be sorry? Sheila snapped.

She said the pains had begun at three in the afternoon. She told Hilary at some point that if they were still going on in the morning they would have to call an ambulance and get her into hospital: she explained in a practical voice that women could haemorrhage and die if these things went wrong. By ten o'clock, though, the worst seemed to be over. There hadn't been any bad pains for over an hour, the bleeding was almost like a normal period. When Neil came upstairs Sheila wanted a cup of tea and a hotwater bottle.

—You'll have to take Hilary out, she told him, —and buy her something to eat.

Hilary had eaten some sandwiches on the coach at lunchtime. She hadn't had anything since then; she didn't feel hungry but she felt light-headed and her hands were shaking.

—I'm fine, she said hastily. —I don't want anything.

—Don't be so silly. Buy her some fish and chips or something.

Hilary was too tired not to be obedient. She put on her mac and followed Neil downstairs, as if their fatal passage round the city had to recommence. At least this time she wouldn't be carrying her case. She waited on the street outside; he said he had to fetch the others.

—By the way, he added, not looking at her. —I shouldn't mention anything. They just think Sheila's got a tummy bug. They'd be upset.

—Okay, Hilary mumbled. Furiously she thought to herself that she wouldn't have spoken to his friends about her sister if he had tortured her. 'You silly little man,' she imagined herself saying. 'How dare you think I care about upsetting them?' She tipped back her head and looked up the precipitous fronts of the houses to the far off sky and cold stars.

She noticed that Neil had put on shoes to come out this time: a pair of gym shoes, gaping without laces. His friend Julian had jug ears and long dyed blond hair; Gus was shy and lumpish, like a boy swelled to man-size without his face or body actually changing to look grown-up. Becky was a pretty girl in a duffel coat, who giggled and swivelled her gaze too eagerly from face to face: she couldn't get enough of her treat, being the only girl and having the attention of three men. She knew instinctively that Hilary didn't count. Even her patronising was perfunctory: she reminisced about her own A levels as if she was reaching back into a long-ago past.

—You've chosen all the easy ones, you clever thing! My school forced me to do double maths, it was ghastly.

—Are you sure you're not hungry? Neil said to Hilary as they hurried past a busy chip shop with a queue. —Only if we don't stop we're in time for the pub. You could have some crisps there.

Hilary gazed into the bright steamy window, assaulted suddenly by the smell of the chips, weak with longing. —Quite sure, she said. She had never been into a pub in her life. There was a place in Haverhill where some of the girls went from school, but she and Sheila had always despised the silly self-importance of teenage transgression. It was impossible to imagine ever wanting to enter the ugly square red-brick pub in the village, where the farm labourers drank, and the men from the estate who worked in the meat packing factory. Neil's pub was a tiny cosy den, fumy light glinting off the rows of glasses and bottles. The stale breath of it made Hilary's head swim; they squeezed into red plush seats around a table. Neil didn't ask her what she wanted, but brought her a small mug of brown beer and a packet of crisps and one of peanuts. She didn't like the taste of the beer but because the food was so salty she drank it in thirsty mouthfuls, and then was seized by a sensation as if she had floated up to hang some little way above her present situation, graciously indifferent, so that her first experience of drunkenness was a blessed one.

When the pub closed they came back to the house and sat around a table in the basement kitchen by candlelight: the kitchen walls were painted crudely with huge mushrooms and blades of grass and giant insects, making Hilary feel as if she were a miniature human at the deep bottom of a forest. Hilary drank the weak tea they put in front of her. The others talked about work and exams. Becky was doing biological sciences, Gus was doing history, Julian and Neil seemed to be doing English. Hilary couldn't believe that they sounded just like girls at school, scurrying in the rat-run of learning and testing, trying to outdo one another in protestations of how little work they'd done. Not once did any of them actually speak seriously about their subjects. Hilary now felt so deeply disappointed in university life that on the spot she made up her mind to dedicate herself to something different and nobler, although she wasn't clear what. Neil and Julian were concentrating upon sticking a brown lump of something on a pin and roasting it with a match. From her indifferent distance she supposed this must be drugs, but she wasn't frightened of that now.

—Don't tell your Daddy the vicar what you've seen, said Neil.

She was confused—did the others know what had happened after all?—until she realized that he meant the brown lump.

—Are you two really from a vicarage? asked Becky. —It's like something out of a book.

—We can't offer the respectability that Hilary's used to, Neil said. —She'll have to slum it here for a few days.

Hilary could see that Neil was the centre of all the others' attention. At least he had not joined in when they were fluttering and fussing about their work; he had smiled to himself, licking the edges of little pieces of white paper and sticking them together as if none of it bothered him. He had an air as if he saw through the sham of it all, as if he came from a place where the university didn't count for much: she could see how this had power over the others. He didn't say much but when he spoke it was with a deliberate debunking roughness that made the others abject, ashamed of the feel in their mouths of their own nice eager voices.

Becky told Neil flirtatiously that he would have to be on his best behaviour, while Hilary was staying. —No swearing, she said. —'Cause I can see she's a nice girl.

—Fuck, he said. —I hadn't thought of that. Fuck that.

Hilary thought of the farm boys at home, who called sexual words when she and Sheila had to walk past them in their school uniform. She had always thought, however much it tortured her, that they had an obscure right to do it because of their work. In the winter mornings from the school bus you could see the frozen mists rising up out of the flat colourless fields, and figures bent double with sacks across their shoulders, picking Brussels sprouts, or sugar beet. But Neil was here, wasn't he, at university? He'd crossed over to their side, the lucky side. Whatever she thought of her life, she knew it was on the lucky side, so long as she wasn't picking Brussels sprouts or meat-packing.

No-one had said anything since she arrived about where Hilary was to sleep. Sheila was supposed to have booked a guest room for her at Manor Hall, but of course she couldn't go there now. When she couldn't hold herself upright at the kitchen table any longer she climbed upstairs to ask what she should do, but Sheila was asleep, breathing evenly and deeply. Her forehead was cool. Hilary kept all her clothes on and wrapped herself in an old quilt which Sheila had kicked off; she curled up to sleep on the floor beside the bed. At some point in the night she woke, frozen rigid and harrowed by a bitter draught blowing up through the bare floorboards; she climbed into the bed beside Sheila who snorted and heaved over. Under the duvet and all the blankets it smelled of sweat and blood, but it was warm. When she woke again it was morning and the sun was shining.

—Look at the patterns, Sheila said.

She was propped up calmly on one elbow on the pillow, and seemed returned into her usual careful self-possession. Hilary noticed for the first time that the room was painted yellow; the sun struck through the tall uncurtained windows and projected swimming squares of light onto the walls, dancing with the movements of the twiggy tops of trees which must be growing in a garden outside.

—Are you all right? she asked.

Sheila ignored the question as if there had never been anything wrong.

—How did you get on with everybody last night?

—We went to a pub.

—Oh, which one? She interrogated Hilary until she was satisfied that it must have been the Beaufort. —We often go there, she said enthusiastically. —It's got a great atmosphere, it's really local.

—When I told them we lived in a vicarage, Hilary said, —one of them asked if we were Catholics.

—That's so funny. I bet I know who that was. What did you think of Neil?

Hilary was cautious. —Is he from the north?

—Birmingham, you idiot. Couldn't you tell? Such a pure Brummie accent.

—He wasn't awfully friendly.

Sheila smiled secretively. —He doesn't do that sort of small talk. His Dad works as a tool-setter at Lucases, the engineering company. No-one in his family has been to university before. His parents don't have money, compared to most of the students here. He gets pretty impatient with people, you know, who just take their privilege for granted.

Hilary felt like a child beside her sister. What had happened yesterday marked Sheila as initiated into the adult world, apart from her, as clearly as if it was signed with blood on her forehead. She supposed it must be the unknown of sexual intercourse which could transform things in this way that children couldn't see: Neil's self-importance into power, for instance. At the same time as she was in awe of her sister's difference, Hilary also felt a stubborn virgin pride. She didn't want ever to be undone out of her scepticism, or seduced into grown-up credulous susceptibility.

—But doesn't he think that we are poor, too? she asked fiercely. —Have you told him? Does he have any idea?

—It's different, said Sheila with finality. —It's just different.

When Hilary drove in the summer with her father in the Bedford van, to pick up Sheila and all her things at the end of her first year, she was waiting for them of course at Manor Hall, as if there had never been any other place, any squat whose kitchen was painted with giant mushrooms. Hilary understood that she was not ever to mention what had happened there, not even when she and Sheila were alone. Because they never wore the memory out by speaking of it, the place persisted vividly in her imagination.

She had stayed on in that house for almost a week: she had arrived on Monday and her return ticket was for Saturday. Sheila rested for the first couple of days, sleeping a lot, and Hilary went out on her own, exploring, going round the shops. On Sheila's instructions she took several carrier bags of bloody sheets and towels to the launderette, where she sat reading Virginia Woolf while the washing boiled. There seemed to be a lot of hours to pass, because she didn't want to spend too much time in Sheila's room; she shrank from the possibility of getting in the way between Sheila and Neil. A couple of times she went to the cinema in the afternoon by herself. They all went out to pubs every evening and she got used to drinking beer, although she didn't get to like it. While the others joked and drank and smoked she sat in a silence that must look gawky and immature, so that she was sure Sheila despaired of her, although Sheila must also surely know that she found the conversation impossible to join because it was so tepid and disappointing, gossip mostly about people she'd never met. Sheila, who had been aloof and not popular at school, seemed to be working hard to make these people like her. She made herself brighter and funnier and smaller than her real self, Hilary thought. She surrounded Neil in particular with such efforts of admiration, prompting him and encouraging him and attributing ideas to him, while he smiled in lazy amusement, rolling up his eternal cigarettes. At least they weren't all over each other, they didn't cling together in public. Hilary even feared for Neil, thinking that he shouldn't trust her sister, he should wonder what dark undertow might follow after such a glittering bright flood.

By the end of the week Sheila was well enough to go to lectures again, and on the Saturday she came to the bus station to see Hilary off. She insisted on carrying Hilary's suitcase, which swung in her hand as light as if there was nothing in it, now that their father's old dictionaries of classical mythology had been unloaded.

—I didn't feel anything, you know, Sheila said as they walked, as if she was picking up on some discussion they had only broken off a few moments before, although in fact they hadn't talked once, since it was over, about what had happened to her. —I mean, apart from physically. Just like a tummy upset. That's all it was: a nuisance.

—All right, if you say so.

For the first time Sheila talked about her studies. She had to write an essay on the *Oresteia* which she said was all about the sex war, female avenging furies and male reason.

—*The gods are disgusted at you*, she said gleefully. —Apollo to the Furies. *Apoptustoi theois. Never let your filth touch anything in my sacred shrine.*

When Hilary was in her seat in the coach, Sheila stayed hanging round outside the window although Hilary signed to her to go, there was no need to wait. They laughed at one another through the glass, helpless to communicate: for the first time they were in tune together as they used to be. Sheila mouthed something and Hilary mimed elaborately: frowned, shook her head, shrugged her shoulders. She couldn't understand. Sheila put her face close to the glass and cupped her hands round her mouth, shouting. She was wearing a woollen knitted hat with knitted flowers pulled down over her ears.

—Give my love to everybody!

Hilary saw that all of a sudden her sister didn't want her to go. She was seized then by an impulse to struggle off the coach, to stay and fight, as if Sheila had after all been abducted by a Bluebeard: she felt focused as a crusader in her opposition to Neil. She even half turned round in her seat, as if to get out. But there was a man in the seat beside her, she would have had to ask him to move, he was settled behind his newspaper. The moment and the possibility passed. The coach reversed, the sisters waved frantically, and then Sheila was gone and Hilary subsided into her solitude, keeping her face averted from the man who had seen too much of her excitement, and whose newspaper anyway would make her sick if she accidentally read any of the headlines.

Above the city buildings the sky was blue and pale with light, drawn across by thin skeins of transparent cloud. Beyond the outskirts of the city everything was bursting with the spring growth which was further on over here than in the east. The tips of the hedgerows and the trees, if they hadn't yet come into leaf, gave off a red haze where the twigs swelled and shone. It seemed extraordinary to Hilary that her life must at some point soon change as completely and abruptly as Sheila's had, so that everything familiar would be left behind. She sat with bubbles of excitement rising in her chest. The scruffy undistinguished countryside outside the coach window seemed to her beautiful. It desolated her to think that when she was dead she wouldn't be able to see it: cows, green hummocky fields, suburban cottages of weathered brick, a country factory with smashed windows, an excited spatter of birds thrown up from a tree. Then she started to see these things as if she was dead already, and they were persisting after her, and she had been allowed back, and must take in everything hungrily while she had the chance, every least tiny detail. □

GRANTA

MARTIN AND ME

Thomas Healy

Thomas Healy with Martin

Martin and Me

It seems now like a different me, the years I spent with Martin, a Dobermann dog, and before he came, another me; it is a new me now, once again, writing this. I would have been dead long ago had I continued to live the way I had before he came. I think someone would have murdered me, given how I drank and the dives that I drank in and that I was an aggressive, angry man. I had no money and no friends. I didn't care, I couldn't have.

How this state of affairs had come to be I don't know. I had been a friendly if timorous boy, not one for trouble. I managed to dodge violence until I was twenty, which was quite a feat where I grew up, but that first fight had a big impact. My opponent was a man named Bull Flannigan. I was working for the railway as a shunter in a yard in Springburn in Glasgow. The job was shifts and there was lots of overtime and I remember that I was able to save four pounds a week, which was a lot of money in 1964. You could buy eleven or twelve pints of beer for one pound then.

I had got into the habit of an occasional pint in a pub that was just under a bridge from the shunting yard. Springburn was a tough district, full of scarred and battered faces: teenage gangs and individual hard men. The man with the hardest reputation was Bull Flannigan. If you were in a pub and he was there, you looked the other way.

When I was working in the shunting yard I would have jumped if a girl had said boo. But I was a good enough shunter and worked all the overtime I could get, and I always had money. I was good for a loan, a couple of pounds to a fellow shunter until payday. I sometimes gave a loan inside the pub, which Bull Flannigan might have noticed, clocked up. Or someone might have told him. There were always people who wanted to keep on the right side of a fellow like Flannigan in Glasgow pubs.

Flannigan was in his thirties and had a close-cropped, too-big head. He was low and squat and wore a buttoned-up black crombie coat. Most of the time he was with two other men who also wore black crombie coats. But not that night.

I had been alone at the bar when, out of nowhere, he was standing next to me. I felt weak to fall by his very presence: a super hard man. I was told to buy him a whisky, and given a push on my chest so that I got the message.

The barman and some customers were looking on. The young railway man and Bull Flannigan: a small drama. I was as frightened as I had ever been, but at the same time I did not see why I should buy him a whisky. The easy way out would have been to have bought the whisky and got the hell away from Bull Flannigan. There was nobody would have looked down on me had I done that, but I could not. Everything in me said no. This bullying hard man in his crombie coat. I told him to buy his own whisky.

A pause. I saw a first doubt in Flannigan's eyes. They were blue, for what that matters. I was taller than him, but he was thicker. They did not call him Bull for nothing. And an insistent bull, that I buy him a whisky. I was now seeing red. Flannigan made to push me again, and I punched him on the nose. Hard. I felt the bridge smash. He stumbled back, his ruined nose and his crombie coat bright with blood. Was this me, the trembling boy of a moment ago? I was a wild man now, hitting Flannigan. It was one-way punches. The first blow on his nose had done for him. And it had done for me, the boy I had been till then.When I left that pub I was a changed person. More a man? I thought so. But I wish now that I had never had that fight, for looking down the years, it did not change me for the better.

From the time of that first fight until I was thirty-nine I was seldom out of fights. My life was a blur of alcohol, flights of fancy, wild, drunken brawls. It is no use kidding here about my drinking habit. I was a paid-up alcoholic. I think the drinking game got out of hand when I was twenty-three, on holiday in Amsterdam. A tour round the bars, the red-light district. I did not feel right until I had had a few Amstel beers. I soon discovered a much stronger brew, stuff that came in small bottles, like half pints. And no wonder: you could get drunk on four or five of them. This was the summer of 1967. The world was swinging. I was rolling, falling down. And I would go on falling for many years to come. No matter how much I drank, there was never enough, and that was the way I was.

In 1983, with forty approaching, I thought to begin anew, to remove myself to London. I had no idea what I would do there, but the place appealed to me, as, over the years, it has appealed to a lot of lost and lonely men. I was assisted in this plan by the offer of a film deal on one of my short stories. I was a writer—not that I was doing much writing then. But in March of that year a man named Martin Harrington offered to buy the film rights to a story of mine. We had spoken on the telephone and agreed to a sum of money. Some hundreds. I thought it enough to get started in London. A couple of days later I got an early morning train, a one-way ticket. I had no intention of returning to Glasgow.

I met Harrington in Euston Station. He had a bald head and a big black beard. We went for drink, and, really, it was no big deal—I had won more money on the horses. Harrington struck me for a cagey guy and I can't say that I liked him. A mutual feeling, I am sure. But I got the money, a bunch of notes in a pub. I had a good drink in me, and I forget how I got rid of Harrington—or how he got rid of me. So far as I know the story was never filmed, or, if it was, it must have flopped. The next I remember I was in the West End, the bright lights.

My new life? It had no chance, there was another fate awaiting me.

I had expected a whale of a time in London, but that night I took a taxi back to Euston and a night train back to Glasgow. I'm not sure why. On the train I was in a queer, blue mood. I longed for the seclusion of a monastery, felt that I had been this way too much, too often in my life. At least it would be the first time in a long time that I had money in my pocket in Glasgow. In the morning, rumpled and hungover, I walked from the Central Station to St Enoch Square, where I got a number 7 bus. It no longer runs, not from St Enoch.

I was staying in my mother's house. Only a mother would have put up with me, for I could swing to violence easily, on a wrong word. I drank morning and night and through the night, and in this dismal state I hated myself for what I was, what I had become, and I had unreal fears and I felt not a little lonely.

It was my habit on drinking bouts to buy the *Glasgow Herald*, an old favourite. I had once written for it, and it is safe to say that booze had cost me a job on it. The job could have turned my life, but it was not to be. I had continued drinking, and I was still drinking. Cans of superlager.

It was April now and a hint of summer, and I hated April and the longer nights, the bright, bright summertime. Reading the *Herald* one day, my eyes fell on the livestock column, pups for sale. I do not know why I paused at an ad for Dobermann pups, which were coloured black and tan and were six weeks old and of a good pedigree. I had not thought to obtain a pet. When I was fourteen or so and still at school, I had acquired a dog, a young cross-breed, that, because he was a golden colour, I had christened Goldie. He came from the city dog pound. But it was a brief affair, for the dog had been sick, I think with distemper; and he had to be put down. I was a mighty sad boy that day, I can remember it yet, my feeling inside when Goldie was no more. And I had only had him for a week or so.

When I saw that telephone number in the *Herald*, all of a sudden I wanted a dog. The Dobermann breed appealed to me, so I telephoned the number. The man who answered told me to come round any time and see the pups, and as he was not too far away I told him that I would be round within the hour. He was tinkering with a motorbike when I arrived. Straight off I did not like the look of him. He was a beefy sort with a scar on his face. He gave a bad impression. 'Are you the guy who telephoned?'

I said I was. I was half drunk and in need of a wash and a clean shirt. He had to think that he had found a clown, a drunken fool. He led me inside a tenement and up some stairs to a council flat. It was the sort of place that you would have thought twice about going if it was night and you were sober.

There were about six pups locked inside an airless room, on a filthy carpet. The rancid room was in need of fumigation. I had expected a more hygienic setting, and I disliked the fat man even more. I think about the only thing that he had done was feed the pups, who despite the filth of their confine, appeared to be bright and full of fun, one tumbling over the other.

I asked where the mother was.

'She's in the other room.'

'I'd like to see her.'

'You must be kidding.'

'I'm not kidding.'

'She'd take off your arm if she knew why you were here.'

'Why, are you going to tell her?'

He hummed and hawed. I almost laughed. Wherever he had got the litter, he did not have the mother. I had got down on my haunches and was quite taken by one particularly bold, aggressive pup. This small creature had fixed itself on to the back of my hand. It had sharp cat-like claws, and would not let go. Nor budge an inch. A show of affection? I thought so, and if it wanted me I wanted it and I decided to buy the pup.

The asking price was £150. There was no way I was paying that, not to him. I was standing again, with the pup on the back of my hand. I offered fifty pounds for it. He shook his head, that it was not enough. I told him he could take it or leave it for I was taking the pup, one way or the other. Afterwards people would think that I had got Martin for nothing, but he cost me fifty pounds.

This was all on a whim, the whole thing. I told the fat guy to phone a taxi for me and my new buddy on the back of my hand. He was all big black eyes and, for all I knew, he could have been a she. It took me weeks to determine its sex, to look.

I was drunk for all of the first week of our new guest's stay. The wee dog—that is what my mother called him—had slept against my chest when I sat drinking, or sleeping, in my chair. Or so my mother told me when I sobered up. She had cleaned up after him and had fed him tins of puppy food. She had no idea how he had come to be in our house, had felt sorry for him. She was none too fond of him, this stranger in her house. I think my mother thought I would get rid of him when I sobered up.

It would be touch and go for a good three weeks if the dog stayed or if he went. I had come by him when I was drunk and without a thought to his wants and needs. That I would need to buy a collar for him, for one thing. As it turned out my mother bought him his first collar, a light tartan affair more suited to a poodle than a Dobermann. He had to have been about three months old by then, when he got his collar.

How he had managed to stay I do not know. There had been times when I could have seen him far enough. The house-training. It had crossed my mind to return him to the fat guy, but I just could not do it. And, one week to two, a month, the longer he was with me, and he was with me all the time, the more I felt that he was my responsibility.

My sister hit on a name for him. 'Tulip.'

'I don't like Tulip.'

'He came in April.'

'What's that got to do with Tulip?'

'They grow tulips in Holland in April,' she said.

They did? But I would not name my pup Tulip. It was not him, not even then. 'You can't have a boy dog with a name like Tulip.'

'Martin, then,' she said. 'Call him Martin.'

It sounded not too bad to me, and a whole lot better than her first choice, Tulip.

'If it hadn't been for that guy Martin Harrington you would never have had him.'

So Martin it was, and I have never heard of another dog called Martin.

On our first few walks I had Martin on a washline rope, and this had to appear odd, as though I had stolen him or something. I had a couple of offers to sell him, and for more money than the £150 that the fat guy had been looking for. But there was never any question, not once I had become accustomed to him, that I would sell Martin.

His tail was docked, and, for a while, I thought he had been born that way, with a short, stumped tail. I knew so much about dogs, the Dobermann breed.

But I was beginning to know Martin. He was a prideful pup and given to sulk, to stay away from me for hours if I had scolded him.

My mother used to say, Martin sitting alone in a corner: 'The wee dog's fell out with Thomas.'

This went on for a time, that Martin could fall out with me, like take the humph and who did I think I was?

I was none too sure. And what was I doing with him? But we went together, somehow. Martin had learned my name before he knew his own. In the coming years there would be a mix-up over this, our names: I was sometimes Martin and he was sometimes Thomas.

For the first few weeks Martin slept at the bottom of my bed. We would get up about ten. After a coffee I would take him out while my mother was cooking the breakfast. I ate fried eggs and sausages, which I would carry though to the living room. We had a glass-topped table and Martin would sit watching me, his mouth dripping.

I used to give him the white of an egg. One morning I went to answer the telephone and while I was gone he ate the lot, my breakfast. I looked at him, he looked at me. What to do? I pretended to have noticed nothing and sat down to eat. 'What's this?' I looked at the plate and then at Martin. 'Who has stolen my food?' I scratched my head as though astonished. 'Did you see anybody?'

Martin's eyes were big and round at my strange behaviour. He had expected an instant scolding; I should have been angry with him. It would have been more like the thing. 'We have a thief in the house.' I tapped my fork against the plate and showed my teeth and shook my fist. 'Come, we will catch him, Martin.' I was up off of the seat and through to the bedroom where I looked behind the curtains and under the bed. 'Where can he be?'

Martin's head was cocked, he had a quizzical look. Had I gone off my head? I think, if he could speak, he would have owned up then that he ate my breakfast.

My mother made a new one. She had got into the act: 'Who do you think it could have been?'

'I asked Martin if he saw anybody.'

'He couldn't have,' my mother said. 'Martin wouldn't let anybody eat your breakfast.'

'Then it will just need to remain a mystery, whoever ate my breakfast.'

'We'll keep an eye open tomorrow morning.'

'You bet,' I said, and I looked at Martin, who looked bemused at all of this. 'We'll keep an eye open tomorrow morning.'

The next day I put my breakfast on the glass-topped table and told Martin, who was about four months old by now, to guard it while I looked out the window.

I had my back to him, but only for a moment. It was enough for Martin to steal one of my two fried eggs. I looked first at the plate and then at him. He looked at me with big guiltless eyes. 'Good boy,' I said, and when I had finished my breakfast I gave him the white of the remaining egg.

This would go on for years, it became a rite that at breakfast time I would turn away and Martin would steal an egg.

We lived in the ground-floor flat in a tenement in a housing scheme and had our own front garden. The garden was helpful when

I house-trained Martin. It had taken less than a week. He had, at this stage, when the egg business had first begun, yet to bark and I had begun to think that he might be barkless.

'Woof. Woof,' I encouraged him, and I cupped my hand behind my ear. 'Woof. Woof.'

But still nothing, or only the usual quizzical look I got from him when I acted daft.

Some teenage gangs hung around near to where we lived, and—I think because they were in a group—Martin used to growl at them. They called me Batman and he was Robin, and the name stuck. We were not a pair to mess with and the gangs avoided us and we avoided them. Or I did. Martin was for attacking them. We were neither of us popular. Martin was hardly a dog to pat. He disliked strangers. I suppose that I encouraged it, for I disliked strangers too.

The teenage gangs thought of themselves as wide boys and were well aware that I sometimes took too much to drink. One evening early that summer, I was much the worse for drink and collapsed in the field behind the house. This was the field where I took Martin every morning before breakfast. It was attached to a school and there was a football pitch, but we kept to the waste ground to the side. This was fenced off from the houses and it was pretty private and, on summer nights, it was a favoured haunt for the gang boys and their girls.

Some of the girls were as bad as the boys and it was their duty to hide the weapons, knives and open razors, in their handbags, until the need arose to use them. This was hardly new. I could remember the same practice when I was in my teens in the tenement Gorbals. When a fight did happen, and it could happen very suddenly, the girls, all shrieks and screams, would urge on the boys to greater deeds of derring-do. I had seen a couple of gang fights when I was in this field with Martin. But I had been sober then.

I was far from sober on this particular summer's evening. I staggered to collapse, pass out. A stricken Batman. Robin, though, was most alert, and when I came to he had his head on my belly and I had a bag of booze beside me on the ground. The gang boys and girls had let us be because they were scared of Robin. I was supposed to be in charge of him, but it had been the other way round that night.

Later that summer Martin took ill. When I brought him to the vet I was told that he had been poisoned. Until then I had let him out into the garden alone, and as it was the only place where he had been alone, it was the only place where he could have been poisoned.

Somebody trying to get back at me? I could think of a few who might want to, due to my past behaviour. I had suspicions of about ten persons, any one of whom could have been the poisoner. After he recovered I never let Martin out into the garden alone again.

It had been a close thing, for a time, if he would recover. The vet thought fifty-fifty. A listless Martin. He would neither eat nor drink. I was given a nutrient that I had to feed him from a dummy teat. By then Martin had shifted out from my bed to a couch that was beside the bed. I had thought it only right that we had separate sleeping quarters. We were still close enough, him on his couch and me in my bed, that Martin did not feel alone. Or, perhaps more to the truth, that neither of us felt alone. And I did not want to be alone again, without him. I think it was then, when Martin was ill, a poorly bit of fur and bone that I nursed all night with the dummy teat, that our bond was formed.

Before Martin's illness, I could not have believed that I would sit with him all through the night and will him to get better. Which I did, and he did. On the third or fourth night I saw the light come back into Martin's eyes. He licked my hand. A dry tongue. I got him water. When he began to lap the water I knew that we had won.

I never found out who had poisoned Martin, and as I was a much different man then than I am today, that was just as well.

Within days of his drink of water Martin was back to his bouncing self, and he had me and I had him. The falling-out days were over.

When Martin arrived my mother was seventy-three. She had white hair and all of that but I did not think of her as old or elderly or that she was even aging. She had always been there and had always been much the same to me. She had always worked and she was still working. She had a job as a cleaner in a bowling club. It was heavy work for a woman of her age, but I can't remember a single day when my mother was sick, laid-up. In any case I did not give a thought to it. What money she earned she tried to save to go on holiday with a group of women she had known for years. They had been to Florida and Italy, the Channel Islands. Unlike me, she was a social person and well-liked. There was nobody ever had a bad word to say about my mother. Wee Mrs Healy, she was barely five foot tall but had a big heart. She had survived my father's death and the death of a baby daughter. Her only two brothers had died on her, each one under fifty. You could safely say she had been through the mill and had known her share of sorrow. She had me for a son, after all. Over the years I must have been a tremendous worry to her. And now, as all of a sudden, I had a pal and my mother did not know what to make of him. Not at first. She had been told that he was a Dobermann and that Dobermanns were fierce guard dogs. Whoever had told her this had also said that you could never trust a Dobermann. 'Are you keeping him, Thomas?'

'That's up to you. I can't keep him if you don't want him in the house.'

'I didn't say that I didn't want him in the house.'

This was after I had just sobered up and before I was fond of Martin. Before she was fond of Martin.

'If you're frightened of him.'

'I'm not frightened of him now,' she said. 'But it might be different when he grows up.'

'I don't think it will be different.'

And neither it was. Martin, a dog you could not trust? We trusted him with our lives, my mother and sister and me. He was a one-man dog and at his happiest with me.

My sister took to Martin straight off. There was no problem with her about his staying. But it was me who had to look after him, she made that clear. 'He's your dog, not mine.'

It would soon become more than obvious to everyone whose dog Martin was. A new side to my nature? It had been a big surprise to a lot of people to see me with a pup. They had not thought that I was a doggy sort of man. Well, neither had I, but we all surprise ourselves sometimes. I suspect they thought it was a fad and that Martin would soon go, that I would kick him out in a drunken rage. They had to be disappointed when, week after week, he still was there. Far from a kick, it is my proud boast that I never laid a hand on Martin. He was never cowed or frightened of me. I encouraged his high spirits, a natural boldness. It was the way he was and why I chose him, or, as my mother often said, he chose me when he had climbed up on to my hand and would not let go.

That autumn my mother and sister went on holiday. It was just me and Martin in the house. My sister had warned me not to drink because of Martin. 'You're all he's got.'

'I know I'm all he's got.'

'You know what happens when you drink.'

'I won't drink.'

'You could lose Martin if you do.'

'I won't lose Martin.' And neither I did, and I did not drink either. I read books and tried to write and took my pal on long, long walks. This was late September. You could feel the winter creeping in. A first frost. I felt to have come a long way since April. I was with my dog and I was sober.

I had been sober for most of that summer. An occasional slip now and then, but nothing compared to my former drinking. I was learning new things about myself. That I was as big a sucker for affection, even from a dog, as any man who ever lived. Martin brought out the boy in me. The surprise was that, in my basic nature, I had hardly changed at all. In many ways I was ten years old in the body of a man. I was not hard at all. My sister could not believe the change in Martin when she returned from holiday. 'Are you sure that is the same dog?'

'No, I went out and bought another one.'

'He looks formidable.'

'In two weeks?'

'I'm telling you.'

'I didn't notice any change in him.'

'That's because you've been with him every day.'

'He's still the same Martin.' But she was right, he was becoming big. A sudden sprout. High and rangy, a gangly look. But he was beginning to form and he had heavy bones and big paws, a promise of great power.

'You didn't drink.'

'Not a drop.'

'Did you miss it?'

'I didn't even think about it.'

'Then you don't need to drink, do you?'

No, I didn't. But a couple of weeks later I did drink and ended up in jail. In a police station in the Gorbals. I had been drinking all day and that night I got into a fight, a bad one. I emerged unscathed but the chances were that I would be remanded to prison for some time.

Inside the van on the way to court I could only think of Martin and what would become of him if I was sent to prison.

In court I was charged with assault. I pleaded not guilty. There were a couple of other guys involved and they pleaded not guilty too. We were all released to appear at a later date. To this day I still don't know why we were not sent to prison.

When I got home Martin almost knocked me down, so eager was his welcome.

The charge against me was later dropped because of insufficient evidence. But I wished I had not been in jail, even for a night. I felt more guilty about abandoning Martin than what they had charged me with.When I should have been looking out for both of us I had been chancing time in prison. I vowed never again for a similar predicament, and I have kept my vow and have had no trouble with the police since that autumn night in 1983.

It had become my habit to buy Martin crisps when I went into a pub for a pint or two. He was no more than a big pup at this time, in November or December of our first year. The pubs we used were far from local. I had never had Martin in a pub where I was known, where there might be trouble. And I was careful too, when I was with him, that I was never the worse for drink. It was a good, high feeling to sit in a pub with my pal right there beside me.

We went into pubs in the daytime only, at the end of a walk. I had Martin on a choke chain now, which was the only way to handle him, to have full control. He was becoming incredibly strong and quick as a flash and I worried that he might break away from a normal lead and get himself run over. He was at that age, not one year old, when he could have easily got run over. Without a choke chain I do not know if I could have managed Martin.

Our pub visits were to come to a sudden stop. This was because of a one-eyed drunk I used to know. I had not seen this guy in twenty years, and I pretended not to notice him. But he noticed me with his one eye. I was reading a newspaper and he decided to surprise me. Which you should not do to a man who has a dog with him, and not to a man with a Dobermann. My one-eyed friend could tell you that, for he almost lost his nose, and I would have lost Martin if he had lost his nose. And all because he was drunk and I was in the pub.

This was the first time I had seen ferocity in Martin. He had always been so playful, a bundle of fun. But not that day in that pub. I had to fight to hold him back, away from the man behind me. Indeed, I had to almost drag Martin out of the pub and away from that man. Such a frenzy! On a blink. He had thought the man was attacking me and had reacted in his nature. Until then I had not thought that it was in his nature to behave like that. It had been a frightful transformation.

I did not tell my mother or sister about our adventure in the pub. They thought, the same as I had, that there was only love in Martin, and I wanted it to remain that way. My big pup. You always hear that it is the master's fault and not the dog's, when a dog gets into trouble, so when I heard about the Dobermann Club I was not slow to take him there. To train me more than him, for there was more to Martin than I thought.

The Dobermann Club was run by a strong-voiced ex-army man who brooked no nonsense. It was a serious business, his training school. He made that clear, and I was glad to hear it. I had not come to the Dobermann Club for a social evening. It took an hour to walk there and an hour back again. We went once a week. I can't say that I liked the trainer but I was not there to like the trainer and I did not care if he disliked me. I was used to people disliking me.

The club was in a hall above a church and you had anything between fifteen and twenty Dobermann pups at any one session. Martin was one of the older dogs, but he was far from being the biggest. There were some brutes of dogs, so called pups, in that place. Martin liked it, but then he liked any place he was with me.

The trainer was good at his job, I'll say that for him. He knew dogs, the Dobermann breed. He would demonstrate with his own dog what obedience should be. I had to admire him and his dog, the level they had achieved. When he told his dog to stay it stayed, not a movement, and it could stay like that—on its belly, on the floor—for the best part of a session.

I could not hope to equal that with Martin. But we were beginning to work together. He was picking up on me and I on him. The Dobermann Club taught both of us that he had to do what I told him, when I told him.

There are no two Dobermanns alike, I learned that too. The trainer's dog and Martin—well, I would doubt that even the trainer could have had Martin stay for half a long as his own dog did. It is all about the temperament of the individual dog. Martin was smaller than most, and other Dobermanns seemed to be more alert and tougher. And he could never compete as a show dog: he was too small and had a rib too many. The vet had told me about Martin's extra rib when he was ill. I had not cared as long as he got better. What is an extra rib, a couple of inches? But there was never any question about his spirit. Martin was the boldest and the most faithful dog at the Dobermann Club. Even the trainer remarked on how close he was to me. We attended weekly for several months, until he was not a pup any more and we had learned all that they could teach. Then we departed on good terms. This was the first in recent times that I left a place where people were without bad feelings.

That Christmas I went to Midnight Mass with my mother for the first time in many years. We sat in a front pew and we would sit in that same front pew for the next nine Christmases. I had no idea where I had been the Christmas before, but it could have been nowhere nearly so good as in the chapel with my mother and Peace on earth to men of good will.

I had known little peace for many years, but was nudging closer. A certain soothing in my heart, my soul? I had asked my mother to come with me to the chapel in a freezing late-night. An odd thing: since Martin, I had become much closer to my mother. I was at home much more, for one thing. Before the arrival of my dog I had been given to disappearing. I could not do that now, with my new responsibility.

There were three priests on the altar saying the mass, and altar boys in white vestments were scrubbed so clean they looked pure and shining bright. My mother knew lots of people in the chapel and I knew that she was proud of me that at last I was with her in the chapel. It had to be a minor miracle.

It was a good Christmas that Christmas, our first with Martin in the house, our new family member. He was not so wee now, but my mother was completely unafraid of him. Had she been afraid of him Martin would have had to go. But rather than afraid my mother was a fierce protector. She would let no one say a word against our dog. We had brought him up almost as a new child in the house.

He was a rebellious one at times. One night that Christmas he was sitting in my easy chair. When I tried to move him off, he did a bit of growling and showed me his teeth. The side incisors were a good inch long and sharp as razors. A touch from them could break your skin. I pointed to him. 'Off,' I said, but he only continued growling. Call me mad, but I found it touching, like he was trying for his self-respect, or that he had his right to be on the chair as I had mine. But I was surprised at this mutiny, and I put it down sharply. A shake of my fist, some harsh words. Martin got the message. His revolt passed over.

We exchanged gifts about two in the morning, my mother and sister and me. My sister had been minding Martin while my mother and I had been at Midnight Mass. A problem with Martin, he would howl for me when I went out. My sister did her best with him but she could not stop the howling. He had been up in my chair and looking out of the window, watching for me. So she said. ' Like a big wolf.'

'He must miss me.'

'You'll never find nobody who misses you more than he does.'

We had a coal fire and a Christmas tree, some Christmas decorations. I forget what gifts I got, but my mother treated Martin to a tin of Pal dog food. I remember that. He was usually fed a dried food that I mixed with water. It was good and nourishing and a fraction of the cost of tinned dog food. (Martin would have eaten six or seven tins of dog food a day and have still been wanting more.) My mother did not want Martin to feel out of things during the gift exchanging. And he had some memory, for the next Christmas and the next he would be looking for his tin of Pal dog food.

We went out that night, Martin and me. It had to be three in the morning. I was becoming a man of the open air, the open field. In stout walking boots and a hooded zipped-up jacket. It is easy to get pneumonia in Glasgow in the winter. A cold can lead to it. Or if you are simply rundown. I felt in robust good health. Stronger than for many a year. I was walking every day, and walking sometimes fifteen or even twenty miles. It is surprising how far you can walk when you are walking with a dog. I didn't think of miles or time, but the time flew in and the miles flew by. A man and his dog. It was a simple life, but it suited me, and Martin had to think that it would go on for ever. □

GRANTA

THE MUSE IN THE CELLAR

James Lasdun

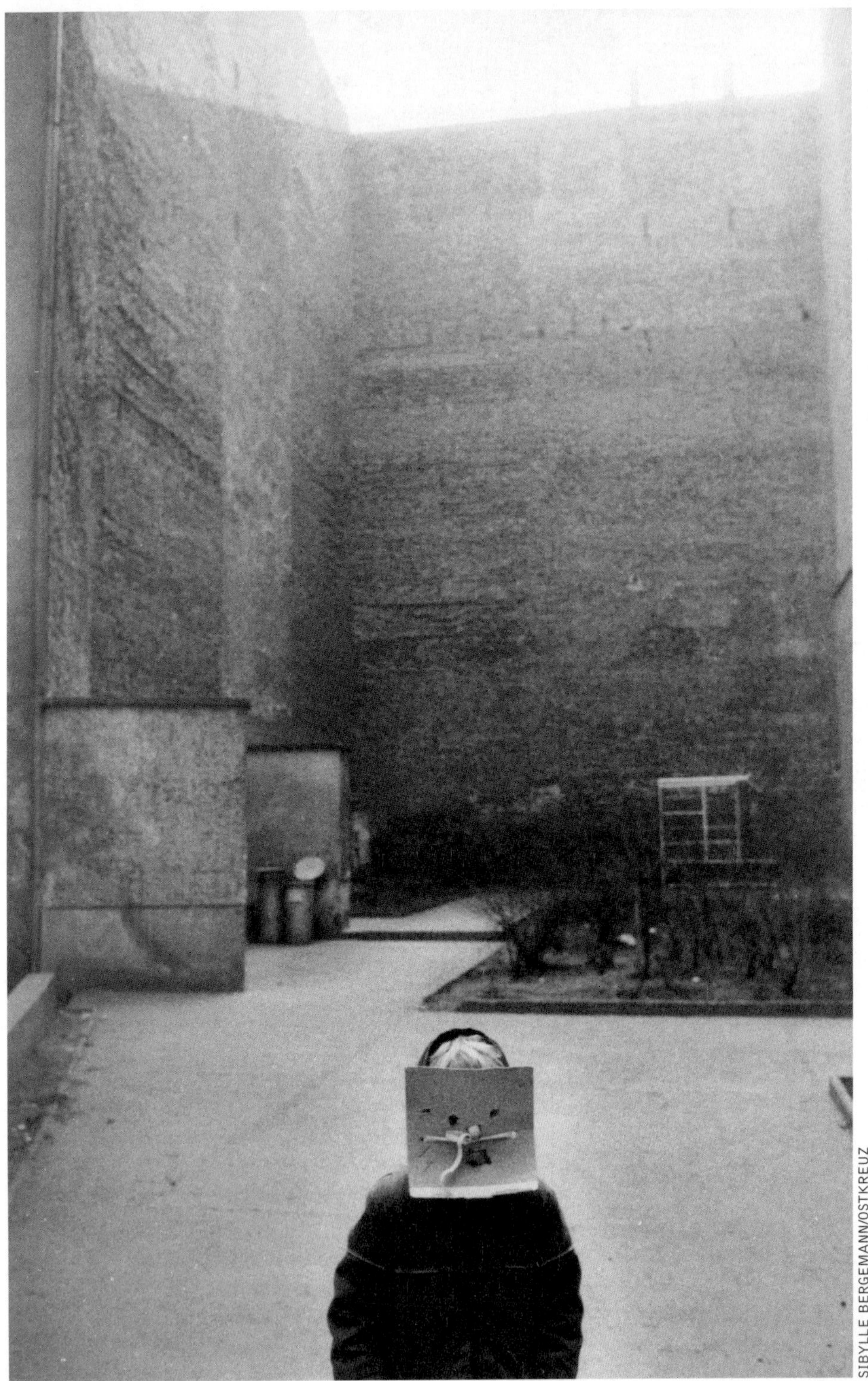

SIBYLLE BERGEMANN/OSTKREUZ

The Muse in the Cellar

The chain of events began in 1974. My father, a lawyer by training, had been quietly consolidating a career in the diplomatic service of the German Democratic Republic, where his speciality was negotiating fine-print details in the Friendship Treaties springing up between the GDR and other countries in the Eastern bloc. It was a humdrum, if respectable occupation, but after the rest of the free world had followed West Germany in granting full diplomatic recognition to our republic in 1973, and the UN itself had opened its doors to us, my father was selected as a junior member on the GDR mission to that august body, and our lives looked set to change.

For a few months he shuttled back and forth between Berlin and New York: kindly, remote, befogged by jet lag and overwork, but always bearing gifts of a radiant strangeness—Slinkies, watches for deep-sea divers, a wireless that woke you with a cup of instant coffee. These little marvels formed the entire body and substance of my image of New York, and as I discovered many years later when I flew in, the picture they had created was strangely accurate: there below us were the toys and gadgets from that brief period in my family's life metamorphosed into an entire city of hooped and flowing steel, of vast, luminous, multi-dialled watches, of buildings like giant radios with towers of glass and streaming water.

My father's visits grew steadily longer. There was talk of a permanent posting, even of our being sent out there to live with him…

New York! America! In those dark ages of absolute division between East and West, the very word 'America' seemed to bristle with dangerous, glittering energies. Like 'Moscow', it named the source of some ultimate fright and power. Bonn was our West German sibling: object of rivalry, contempt, occasional jealousy; but America and Russia were parental figures, and upon them we projected all our fantasies of supernatural and possibly cannibalistic strength. Nominally, of course, one was our friend, the other our enemy, but both gave us the same peculiar excitement to contemplate.

For my mother, the idea of our living in New York played directly to her sense of our family's innate superiority. She and her brother—my Uncle Heinrich—were of blue-blooded Silesian descent. Naturally this was not something to brag about in communist East Germany, and they had been quick to drop the 'von' from the family name after the war. But in their quietly indomitable way, these two had maintained a sense of themselves as somehow ineffably superior to other people, and moreover they had managed to transmit this sense to those around them, not by any crude arrogance or self-aggrandizement, but by a certain aristocratic froideur; a mixture of haughty reserve and sudden graciousness, which bewildered people, intimidated them, and filled them with a kind of strained awe. My mother in particular was an expert in that form of psychological control which consists on the one hand in withholding, or at least delaying, a smile or word of kindness when the situation seems to call for one, and on the other in bestowing her approval of something—when she chose to do so—with a magisterial impersonality, as if she were merely the channel for an objective fact that had been handed down to her by some celestial source of judgement. The effect of the latter was to make one feel elevated, officially congratulated as it were; as if a medal with the head of Lenin on it had been pinned to one's chest.

You might imagine that in a socialist society a personality such as hers, with the distinctly unegalitarian idea of life that it projected, couldn't possibly thrive. But somehow she managed to short-circuit the mental processes by which people might form a criticism of her in political terms, and confront them instead on a more intimate and primitive level of the psyche, where authority, if it succeeds in imposing itself as such, is unquestioningly believed in and—how shall I put it?—quaked before.

She was no beauty, with her sturdy little frame clad always in the drabbest brown and grey clothes. Her crooked, slightly jagged-looking front teeth dominated one's initial impression of her face, and made even her oldest acquaintances prefer to shake hands with her rather than exchange kisses. But there was something forceful, even magnetic in her appearance. Her dark brown, slightly protuberant eyes, encased in folded, lashless lids, possessed an unusual mobility and expressiveness. As they narrowed attentively, tilted to admit a faint sardonic lightness, gathered into their corners the traces of a codified smile, flashed with anger or coldly averted themselves from your gaze, drawing behind them an almost visible portcullis, one felt—with the fascination of seeing anything naked—that one was observing the fluctuating movements of the very organism to which the names Frieda, Frau Vogel, Mother, all referred. For as long as I can remember there was a patch of pure white in her greyish-brown hair, such as you see in certain city pigeons, and this too seemed the mark or brand of some quality that set her apart, though I was always uncertain whether it represented something done to her, or something she was liable to do unto others.

All of this—the haughtiness of her manner, the crooked teeth, the naked, imposing eyes, the little arctic patch on her head—was contained in, and to some extent tempered by, an overall burnish of tragedy; a kind of final, stabilizing layer that had been added to her portrait during the middle part of the 1970s. This was the tragedy of thwarted ambition, and my father was to blame for it.

In his profession hard work and competence landed you in Hungary or, god help you, Romania; above average skills might get you as far as one of the West European Permanent Representations; a certain type of well-connected career lackey would end up in Moscow. But in the private hierarchies of my mother's imagination, a mission into the *Imperium Americanum* was an acknowledgement to those entrusted with it that they were the very crème de la crème, the crack troops, the elite. As our posting there grew more certain, all the chilly potency of that vast opponent seemed, by virtue of our association with it, to decant itself into our lives, and for several weeks we emitted an eerie glow among our friends, like that of immortals from legend, imprisoned for a term among mankind, but now at last able to reveal their true lineage.

Naturally my mother pretended to make light of these developments, even to disparage them. At the mention of America, or New York, or the United Nations, her lips would purse with a look of involuntary annoyance, as if some ancient personal grievance were being referred to, after which she would rather affectedly change the subject. Nevertheless she saw to it that people were told of our imminent elevation. Allusions to my father's jet lag were dropped nonchalantly into conversations with our neighbours. Our friends in the Politburo, the Gretzes, were invited to dinner with Uncle Heinrich, who could be counted on to raise the subject with a twinkle of indiscretion, and thereby ensure that they were properly confounded. Heinrich himself, whom my father had helped get a job in the office of the Chief of the People's Police, spread the word among our acquaintances in the security community.

Once, to my chagrin, my mother made an appearance at the school my brother and I attended, asking to be allowed to sit in on my history class. The subject was a comparative analysis of the emancipation of the serfs in Russia and the abolition of slavery in the United States. The idea being instilled in us was that the Americans had had no ideological interest in freeing the slaves, and only happened to do so by accident, whereas the Russians, as their subsequent history showed... et cetera. My mother sat at the back of the classroom with a stern expression. Halfway through the class she stood up and called to me in a quiet voice:

'Stefan, come with me would you please?'

Writhing inwardly, I rose and made my way towards her under the puzzled eyes of my teacher. We went to the office of the principal, whom my mother proceeded to harangue about the poor quality of the class.

'I don't see that the interests of our children are well served by quite such a crude portrayal of the Western powers,' she declared. 'I hardly think that those of us obliged to have direct contact with the capitalist system,' placing a hand on my arm, 'are likely to benefit from being taught about it in terms of caricature...'

I stood beside her; oppressed, heavy, numb; assuming the posture that now seems characteristic of my entire adolescence: hunched, eyes averted, blank-faced; a kind of permanent, petrified shrug.

The principal eyed us shrewdly from beneath her portraits of Marx and Engels. She must have been trying to decide whether my mother was raving mad, or was perhaps privy to some new educational policy development forming itself in the higher echelons of the Party. Luckily for us she seemed to choose the latter. She promised to investigate the matter personally and see to it that the teacher in question was properly reprimanded. With a curt nod my mother thanked her and we departed.

The culminating act in her folie de grandeur (it amounted to that) came one evening while my father was away in New York. She, my older brother Otto, myself and our 'lodger' Kitty (our maid in all but name) were seated at the dinner table, which, as usual, Kitty had covered with a cotton cloth before laying, when my mother suddenly exclaimed, 'The linen! The von Riesen linen! We'll take it to New York!'

It turned out that a trunk full of family belongings had survived not only the war but also the upheavals following Yalta that had left my mother and her brother orphaned and penniless in what became East Germany. The trunk was in my mother's possession, stored in the basement of our apartment building. Among other things it contained a full set of Irish linen, including tablecloths and napkins, every piece embroidered with the von Riesen initials and family crest. Upon some fantastical new whim, my mother had taken it into her head that this linen, spread on a communist table in New York (I suppose in her imagination she saw herself as some sort of society hostess in the diplomatic world) would strike just the right note of mystery and coolly ironic humour, while at the same time impressing people tremendously.

'Nobody will know *what* to make of us,' she declared. 'And we won't explain. Just—' and she gave a sort of aloof shrug as if indicating to some fascinated enquirer that she personally had never troubled her head to wonder about anything so trifling as a set of initials that happened, yes, since you ask, to coincide with those of her own maiden name. On these rare occasions, when the outward guard of her demeanour was let down, to reveal the rather childlike cravings and fantasies it served to advance, there was something endearing about her. Our hearts went out to her then; we felt we were being gathered into some rich and vulnerable conspiracy, and our loyalties were aroused.

Otto and I were sent down to fetch the linen as soon as dinner was over. To do this we had to get Herr Brandt, the janitor, to let us into the storage room.

'Try to keep Brandt from poking his nose into our things would you?' my mother asked. 'Not that we have anything to be ashamed of. But he can be a nuisance. Here, take him one of the miniatures and ask for the keys to let yourselves in. Tell him you'll give them back to him when you're finished.'

It went without saying that Brandt was a police informer, and my mother was probably right in imagining he would think it his duty to make a report on something even so trifling as the retrieval of a set of initialled linen from a trunk. It was also known that he could make himself obliging over practically any matter in return for small gifts, preferably alcoholic. He was especially partial to the Schaad-Neumann brand of aquavit, impossible to get hold of in the GDR, and my father made a point of bringing back a set of miniatures whenever he went to the States, for the express purpose of lubricating Herr Brandt. Thirty or forty of them were lined up in a double row at the back of a shelf in our larder.

Taking one of these frosted, cylindrical bottles, Otto and I went down to Herr Brandt's headquarters on the ground floor.

Ours was a modern building, constructed from the cheapest materials, but well-maintained, and with a few grandiose trimmings, as befitted its inhabitants, who were mostly Party officials of one kind or another. Four white pillars stood incongruously in the middle of the brick front, marking the entrance. The lobby was floored with polished slabs made of a pink and white agglomerate, like slices of vitrified mortadella. A bronze bust of Lenin, looking oddly piratical, stood on a plinth by the elevator, which generally worked. On every floor was a plastic indoor plant, the leaves of which Herr Brandt could be seen laboriously squirting and buffing on Sunday mornings. A powerful odour compounded of floor polish and boiled meat pervaded the stairwell, and there was a more or less constant sound of toilets flushing.

Brandt was in the glass-walled office to the side of the main entrance, surveying the empty lobby with his usual dull stare. He wore a crumpled brown jacket over a sweat-soiled undershirt in which his womanly breasts and very large stomach bulged and sagged like pumpkins in a sack. Black stubble glinted on his whitish skin in the artificial light of the little booth, and the bulging roil of scar tissue between his throat and ear gleamed like satin. This scar, so he claimed, was from a grenade wound received during some battle on the eastern front. To my youthful and admittedly subjective eye, it was a decidedly unheroic looking scar, and in fact had something furtive and guilty about it, like some malignant companion that had attached itself to this otherwise vague and uninteresting person. It was the scar—it seemed to me—that compiled reports on the comings and goings of the inhabitants of our building; the scar that had to be propitiated with bottles of Schaad-Neumann aquavit. Brandt himself gave the impression of living under its tyranny. For his own part he would have been content to pad around the place keeping the plants shiny, the floor waxed, supplying the tenants with cheap eggs from the poultry cooperative where he had a special concession. But some incomprehensible malignancy had settled upon him, and he was now its servant.

Once, when I was quite young, I had seen him carrying a parcel to the door of an elderly couple who lived on our floor. The parcel, which evidently contained either a mirror or a framed picture, slipped from his hands and fell to the floor with a smash and tinkle of breaking glass. He stooped down at once to examine it, prodding the wrapping with his fingers, an expression of grave concern on his face. Then all of a sudden a most extraordinary cynical sneer took possession of his features. Fully aware of me looking at him, he dumped the parcel at the door of the elderly couple and padded off, shrugging as he passed me by, as if to say 'nobody will know it was me who broke it, and even if they suspect, there's nothing they can do about it.' Furthermore, he seemed to convey that my having witnessed it, far from alarming him, in fact implicated me in the deed itself, making me no better than him. And the strange thing was, I did feel mysteriously implicated, and guilty too. It was the first time I had seen an adult do something patently and knowingly 'wrong', and the idea that such a thing could be came as a profound shock. From then on, whenever I ran into Brandt on my own, he would give me a contemptuous, almost taunting look, as though to say that he and I knew each other too well to have to pretend to be respectable citizens.

Otto told him we needed to get into the storeroom. He rose with a lugubrious sigh, evidently meaning to accompany us.

'No need for you to come,' Otto said suavely. 'Just give us the key and we'll let ourselves in. Here, this is for you. Compliments of the house.'

Brandt hesitated, holding the bottle in his hand as if he didn't know what to do with it. Then he winked unpleasantly—or rather it seemed that his scar winked—and unhooked the key from the ring at his belt.

The storeroom occupied a large area of the basement and consisted of a series of open cubicles behind a single steel-mesh fence with a padlocked door in it. We opened this door with the key Brandt had given us, and by the dim light of a couple of naked bulbs found the cubicle that corresponded to our apartment, picking our way between the many glue-traps Brandt had set out, in which insects and the occasional mouse lay in odd contorted positions, some of them still twitching with life.

There in our cubicle, among bits and pieces of old furniture which we no longer used, lay my mother's trunk: not so very large, but with ornate hasps of tarnished brass at every corner and great florid brass buckles that intimated a world of strange and remote ceremoniousness. I suppose I must have seen it before, but I had never taken much notice of it, and certainly never looked inside.

A sweet, mildewy smell rose as we opened the heavy lid. It was neatly packed, everything stowed in small boxes or bundles. The linen was in one corner, in a rust-coloured cotton sack, itself monogrammed with the intertwined initials and three falcons of the von Riesen crest. My brother looked on impassively, apparently less intrigued than I by this faintly mouldy-smelling exhumation of our family's past, while I poked around, turning up a set of silver spoons, an old marbled photograph album, and a case of pocket-sized books beautifully bound in dark green leather.

'Come on,' Otto said, grabbing the pile of linen, 'Mother'll start fretting.'

I looked at the case of books. Of all things, it was a set of poetry: *World Poetry in Translation,* Volumes I to VI. I didn't know or for that matter care very much about literature, but I had an instinct for contraband, and the thought of anything—poetry included—that might not be officially approved of, automatically excited my interest. I opened one of the books: poetry on one side, German prose translation on the other, but Otto was growing impatient.

'Let's split,' he said, 'it gives me the creeps down here.'

Closing the trunk, we went back upstairs, Otto waiting for the elevator with the linen while I returned the key to Herr Brandt.

Seeing me alone, the man immediately relaxed into that familiar contemptuous expression.

'So did you find what you were looking for?' he asked.

I muttered that we did.

'And what was that?'

I looked at him, more surprised perhaps than I should have been by this flagrant reneging on his tacit contract to turn a blind eye: here after all was a man who had obviously broken every bond of decency with his fellow human beings. His face, or rather the swelling tissue at his neck, seemed to stare at me with a brazen leer as if to say 'so what if I accepted a bribe to mind my own business? *You* know me better than that…' However, it was apparently out of personal amusement, to remind me that we were both contemptible creatures, that he asked, rather than any real interest, for when I said, 'Oh, just a few odds and ends,' he merely gave a chuckle and let the matter drop.

Upstairs my mother and Kitty unpacked the linen. It had lain so long in the trunk that the folds seemed to have made permanent creases in the material, and the creases themselves had discoloured slightly, forming a grid-like pattern over everything we unfolded. But the silk-embroidered monograms were intact on every corner, shiny as the calm areas on ruffled water, and in spite of the poor state of the linen itself, my mother still seemed entirely satisfied with her idea.

She and Kitty spent the next day washing the linen and wringing it through the mangle. The following morning, when my father returned from New York, he found them ironing it in the kitchen.

It was evident that all was not well with him. Normally he was fastidious about his appearance, careful to keep his wavy black hair well-combed, aspiring to a well-groomed anonymity in his dark suits, plain ties and clean white shirts. Even after his all-night flights back from New York he would look spruce and tidy, if a little tired. But this time there was a strange raggedness about him; his tie loose, his shirt dishevelled, his jacket crumpled as if he had used it for a pillow. Most unusually, he had not shaved at the airport. And there was a haggard look in his red-rimmed eyes as they roved around the pieces of linen draped all over the kitchen.

'What's this?' he asked, turning up the corner of a tablecloth and examining the embroidered initials.

My mother told him. 'I thought it might come in useful when we go to New York.'

'Put it away. Get rid of it.'

It was extremely rare to hear him speak sharply to my mother. She retorted at once—'What's the matter with you, Joseph? Didn't you sleep on the plane?'

'Kitty, leave us would you?'

Kitty slipped out of the kitchen. My father waited till he heard her close the door of her room.

'Are you out of your mind?' he asked my mother.

'Joseph, please don't speak to me in that manner.'

'As if your family isn't enough of a liability already, you have to go flaunting your ridiculous heirlooms in front of strangers…' He waggled the embroidered corner at my mother: 'von Riesen… What do you think this is, the Hapsburg Empire? The court of King Ludwig? Are you crazy?'

'I would hardly call Kitty a stranger.'

'You have no idea who she talks to.'

My mother's eyes gleamed dangerously. She asked in a tone of deadly self-control: 'Joseph, what is the matter? Did something happen in New York?'

'No!' he shouted. He seemed to quiver. And for a moment a look of fear crossed his tired, careworn face.

For my mother was right. Something *had* happened in New York. It appeared my father had made a blunder. What he had done, I learned later, was to have slightly overestimated his own licence to make concessions in the finer detail of an informal round of arms negotiation; a minute conciliatory gesture that he had believed himself empowered to offer, but which had been relayed to a member of the Soviet SALT II negotiating team stationed in Geneva and promptly aroused that personage's imperial ire. On the diplomatic stage at that particular moment in history, when the two sides of the globe had worked themselves into an inflammable sweat of paranoid terror about each other's intentions, the smallest things were charged with an exaggerated significance. There was the well-known incident of the Soviet official who forgot to remove his hat when he greeted President Nixon in Moscow for the signing of the SALT I treaty. The negligence was interpreted by the Americans as a deliberate affront, and the newspapers spent many days speculating on what precise grievance was being symbolically expressed. Given that this year, the year of my father's blunder, happened to be the very year in which our state was prevailed on to change its constitution, and proclaim itself 'forever and irrevocably allied' with the Soviet Union, my father had good reason to be worried. History doesn't relate what happened to the official who forgot to take off his hat, but there is little reason to believe that he was forgiven for his error.

At any rate my father wasn't. A few days after his return he was told that he had been removed from the UN team.

My father must have guessed that that was to be his last trip; in addition to the usual case of miniatures for bribing Herr Brandt, he had brought with him presents of an especially poignant 'Americanness': a raccoon-skin hat for my mother, a New Mexican turquoise pin for Kitty, a calculator for Otto, and for me a set of metal ballpoint pens, each in the shape of a famous American skyscraper. These joined the other knick-knacks and gadgets he had brought home on earlier trips, and because they were now part of a finite series, never to be further augmented, they acquired a hallowed quality in our household. They were the sacred relics of a brief, visionary connection with a reality larger than our own; one that had tragically eluded our grasp.

So much for my family's glorious ascent into the international political elite of New York.

To my mother's credit, she never directly reproached my father, but the tragic aura she assumed from then on must have been a living reproach to him, and even if it wasn't, he certainly subjected himself to enough reproach of his own. Quite a rapid change came over him: he continued to work hard (he was sent back to the Friendship Treaties, and the subsequent agreements on technology-sharing with other Warsaw Pact countries), but under what seemed a steadily thickening glaze of failure. He wasn't the type to respond to the criticism of his superiors with defiance or counter-criticism. What he seemed to want were opportunities to show his loyalty and diligence, if not in order to be reinstated, then at least to be acknowledged as a faithful servant. At the same time though, he had obviously lost his self-confidence, and with it the air of quiet capability that had once impressed people, so that even if his blunder had been forgiven, he was clearly no longer suitable for a high-level career in the diplomatic service. His appearance grew shabbier. He aged. There was something distracted and disconcertingly meek in the way he smiled.

As for my mother's 'tragic aura', it was a complex thing; a hybrid, I believe, of real disappointment, and a kind of tactical reorganization of her forces. There was humility in it—just enough to deflect the Schadenfreude or downright vengeful delight of her acquaintances, and to convert what had formerly been a rather too flagrant haughtiness into something more subtle and sombre and dignified. If she could no longer intimidate people by the suggestion of hidden powers in her possession, she could make them respect her out of consideration for the magnitude of our loss. She made a point of telling our friends and neighbours what had happened, always in a tone of sad but unselfpitying acceptance of our misfortune, thereby establishing the event in terms that were acceptable to her, and gaining control over people's reactions to it.

It was during this period that the word 'intellectual' first entered her active vocabulary. Pretty soon it was joined by other, similar words such as 'cultural' and 'aesthetic'. 'So and so is an *intellectual* fraud,' she might be heard saying, or 'so and so has no *aesthetic* sense whatsoever.'

At first these remarks had a tentative quality, like somebody trying out a new way of dressing, and pretending not to be anxious about what others might think. But people seemed to accept them without protest, and the self-consciousness soon left her. Before long it was apparent that she had constructed a new hierarchy of values by which to organize the world in a manner that once again accorded with her invincible sense of our family's worth. If we were not to take our place in the inner circle of the political elite, then so be it: we would dazzle and confound others from our eminence in the sphere of *real merit*, which was to say the sphere of culture and ideas and above all, *Art*.

Given that none of us had accomplished anything at all in this sphere, her successful transformation of our whole tone and image as a family must be counted as quite a triumph. Her own education had been a ramshackle affair, interrupted by the war (though she claimed to have had a tutor at the age of eleven who had made her read 'everything'), but her brother Heinrich had been through university, and at one time contemplated a career as a man of letters. He still subscribed to the official literary publications, and in his position as senior counsel at the office of the Chief of the People's Police, he had easy access to the best artistic circles, which from time to time he still frequented. Naturally my mother enlisted him in her new project. And doting on her as he did (he had no family of his own), he was happy to oblige.

A new phase of our life began. Heinrich introduced my mother to a number of officially recognized writers and artists of his acquaintance. We dutifully made the round of their plays, concerts and exhibitions, mingling with them afterwards, and before long they began appearing at our apartment on Micklenstrasse. Naturally obsequious as a breed, and knowing of my mother only that she was the sister of an important government functionary who took an interest in the arts, they were never difficult to entice. In a remarkably short space of time, through sheer force of will, as well as that curious hypnotic power of suggestion that gathered people like sheep into her private fantasies, she turned our household into a gravitational centre for artists and intellectuals of every stripe. My father acquiesced in his meek way. Once, timidly, he asked if she was sure she wasn't going to 'receive disadvantage' for associating with the wrong types, but he was quickly silenced by her acid retort that she hardly thought her brother would be introducing her to charlatans of the kind he was obviously referring to.

The apartment itself underwent a transformation. Framed prints and reproductions went up. In time, as my mother's patronage grew, artists began presenting her with original oils and watercolours, and these joined the reproductions on the walls. There were even some sculptures which, like the paintings, were both representational and at the same time sufficiently unrealistic in their distortions and bulbous excrescences to indicate that their creators were fully abreast of the latest developments in modern art. Furthermore, they were uniformly of what I would call an 'aspiring' tone. Eyes and hands were often raised upward in a slyly sublime manner. The darker, more turbulent works were sure to have gleams of light peeping over some horizon in the background.

The most 'aspiring' of them all was a life-size bronze statue representing a naked female dancer reaching towards the heavens. Her arms and hands were immensely thin and elongated, as if the intensity of her 'aspiration' had literally stretched her about five inches. Her thin legs were more like a flamingo's than a human's. Interestingly though, as if distracted from his lofty purpose by a momentary lasciviousness, the artist had endowed her with full, upward-curving, gravity-defying breasts, which he had very carefully modelled to show the nipples and areolae in minute detail. Otto in particular was fascinated by these breasts, and when our parents were not about, he would entertain me by slinking up behind the girl and grabbing hold of them, murmuring delirious blandishments into her bronze ear. Kitty was embarrassed by her, and could be made to blush when circumstances forced her to acknowledge her presence. My father also objected to her, ostensibly on the grounds that she occupied more than her fair share of the living room. But my mother had pronounced this figure an 'aesthetic triumph', and we were given notice that anyone who criticized her ran the risk of being stigmatized as 'visually blind'; one of her most deadly put-downs at this time.

It was during this period that I first heard myself being referred to as the family 'poet-intellectual'. It was done so casually that I didn't consciously notice it until it had insinuated its way into my own image of myself. I therefore didn't react to it with the suspicion or perplexity I should have. As our artistic gatherings consolidated themselves into regular soirées I heard my mother introduce me as our 'literary man', our own 'poet-intellectual', often adding, 'he reads *all* the time. It's impossible to drag him away from a book once he's started; just like I was at his age.' I felt it as one of those immemorial truths about oneself that are so well-established they are almost too boring to mention. It was as if she had said 'he's rather small for his age', or 'he's always had a sweet tooth'. The fact that I had never written a poem, and that I never read a book unless I had to for class, was neither here nor there. The idea was like one of those cloud-forest plants that subsist on air and light alone. It appeared to require no nourishment from reality in order to grow, either in my own mind or in the minds of our acquaintances. Before long it became absorbed into the conversational ritual at our monthly soirées, where guests suffering from the slight awkwardness entailed in talking to the adolescent children of their hostess, could now enquire after my poetry. 'How's the writing going?' they might say with a look of respectful concern, or—more facetiously, with a little motion of their wrists, 'still scribbling away?'—to which I would respond with a vague nod and what I hoped was a tantalizingly elusive smile, before changing the subject.

There was an upright piano in the corner of the living room, and from time to time there would be music at our gatherings; a solo recital by some budding young pianist, or a trio or quartet if others brought instruments. Given the obdurately stiff, formal, frosty tenor of the conversational part of the soirées, these interludes were a relief to the company and always greatly appreciated. One day a lull descended on the room when there happened to be no musicians present. A writer named Franz Erhardt stepped forward and 'begged permission' to read us something from his novel, which he had brought with him. Permission was granted, and he began to read.

He was a small, sallow man with a forked beard and light-blue eyes that always seemed to be at work on some caustic or double-edged little observation. My mother had found him a job at the state TV company, and he told me once, with a strange sort of rueful sneer, that he occasionally dreamed of her 'just as the English dream of their queen'. I understand that he went on to become quite a success in the literary world of the GDR, and that by the time the Wall came down he was a top-ranking bureaucrat in the Writers' Union, with guaranteed sales of 100,000 of every novel he wrote. A few years ago I read in the *New York Times* that he had hanged himself after his Stasi file had been opened, revealing that he had been an informer for most of his adult life. I remember that the novel he read from that evening was a strange sort of satirical spoof, unusual in those days of solid socialist realism, taking as its premise President Kennedy's famous statement '*Ich bin ein Berliner*' and imagining a patrician American with Kennedy's decadent appetites and corrupt ideas getting stuck in East Berlin, and suffering a series of instructive mishaps that finally turn him into a good and happy socialist.

Judging from the hearty laughter that filled the room, it had plenty of funny jokes. I myself was too young to understand them. Besides, I was distracted. There was something about the very fact of this reading—a novelty in our drawing room—that was making me uneasy. I noticed my Uncle Heinrich staring at me pensively once or twice across the room. For some time I had been dimly aware of his interest in me growing more intense, as if my 'writing' and his own former literary ambitions made us kindred spirits. He would often talk to me about writers he admired, sometimes discussing his own youthful efforts, and telling me how much he looked forward to reading something of mine. For my part the whole subject occupied such a dreamy, subterranean part of my consciousness, that I find it almost hard to accuse myself of active hypocrisy in allowing him to continue in his delusions about me. But as I watched him now, his cropped head with its elegant, gaunt features and silver-grey eyes roving attentively between Erhardt, the enrapt guests, and myself, I had a faintly sickening sensation that some hidden and intimate area of myself that I had until now considered inviolably private was about to be forcibly exposed to public view.

Sure enough, as soon as the reading was over and the applause had begun to die down, I heard my uncle's rather high-pitched voice with its clipped enunciation calling to me from across the room.

'Stefan, young fellow, what about you? Why don't you read something of yours now?' He was looking at me with a kindly expression—there was always something very proper and clean and good-natured about him; *merry*, one might almost say—but at that moment his smiling face seemed to me full of menace and barely concealed cruelty. I remember observing the same dignified and innocent expression of warmth on his face, and feeling the same chilled response in my own heart many years later when I was brought to him in his comfortable rooms at the office of the Chief of the People's Police, where once again I found myself at a loss to circumvent some request that from his point of view was wholly reasonable, while to me it seemed to stretch the already abused fabric of my soul to the point of ripping it altogether in two.

His suggestion was immediately taken up by the other guests.

'Yes, what a good idea,' a voice cried out, 'Frau Vogel, ask your son to read us one of his compositions.'

'I—I don't have anything prepared,' I stammered. But my apparent modesty merely fanned the flames of their interest, and I soon found myself at the centre of a chorus of bantering remarks about my shyness and lack of spontaneity. 'Come on Stefan, read us something from this great work we've been hearing so much about,' someone called, while another, to my mortification, said, 'Otto, fetch your brother's poems. He's too modest to get them himself.'

Otto turned to this speaker with the look of surly impassiveness that he had been perfecting over the past year. He too had been a target for my mother's 'artistic' reinvention of our family. Since he had always been good with his hands, he was chosen to represent the pictorial muse. He had been sent to drawing classes and presented with a box of high-grade French charcoals and some handmade paper sketchbooks finagled by my mother through our surviving connections in the higher levels of the *privilegentsia*. After the first few classes he had abruptly refused to attend any more. My mother tried to change his mind, but he stood his ground. Even when she rather unsubtly attempted to pander to his burgeoning interest in girls by offering to find him a class with live nude models, he resisted. And when finally she threatened to punish him if he didn't keep at it, he broke the charcoals, ripped the sketchbooks to pieces, and exploded at her with such savage virulence that she—even she—had been forced to back down. Otto now occupied an anomalous, private, decultured zone within the family; tolerated, but not much more.

I'm not sure whether I simply lacked his courage to be himself, or whether I had allowed myself to become tainted by the thought that I might actually be that potent and glamorous thing, an artist. Perhaps despite my shyness and horror of exposure, I secretly craved the kind of attention that had just been lavished on Franz Erhardt. Instead of coming out and confessing that I didn't in fact have anything to read to the assembled company, I merely stood there, inwardly writhing, unable to speak, while the guests continued baying at me from all corners of the room.

It was my father, to my surprise, who saved me, though it would certainly have been better for me in the long run if he hadn't.

'Perhaps next time, Stefan, eh?' he said quietly. 'That way you'll have time to prepare something for us.'

It was so rare for him to assert himself in any way at these gatherings, that I think people in their uncertainty attributed more authority to him than he actually possessed. He was deferred to: the baying stopped, and with a few waggings of fingers and stern warnings not to forget, I was given a month's reprieve.

As the days passed, the question of how I was going to acquit myself at the next soirée grew rapidly from a faint unease to a consuming preoccupation that soon formed the single focus of my life. Theoretically it would have still been possible to own up to my lack of material and back down, but as I have often felt when faced with a choice between a healthy and a harmful course of action, I had the distinct sensation of the harm having already been done, without my conscious consent or even participation, so that the apparent choice is in fact no choice at all. At any rate, the thought of making a clean breast of things, disgracing myself before my mother and looking foolish in front of her friends, barely crossed my mind. With the same odd mixture of submissiveness and furtive ambition, I lay awake at nights, next to my sleeping brother, racking my brains for a solution. I had tried the most rational thing: to sit down and write. But it had become painfully clear to me that whatever faculties of imagination and verbal ingenuity were required to bring something even remotely coherent, let alone interesting, into existence on a blank page, I was entirely devoid of them. The feeling I'd had as I sat at my table trying to coax words out of myself, was more than simply one of impotence; it was a kind of vast, inverted potency: the sheer inert mass of blankness that I had attempted to breach reverberating violently back through me, as though I had tried to smash through a steel door with my fist. I soon gave up.

It was on a morning a few days before the soirée that my anxiety, roused by now to a condition where it actually functioned as a kind of substitute imagination, formed the first in what turned out to be a long series of dubious solutions, each of which immediately raised new and more serious problems.

As Kitty opened the larder in search of some jam for my mother's toast, I happened to glimpse the double row of aquavit bottles at the back of the top shelf. Unreplenishable since my father's fall from grace, these had now acquired the value of precious heirlooms, and my parents were extremely sparing in their use of them as bribes. From the sight of these bottles, my mind turned to Herr Brandt, and from him to the last expedition Otto and I had made to the basement, in search of the von Riesen linen. And suddenly I remembered those leather-bound volumes of *World Poetry in Translation.*

That afternoon, during the quiet hour after my return from school, when my parents were both out and Kitty was in her room enjoying a moment of leisure before preparing our dinner, I stole one of the little frosted-glass bottles from the larder, and went downstairs to ask Brandt for the key to the storage room. He stared at me, for so long, and with such vacant dullness, that for a moment I wondered if he now considered it so far beneath his dignity to acknowledge me that I had actually become invisible to him. But eventually he gave his weary sigh, and got up to accompany me.

Doing my best to imitate my brother's confident, worldly tone, I told him I could manage on my own, if he would just give me the key. I took out the aquavit bottle and nonchalantly offered it to him.

'Here, this is for you. Compliments of the house.' A glint of something approaching amusement appeared in his eye. My contemptible absurdity had apparently just sunk to new depths of preposterousness. He took the bottle with a disdainful shrug of his heavy, soft shoulders. I waited for him to give me the key, but he merely looked at the bottle, wiping the mist from the frosted glass with the pad of a thumb so fleshy and nailbitten it looked like one of those pastries where the risen dough all but engulfs the dab of jelly at its centre.

'Could I have the key please?' I asked, attempting to control a faint tremor in my voice. Herr Brandt smiled and raised two obese fingers. '*Zwei Flaschen,*' he said, 'one for privacy, one for the key.' It struck me that the peculiar warped affinity that existed between us had somehow made it apparent to him that I was here on personal rather than family business, and with his lugubrious but unerring instinct for such things, he realized he had found an opportunity for extortion. Aware of my own powerlessness as well as the jeopardy I had placed myself in, I swallowed my protests and went silently back upstairs for a second bottle.

Kitty was now in the kitchen peeling potatoes. It was imperative that I get her out immediately: I sensed that if I were gone longer than a minute or two Brandt would consider himself justified in renegotiating the terms. I could picture exactly the ponderous way he would look at his watch and shrug off any attempt to hold him to his word. As is often the case with me, acute necessity brought forth invention—or at least a short-term expedient. I remembered that Kitty had been unhappy a few weeks ago when some man she had been seeing had suddenly vanished. Tearfully she had admitted to my mother that the man had been a member of a group that met once a week in a church to discuss world peace. Thinking he had been arrested, she had begged my mother to use her influence to help him. My mother had retorted with a stern lecture on the impropriety of a member of our household having anything to do with such a person, and that was the last I had heard of the matter.

'Jurgen's outside,' I told Kitty. 'He asked me to come and get you. He's in the alley by the coal-hole. He looks like he's been living rough.'

Gasping, Kitty ran out of the room, her hands still wet from the potatoes. I took the second bottle, rearranging some canned celery to fill the space at the end of the row, and with a feeling of venom in my heart, went back downstairs.

This time I was careful not to give Brandt the bottle until I had the key. Even so, he managed to make me jump through one more hoop. Instead of actually handing me the key, he merely pointed to the bunch hanging at his waist, and told me to come and unhook it myself. This I did, reluctantly, but feeling that I had no choice. As I fumbled with the key ring, I was unpleasantly aware of his sour smell and the soft paunch of his stomach wobbling against the back of my wrist.

With the key finally in my hand, I went down to the basement. Only one of the two bulbs hanging in the storeroom worked, and the place was gloomier than ever. The trunk's brasswork gleamed faintly among the shadowy bric-a-brac of our cubicle. I opened the lid, releasing the familiar musty odour, and took out the six volume set of *World Poetry in Translation*. There was no question of bringing these upstairs: even if I had found somewhere to hide them, they would have been discovered. My mother had once discovered a West German comic book under Otto's mattress, and since then she had been in the habit of regularly turning the place upside down. I had brought a pencil and paper with me, my plan being to copy out one of the prose translations down here, and convert it into poetry upstairs. If anyone saw the copied-out translation, I would claim it was 'notes' for a poem.

With this in mind, I tipped one of the volumes to the light and began looking through it. I was searching for something that conformed in spirit to the quasi-abstract but unequivocally 'upward-aspiring' tenor of the art works favoured in our home. I read quickly, aware that the longer I took, the more likely it was that I would have to account for my absence. Many years later, I heard a literature professor on the radio declare that the only valid criterion for judging a piece of writing was whether it could 'save your life'. Remembering my feverish ransacking of these volumes in the grainy darkness of the storeroom, I felt that I understood exactly what he was talking about.

I found what I was looking for, copied it out, put away the volumes, and ran back upstairs, returning the key to Brandt.

Kitty was back. So, fortunately, was my mother, making it

temporarily impossible for Kitty to question me about my alleged encounter with Jurgen. She gave me an anguished look, which I ignored. Just before dinner, I found her waiting for me as I came out of the bathroom. 'He wasn't there,' she whispered. I tried to look surprised. 'Maybe someone recognized him. He seemed nervous.' 'You said he looked—' Kitty managed, breaking off guiltily as my mother came out of the kitchen.

She regarded us for a moment. The notion of Kitty and myself having any kind of relationship independent of the rest of the household, let alone something to whisper about, clearly both surprised and disturbed her. With a little movement at the back of her protuberant eyes, suggestive to me of a camera shutter opening and closing, she seemed to absorb the situation and store it away for further reflection, before ushering us on into dinner.

It was our custom to sit in the living room after dinner, and listen to the latest instalment of one of the Russian novels that were continually being serialized on the radio. My father would sit back in his armchair with a glass of plum alcohol and pass into what seemed a state of innocent, genuine contentment. My mother fidgeted, torn between a sense that there might be something not altogether highbrow about this method of ingesting culture, and the relish she took in telling people that this was how we passed our evenings as a family. (When she did this, she would deliberately stress the humble nature of the entertainment, implying, with her genius for suggestion, something simultaneously populist and austere in our tastes.) Perched restlessly on her chair, she would nod gravely at the passages of sententious generalization, smile mysteriously at odd moments, as if to suggest an attunement to notes of humour too rarefied for the rest of us to catch, and sometimes sigh, 'Ah yes,' apparently remembering a passage from her numerous readings of the book in her youth. Otto and I sat for the most part stupefied with boredom, though lately Otto had begun paying more attention. Since entering adolescence, he had made a private cargo cult out of any scraps of drama that could possibly be construed as erotic, hoarding them away for use in his private fantasies, and continually on the lookout for more. Kitty was seldom present: she usually went out in the evenings; if not, she stayed in her room.

That evening I announced that I would not be joining the family in the living room. I waited to be asked why, and with a joyful sense of momentousness, answered that I needed to work on one of my poems. A bright, shining truth that seemed to bathe me in a fluorescent aura as I uttered it. I was immediately excused.

In my room, I took the prose translation from my pocket, and set to work. The name of the poet I had stumbled on, and who, in the company of one or two others, was to prove so fatefully useful to me over the next few months, meant nothing to me at the time. But just as our janitor had for many years provided me with my mental image of the West German chancellor, simply because he bore the same name (leading to a great pang of bittersweet surprise when I first saw the exquisite, civilized, elfin face of Willy Brandt in the newspapers on the occasion of his momentous visit to Erfurt in 1970), so between Walt Disney (a controversial, if not actually unmentionable name at that time), and the word *witz*, meaning joke or wit, I formed the image of my stolen poetic persona as a kind of goofy, playful, disreputably capitalistic character. Though I couldn't read English, I had noticed that his lines were long, uneven, and unrhymed. On a whim, I decided to reverse each of these qualities. Almost as soon as I began, I found myself strangely enjoying it—not that I discovered any great talent for producing short, regular, rhyming lines—but the very process of this weird inversion had a peculiarly natural, almost familiar feeling about it, as though I had already been doing it for years.

While I was happily working away, the door opened and Kitty came quietly into the room. Needless to say, she was after more information about her beloved Jurgen. What exactly did he say? What was his tone of voice? What had he been wearing? I sensed that she wanted the truth to match the romantic quality of her own feelings for the man. Since I was the sole source of this 'truth', I had it in my power either to bestow or to withhold what she wanted. It was unusual for me to find myself in a position of power over another human being. I was aware of it not so much in the Brandt sense of something to gloat over and exploit, as of a kind of transformative agent; a means of introducing a sudden and extreme volatility into a hitherto static situation. 'Well, his exact words were just "ask Kitty to come down and see me",' I told her, 'but the way he said them was as though seeing you was the most important thing to him in the world.' I remembered she had knitted a red scarf for him, and I added that he was wearing that. A look of ardent longing came into her eyes. Gratitude also. She was perhaps twenty-six, not well-educated, but in her quiet way fuelled by a passionate vitality that made her presence in a room always a positive enhancement. I knew that Otto had reassessed her lately from the point of view of his emerging sexuality, and found her to be desirable. As she looked at me, her eyes brightening with everything I said, I felt a kind of vicarious desire—as if I were Otto—and a corresponding rise in the value of the power I was wielding. Had I actually been Otto, I could surely have turned this situation to my advantage. Not least because Kitty, unsophisticated soul that she was, seemed at some level to be confusing me—the conveyor of pleasurable tidings—with Jurgen himself. For a moment the room seemed to brim with potentialities, as the two of us populated it with emblems of ourselves, each other, Otto and Jurgen, all conversing with one another. I felt that I was being given a foretaste of the world of adult passions, and a strong excitement came into me.

Footsteps approached. Kitty abruptly left the room. I heard my mother say, 'Hello, Kitty,' in a bemused tone. She then appeared in my doorway.

'What are you two up to? You seem to be whispering like a pair of conspirators whenever I see you.'

She was smiling with her mouth open. She had two smiles: a closed-mouth smile for formal occasions, and an open-mouthed, vulnerably toothy smile for when she was being a mother on intimate terms with her children. I sensed, however, something duplicitous in her choice of smile now, as though she felt guilty about her compulsion to pry, or at any rate was trying to disguise it as innocent curiosity.

'What were you talking about?'

'Oh, nothing serious,' I said, racking my brains for something to tell her when she questioned me more forcefully, as I knew she would.

'Please tell me what you were talking about.'

'Kitty wants to knit something special for your birthday,' I managed to lie. 'She was asking me what I thought you would like.'

This silenced her for a moment. Seizing the advantage, I told her that Kitty had wanted the gift to be a surprise, and that now we had spoiled that. My mother looked uncomfortable, distressed even, and for a moment I felt an almost overwhelming urge to confess to all the absurd, trivial, but increasingly exhausting deceits her encouragement of my poetry had engendered.

'All right,' she said, 'we won't say a word to Kitty, and I'll act completely surprised on my birthday. Tell her to make me a matching hat, scarf and gloves. Blue, with white falcons on.' And so that subsidiary chain reaction of unpleasantnesses finally petered out. Except that Kitty had to spend all her free time over the next few weeks knitting woollens for my mother.

Meanwhile the main sequence continued. The month passed, and preparations began for the next soirée. Eggs were hardboiled and sprinkled with paprika. Chunks of canned Cuban pineapple were rolled in slices of ham. 'Plain, honest fare,' my mother would say as she served various combinations of these things. 'None of your Central Committee foie gras in *this* household.' As always in her assertions of humility, family self-esteem was maintained by the unstated, countervailing facts of the matter, which were that for most of our visitors, even these relatively modest items represented a gastronomic treat.

It was November—windy and wet. Out of the bleary Berlin night guests began arriving, stamping their chilly feet in the hall, hanging their water-absorbent GDR raincoats on our iron coat rack.

I was in an agitated state. The idea of actually having to stand up in front of these people and reveal the fruits of my dubious labours was suddenly beginning to fill me with fear. For the first time it struck me that somebody might expose me as a fraud.

Uncle Heinrich hadn't arrived—his work often kept him late. I moved among the guests with waves of tension floating through my stomach. To my surprise, no one mentioned the performance they had made me promise to give. Either they had all forgotten, or—as I began to suspect—they had reached a tacit agreement among themselves to let the matter drop. Did they feel sorry for having pressured me? Or was it that they were really not very interested in hearing me read after all? Despite my anxieties, I found myself strangely resenting both of these possibilities. After an hour or so, I saw Uncle Heinrich's official limo—an old Czech Tatra—pull up on the street below. He came in, his usual kindly self, apologizing for his lateness with a humility that never failed to flatter these people, any one of whom he could have destroyed with no more than his signature on a piece of paper.

He greeted me warmly, but he too failed to mention my promised reading. My deepening stage fright was compounded by a new anxiety, that I might not actually be called to the stage at all. The milk of human kindness may not have flowed in our household, but the milk of judicious approval for prowess in sanctioned fields could occasionally be made to trickle. It was the only nourishment going, and I evidently thirsted for it.

Across the room I saw Franz Erhardt speaking with my uncle. I drifted over. Erhardt watched me approach, smiling thinly as I arrived, without pausing in his talk. I felt sure that he of all people could not have forgotten my reading, and was deliberately avoiding the subject out of professional rivalry. I could feel him willing me to leave, but I stood my ground. Eventually I looked at my watch, and sighed so ostentatiously that they were obliged to notice.

'What is it, dear boy?' my uncle asked, concerned.

'Oh, nothing. Just that—well, I suppose I'm going to have to get those poems out. I've been dreading this.'

'Poems? Oh! of course! Your reading!'

'I'd really rather not do it, Uncle Heinrich.'

'Nonsense! No backing down now!' He wagged a finger at me, and summoned my mother over.

'Stefan promised to read to us. I'd quite forgotten. Now he's trying to wriggle out of it again.'

My mother looked at me. It seemed to me there was a little movement, a vague twinge of guilt, in the expressive depths of her eyes, as if she were at the point of supporting me in my alleged reluctance, as my father had the month before. Before she could speak, though, I shrugged my shoulders and said with an air of defeat: 'All right, I'll read them, if that's what you all want.'

I went to fetch the pages from my room. When I returned, the guests had been assembled in a circle around the piano, where Erhardt had read the previous month.

I had never addressed an audience before. My mouth had gone

dry and my heart was pounding in my chest. The rows of people before me resembled nothing so much as the teeth of a gaping shark, ready to tear me apart. I wanted to flee from it, but it seems I also wanted to put my head in its mouth.

I managed to recite what I had written. The guests listened in silence, and when I finished there was applause.

For the record, the English equivalent of the lines I concocted would have sounded something like this:

> I celebrate myself, myself I sing
> And my beliefs are yours, as everything
> I have is yours, each atom. So we laze—
> My soul and I—passing the summer days
> Observing spears of grass...

And so on—an anodyne burble that was clearly too boring to raise suspicion. At any rate, nobody unmasked me.

But I realized almost as soon as it was over that not everything was as it had been before. The room may have been the same—the atmosphere of simulated conviviality certainly felt unchanged—but I myself was changed.

At first I didn't understand what had happened, but as the evening continued, with every guest obliged to make some kind of congratulatory remark, I realized that my attitude towards other people had undergone a radical alteration. Quite simply, the straightforward relation of cordial respect, or at least neutral interest, that is supposed to exist between people who have no prior reason not to respect each other, was no longer available to me. It was gone, as if a cord had been cut. In its place, it seemed, was an intricately shuttling machinery of silent interrogation and devious concealment. Everyone I spoke to seemed newly illuminated by what I had done. Depending on certain minute signals given off by the movement of their eyes or the inflection of their voices (I felt suddenly attuned to these things), they were disclosed either as fellow hypocrites in whom the cord had also been cut (they had seen through my deception but weren't saying so), or else as innocent fools (they hadn't the guile to see through my deception). I was no doubt wrong in most of my individual diagnoses, but the idea that such a division might exist—

between those in whom the cord has been cut, and those in whom it remains intact—was a revelation, and I still find myself appraising the people I meet on that basis.

My Uncle Heinrich, whose voluble enthusiasm for my performance led me to categorize him among the innocents, proposed that I should give another recital soon, since this one had been such a success. The proposal was immediately seconded by the person he was talking to, and by the logic of escalation that prevails in circumstances where power alone has meaning, someone else then had to suggest that I do it the very next month, only to have someone else trump them by saying I should do it *every* month. 'That way we'll all be able to witness first-hand the development of your young prodigy, Frau Vogel.' And before I knew it, I was looking at the prospect of my little act of stealth, which I had thought would now be cast off into the backdraught of history, having instead to be repeated, month after month after month.

There was one small upset before the soirée ended. A guest went into the bathroom and discovered Otto slumped on the floor, dead drunk. He had passed out while throwing up into the toilet.

Otherwise, the evening was considered a triumph, and for the next period of my life I devoted most of my energies to maintaining the facade of 'poet-intellectual' that my mother's warped pride had created and that I now began to half believe in myself.

It was a peculiar kind of drudgery—exhausting, depleting, and yet somehow compulsive. Like an inhabitant of hell—the hell of Sisyphus and Tantalus—I had a task, a labour, all of my own, and I felt inextricably bound to it. In its service, life became a series of furtive routines. The stealing of the aquavit. The concealment of the theft. The bribing of Brandt. The removal of the key from his waist. The dark half hour in the storage room where I opened the trunk and copied the selected pages. The turning of the pages into 'poetry'. And then finally the nacreous glory of my monthly soul-bath in that crowd of admiring, captive faces.

A few years later, when I was making a private study of the career of Joseph Stalin, I came across descriptions of his seventieth birthday: the enormous portrait of him suspended over Moscow from a balloon, lit up at night by searchlights; the special meeting of the Soviet Academy of Sciences honouring 'the greatest genius of the human race...' The festivities culminated in a gala at the Bolshoi Theatre where the leaders of all the world's Communist Parties stood up one by one to make elaborately flattering speeches to Stalin, and lavish him with gifts. One can imagine his state of mind as he sat on the stage receiving these tributes—the absolute disbelief in the sincerity of a single word being uttered; the compulsive need to hear them nonetheless; the antennae bristlingly attuned to the slightest lapse in the effort to portray conviction...

It seems to me that at the age of thirteen, I had already developed the cynicism of a seventy-year-old dictator. □

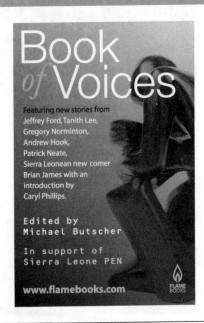

GRANTA

THE GAME OF EVENINGS

Adolf Hoffmeister

TRANSLATED FROM THE CZECH
BY MICHELLE WOODS

James Joyce, drawing by Adolf Hoffmeister

James Joyce met the Czech writer Adolf Hoffmeister in Paris several times in 1929 and 1930. Joyce was writing *Finnegans Wake* under the title *Work in Progress* and had completed the 'Anna Livia Plurabelle' section of the book. A Czech translation by Hoffmeister, Vladimír Procházka and Marie Weatherall was published in 1932. In the introduction to an excerpt published a year earlier in *Literární noviny*, Hoffmeister and Procházka wrote: 'The complete *Work in Progress*, will never be translated, because no one would be able to translate it, taking into account the average life-span... We are fully aware that we are doing work which will not be understood and will go unrewarded... Our translation will never be a precise mirror of the original. But...we are clear that we have attempted a translation of beautiful poetry, one which extends the vault of the sky over the world of man.'

Hoffmeister's interview with Joyce which begins on the facing page was published in *Rozpravy aventina* over two issues in 1930–31. The conversation was conducted in French. This is its first full publication in English.

The Game of Evenings

In August of this year [1930], Joyce was passing through Paris. His apartment had the emptiness of holidays and the doorbell echoed resoundingly in the curtainless and carpetless room. In the scene as I imagined it, our movements were very ceremonial and solemn. I was wearing tails and a high collar, a beard and a top hat. Joyce wore a white ermine cloak and a laurel wreath. We floated, as if in a newsreel, slowly and elegantly through marble colonnades. With a graceful movement I handed him the first Czech translation of Ulysses. *Music was playing. There was a fanfare of trumpets. In reality, we sat down in the flat which had just been spring-cleaned. The furniture reminded me of a museum space being prepared for an exhibition. Joyce stroked the four-volume translation of his work. Around our movements, emptiness.*

Joyce: That's a cobalt blue, isn't it?

'Yes.'

The colour of the book. Nowhere in the world is there anything as blue as this. It is strange, Mr Hoffmeister, that all the moments of this summer seem more sacred to me.

He grabbed me by the hand, pulled me towards him and looked me in the eyes.

Today is the first day I have seen you although we have met many times before.

'I am very happy that your sight has got so much better. There was a lot about it in the newspapers in Paris.'

I visited a wonderful doctor, who carried out a complex operation on my eyes. I am going to see him again in September in Zurich. I am indebted to him for saving my eyesight and my life. He is Professor Alfred Vogt in Zurich. I can see. I can see.

Joyce can see, he can make things out, but unfortunately not yet well enough to walk around the room completely confidently, without colliding into a table or the corners of the furniture. He writes illegibly and messily, but life is returning to him through his eyes and with it a new resolve. Meetings with Joyce could take place in the most unpredictable parts of the city. At the childrens' afternoon show at the Palais Royal, in a factory canteen, in a tiny suburban cafe, at a big fashion-house show. He walked around the city, finishing his journeys with wine. He wandered without purpose, without direction, without a sense of time. For such wandering sight is of course necessary. He was afraid that he had lost it for ever.

I wanted to finish my latest piece *Work in Progress*. It is ready. But I never finish any of my work, I always want to rewrite it. From *Dubliners* onwards, everything has been a work in progress, work for which names cannot be found. *Ulysses* is the most unfinished. The fragments from *Work in Progress*, which have been published in various places, have changed and are still changing. 'Anna Livia Plurabelle' in the 1925 *Le Navire d'Argent* edition is substantially changed from the most recent version, which was published by Faber & Faber in their *Criterion Miscellany* [1930]. In between those two, I published another version in *transition*, number eight [1927]. My work is a whole and it is impossible to divide it into the names of books. *Ulysses* is, of course, a day in a life, but it could even be the life of a second. Of course, time is measured by beginnings and endings.

'I think the critic Marcel Brion, in a wonderful article on the concept of time in your work, came up with the hypothesis that it is possible that the difference between God and man is only a question of time.'

Yes, he compared me with Marcel Proust. For Proust, time is the centre, the *Ding an sich*. This Mr Brion discovered the principle of relativity in my work. For him, my work reads as badly as Einstein's writing.

A number is a mystery, which God solves. With Samuel Beckett, a small Irishman and my great friend, we discover the numeracy of life and history. Dante was obsessed by the number three: he divided his verse into three *cantiche*, each written in thirty-three cantos and in terza rima. Why do we depend on the number four? Four legs on a table, four legs on a horse, four seasons and four provinces of Ireland? Why are there twelve pillars of the law, twelve apostles, twelve months, twelve of Napoleon's marshals? Why was the armistice of the Great War sounded at the eleventh hour of the eleventh day of the eleventh month? Number as a measure of time is indeterminable. The ratio of these numbers is relative to place and content. In a portion of time, it is possible to realize one thing through abstract thought, but even if we eliminate one thing, by replacing it with a copy, a laborious duplication arises, which loses the proportions of reality. To describe in detail the ceaseless motion of man calls for such time and such space that the endlessly slowed down motion would be the same as stillness, as if eternity when measured does not distinguish between the two. The lives of Bloom and Stephen are not the lives of real people, nor a description based completely on living Dubliners. They are perhaps bound to human life, and so are measured by time—by the hours, that is, of June 16, 1904.

It is true it is Bloom's life, and it is the whole of Bloom's life which gave rise to the day in Bloom's life, in *Ulysses*, a book of seven hundred and thirty pages: perhaps it could be that a minute of a life could be described in a bookcase of books. A look at *Work in Progress* is the first look into the bowl of creation. At the beginning was chaos. But there is chaos at the end, too. The reader participates in the birth or the end of the world when it happens. Everyone is anyone and every moment is any moment. The fall of the angels mixes with the battle of Waterloo and HCE [Humphrey Chimpden Earwicker] is a person who changes as many times as his name changes in the narrative.

It is said that a person flying at the speed of light would experience in a short time the history of the world: anyone who accelerates to the ultimate speed of their flight, would behold the impact of what was, is and will be. Time is so powerful in *Work in Progress*, that its difference is not marked in its ideas.

'This kind of simultaneity does not exist in Ulysses. *Each hour in it has its own meaning and image.'*

Of course. The colour of the day changes with the passing of time. The chapters of *Ulysses* are illuminated in different ways. Stuart Gilbert drew up a table. It is a schedule of the hours of *Ulysses*. Have a look at it. I think that it is an important book for readers.

'I have the book, it is quite perfect. The detailed games and shadows of Ulysses *became clear to me when I first read it.'*

You know, the writer Valéry Larbaud praised *Ulysses* with an exaggeratedly beautiful metaphor. He compared it to a starry sky: when you look at it long and carefully, it becomes more beautiful as new, uncounted stars reveal themselves.

Gilbert divided *Ulysses* into chapters by places, times, authorities, scholarship, colours, symbols and modes of deliveries. It is a mathematics of literary history.

What kind of moral response did the Czech editon of *Ulysses* receive?

'It was published privately. It did not become a newspaper sensation or a sensation in the gutter press. I think the fact that the edition sold many copies can be explained by "pornobibliophilia", which has attracted people to such a sublime book.'

The Anglo–American attitude to *Ulysses* bears no relation to the underlying interests of readers and what they are really scandalized by. The realistic form which follows a day, the rhythm which fills the book with general truths or universal symbols is ignored by the focus, on a few places, of unconventional language about things and thoughts which are usually unsaid. I think that the animal nakedness of human nature in *Ulysses* is depicted faithfully and with balance. The Irish censors considered these paragraphs as 'anything calculated to excite sexual passion'. Obscenity fills the pages of life, too, and a book cannot wholly avoid the reality of thoughts and deeds, even if it can't be written about without resorting to cowardice. No book—starting with the Bible—has been able to do this, not one. Some Frenchman [Emile Pons] wrote about Swift, with whom he compared me, and whose influence I do not deny, that he was capable *d'une sérénité dans l'indécence.*

'Can you tell me, what are the connections or the differences between Ulysses *and* Work in Progress?'

I don't think there is a difference. Starting with *Dubliners*, there is a straight line of development in all my work. It is almost indivisible. Only the level of expressiveness and technical complexity has changed, perhaps even a little dramatically. Of course, I was twenty when I wrote *Dubliners* and between *Ulysses* and *Work in Progress* there is a difference of six years of painstaking work. I finished *Ulysses* in 1921 and the first fragment of *Work in Progress* was published in *transition* six years afterwards. The difference then is down to development. The whole of my work is still in progress.

'I know that our readers cry out together with Mr H. G. Wells: it is a great work, but we don't understand it.'

I don't agree that difficult literature is necessarily so inaccessible. Of course each intelligent reader can read and understand it—if he returns to the text again and again. He is embarking on an adventure with words. In fact, *Work in Progress* is more satisfying than other books because I give readers the opportunity to supplement what they read with their own imagination. Some people will be interested in the origins of words; the technical games; philological experiments in each individual verse. Each word has all the magic of a living thing. Each living thing can be shaped.

In *Dubliners* I wrote in the first story that the word 'paralysis' filled me with horror and fear, as if it were the name of something evil and sinful. I loved this word and whispered it to myself at night at an open window. It has been pointed out to me that some words are created under the influence of the impression of a world that I have not seen. My weak sight is perhaps to blame for this, so my thought escapes to images from words, and it is of course the result of my Catholic upbringing and Irish origin.

'Your nationality is very prominent in your work.'

Each of my books is a book about Dublin. Dublin is a city which has about 300,000 inhabitants and it became the universal city of my works. So I looked at the people around me. *Portrait* was a picture of my spiritual self. *Ulysses* reshaped individual impressions and what was generally acceptable. *Work in Progress* transcends reality, individuals, eternity and thought and enters the sphere of absolute abstraction. Anna and Humphrey are the city and its founder; the river and the mountain; male and female. There is no linear action in time… Wherever the book begins, there it will also end.

'Do you think that critics can understand your books, or these commentators?'

All of my work has been discovered by just as many well-known commentators as by arch-evil critics. Rebecca West's article in *The Bookman* in New York raised a huge storm. I am very curious how *Ulysses* was received and what is being said about *Anna Livia Plurabelle* in Czechoslovakia.

'I have not yet read any reviews of Ulysses *there. I think this is only because our critics have not yet been brave enough to read the book.'*

I think that it takes great courage to want to publish even a fragment of *Work in Progress*. It is an even greater responsibility for the translator. I did not want to have to decide about the publication and translation of the book, especially when it involves no ordinary translation, but the creation of a new poetry in Czech. The difficulties which you will encounter are vast. *Ulysses* was testing and tough work for a translator but it is nothing compared to *Anna Livia*.

'I would like to hear your final decision. I would like to come away with your permission to our translating Anna Livia.*'*

I know, but let's leave it for now. We will talk about it more later. I have invited the potential French translator here for the sixth time. Like ancient gladiators: *Translaturi me salutant.*

Could you open the shutters a little? It is already quiet on the streets and the sun is not beating down. I am here only on a short visit. I may go to Etretat for the weekend and then I will come back to Paris for a few days.

Joyce sits in a deep armchair. Tall, thin, and wearing a white shirt, his hair is turning grey. His expression is contemptuous and his lips are pursed tightly shut. His wife Nora excuses the state of the flat. His way of living is reflected in the mystery of his personality. Paris is now quiet. We do not speak. The room is blue, the colour of blue eyes.

Cobalt.

Joyce likes to declaim words, the sound of which illustrate the progress of his thoughts.

Cobalt.

Without connection and without direction, these isolated words fall into the silence which echoes throughout the room. Into the silence of the room lifeless from the holidays, into the room where he does not live. The silence is wide and clear. The furniture is covered in dust-sheets and everything which has not been locked into cupboards and remains in its place, sleeps. To speak in this kind of silence, one must have the courage to listen to oneself. Otherwise the words circle the room like startled pigeons, which change into bats when the words have died away, their ideas flying unheard over the white dust-sheets and poisoned bread which has been laid out for the mice. I did not care to speak. I waited for Joyce to break the silence, but I did not expect to hear, without introduction and in a perfect accent and in clear Czech:

České Budějovice.

I was genuinely startled.

Živnostenská Banka.

'Have you learned Czech since we last met?'

Oh no, it is just that I have discovered some interesting roots in your language and in mine. I know the rhythm of your language, naturally.

'Have you been in Prague?'

No. But my brother-in-law was Czech. My sister Eileen met a man in Trieste, whom she married. He was called František Schaurek and he was a cashier in a branch of Živnostenská banka in Trieste. At that time we lived together at my brother Stanny's, a language teacher. Schaurek was Czech, his family still lives perhaps in Prague, in Žižkov. He spoke perfect Czech, German and Italian. After the war, the Schaureks moved to Prague. František Schaurek later shot himself and my sister now lives in Dublin.

Would you be so kind as to send her a specimen of the Czech translation? I doubt that she has read the English original, but perhaps she will be able to capture the sense of the sentences in Czech…

'I didn't imagine that there was such a tie between you and Prague.'

It is only a family affair which I don't like to talk about.

The West of Ireland is Joyce's country. The Joyce family come from there, from an old noble family. James Joyce's father was a wonderful, typical Irishman of uncertain employment. They had a lovely home in Dublin and lived a happy life despite the ups and downs of success and penury. The days of feasting came with weeks of hardship. The concept of money and of responsibility towards the future is not in the character description of the Irish. The Joyce family was large. There were thirteen or perhaps even fifteen children. [In fact, there were nine] *Most are still alive. Two of his sisters are nuns: one in a Loreto convent in Dublin, the other in a Chinese mission or somewhere else in the East. The father was big, blue-eyed and had a lovely voice. The mother loved Jim (James Joyce). Whenever she was in pain, she asked Jim to play the piano. German critics attacked Joyce because he composed and played on the piano in the room next to the one in which his mother was dying. Joyce's sister confirms that it was his mother's wish that he played.*

The whole family was very musical. When Joyce returned from concerts, they sat in a circle and Jim would analyse the work and the performance in long debates taking the piece apart movement by movement, bar by bar. These night-time sessions of endless rumination and serious deliberations about the minutest details of a second, or even of work of transient importance were Jim's hobby. They didn't always concern music. He would go to antique dealers and bring home statues, artefacts and art and speak about them all night. His voice, like the voice of a poet, inspired respect and terror. His family weren't happy that he wrote. They were even less happy about what he was writing. Dublin, which he has so often celebrated in his work of unquestionably Irish temperament and morality, shunned him. After the publication of Dubliners, *Joyce abandoned Ireland. Some scandalized, philistine Dubliners wished him good riddance from Ireland, seemingly for ever. He now travels rarely even to England and goes almost incognito. In Ireland his name is anathema.*

Mr L[éon], Joyce's secretary, a Russian Jew, came in. We talked more about the possibility of translating Work in Progress *into another language. It was a combative meeting, and I felt rather like a pupil who is only starting to make headway. Joyce stood up and disappeared into a neighbouring room. He returned holding the slender volume of* Anna Livia Plurabelle *in his long fingers like a strict teacher, a tall figure hidden behind the magnified lenses of his glasses. His thin clenched lips pulled back into a smile, perhaps from pleasure at the thought of the strange suffering of school where you are punished with the cane, in an abandoned old manor house filled with anticipation of depraved horror. The scene reminded me of the chapter in Robert Desnos' banned book,* L'amour et la liberté: *La scène de correction commença. Leon and I sat in silence on the edge of our chairs.*

Joyce: Who is going to translate?

We both answered in unison:

'Mrs Weatherall,
Dr Vladimír Procházka,
Vitezslav Nežval
and I.

'Léon Paul Fargue
Eugène Jolase
Phillippe Soupault
Valéry Larbaud
Iwan and Claire Goll.'

And you know that it is impossible to translate.

'We know.'

It is possible to make it into poetry—poeticize it with the greatest poetic freedom that you can give it. *Work in Progress* is not written

Joyce by Hoffmeister

in English or French or Czech or Irish. Anna Livia does not speak any of these languages, she speaks the speech of a river.

It is the river Liffey. That is a woman, it is Anna Liffey. She is not quite a river, nor wholly a woman. She could be a goddess or a washerwoman, she is abstract. 'Plurabella' is for her humorous possibilities of tributaries and the diversity of her beauty.

Anna is of course a simple corruption of the Latin for river, *amnis*. Anna Liffey on the old maps is Amnis Livius. From this I then turned her name by analogy into a series of Saint Annas from different countries. Like Anna Sequana, Annie Hudson, Susquehanna etc: the names of women or rivers.

Opposite her stands Humphrey Chimpden Earwicker (Here Comes Everybody) or HCE, the male character of the story. He appears under many names, most often as Persse O'Reilley, which is from *perce-oreille* (earwig). Initials hint at the main character, when he appears in various guises in the course of the story. As for instance *H*ic *c*ubat *e*dilis. *A*pud *l*ibertinam *p*arvulam (H.C.E.A.L.P.). And out of the other characters, who appear in *Work in Progress*, come part of the whole. Finn Mac Cool, Adam and Eve, Humpty-Dumpty, Napoleon, Lucifer, Wyndham Lewis, Archangel Michael, Tristan and Isolde, Noah, Saint Patrick etc. Hircus Civis Eblanensis… Well, you know *Anna Livia*?

Joyce recites one of the first sentences of the fragment.

Anna Livia Plurabelle is a completely hermetic little work, which can be read separately from the whole of *Work in Progress*.

It is a question of the coupling mountains to rivers, and the founding of a city. I think that a translator needs to be a poet to understand the speech and to understand the river. Valéry Larbaud called his massive and amazingly precise translation of *Ulysses* a '*divertisement philologique*'. I think that perhaps *Anna Livia* is not about expression. It will be terrible work to undertake.

'We will prepare for the translation with great thoroughness.'

You will need half a year for these thirty pages. I do not want to make trouble for the Czech translator, I do not want to supervise you like a grump and a pedant, but I am afraid for my work. I do not want to be translated, I have to remain as I am, only explained in your language. I am giving you the every possible freedom in the transformation of words. I depend on you. In your country there are many rivers. Take your rivers: Vltava, Váha, Úslava and Nežárka.

Joyce has a surprisingly detailed knowledge of the names of Czech rivers.

It is possible to break them up into living words, which they were at the beginning, when God was the Word. Create a language for your country according to my image. Viktor Llona in *transition* posited the thesis: language can be made by a writer. In this case, also by the translator. Europeans make a comparison between my work and that of Rabelais in philological terms. Rabelais is a robust joker with language.

Stendhal in his *Memoirs of a Traveller* writes: 'Mr L., you are used to speaking Spanish and English in the colonies, using many words from both these languages, since you understand that to be more practical.' Stendhal continues, 'More practical, of course, but only for those who speak English and Spanish.' This kind of voice follows me around. People prefer to proclaim me an idiot, instead of trying to understand me.

'People are resentful, because you expect too much knowledge from them.'

I have received several amusing letters about my work from ordinary readers. One of them compared me to Gertrude Stein: 'Miss Gertrude Stein experiments in the same way, but to this very day, she is satisfied with a sort of hyper-normal foolishness, which we must connect to the use of already existing words. But Mr Joyce trumps her and invents his own words, as far as you can then honour them with this name.' Another letter-writer attempts to imitate me and considers playing with words as a form of after-dinner entertainment, calling me Germ's Choice and asserting that my work is Uncle Lear (Unclear) for him.

'I once translated a piece of Gertrude Stein's work. It was an unbelievable game with words.'

Perhaps you could read that translation to me.

'You would not understand it.'

My secretary, Mr L., understands Czech well.

'It went like this:

'Their women in their place were, when suddenly they were at the cashier. There is no one there for certain, with the clearly chosen which is there, is not which is there, but what was there.

'Or elsewhere: Whether it is more to want from them more than

to want from the most of them, then this is more an advantage than a mystery, and so on.

'It's not for nothing that I translated The Making of Americans. *It is the thickest volume of the music of words I know. It is an opera or a symphony of grammar. It's the reason I know I will not manage to translate the whole of* Work in Progress *by myself.'*

I think that you would need to be alive longer than you will be. Please, gentlemen, translate a piece for me, and then we will see whether it is possible to navigate *Anna Livia* in another language.

He became quiet, reminding me of the tense silence before an exam. Now that I was being tested, it seemed to me that I couldn't offer up even the smallest word. My heart and soul were quivering as if a school bell had just rung.

Please look at the top of page thirty, sixth row down.

It reads: 'It's that irrawaddyng I've stoke in my aars.' And so on. We tried to translate it.

'But what is this irrawaddyng?'

'Irrawaddyng' is from *waddyng* (= Watte, vata) with a common use in Ireland. Mainly of course Irrawaddy is a river in India. [In fact, Burma.]

Stoke is a verb of intense movement. It is taken from a dictionary of railroadmen. A stoker is the man who feeds the fire; contained in this word is a suggestion of great intensity and physical rowdiness, with which this girl pushes cotton-wool into her ears, like so, until they are ringing; the long 'aa' is repeated in this sudden feeling of wide bubbles, in the quiet of the ear or the skull, which it wouldn't have been if I'd used 'ears'.

We tried the translation. 'Irrawaddyng' was an insurmountable obstacle.

Or on page five at the bottom. 'My wrists are wrusty rubbing the mouldaw stains. And the dneepers of wet and gangres of sin in it.' The language of fluvial washing is full of fluvial expressions. In your translation, do you think that you can find a similar expression for 'mouldaw stains' in the river Vltava, just as 'dneepers of wet' recalls the Dnepr [the Russian river] or as 'gangres of sin' recalls the Ganges?'

'It will be the game of evenings. We all want to do it.'

We were suddenly obsessed by the longing to lose ourselves in this maze of suffixes created from the roots of words.

Try to translate the correspondence of words, for instance…'the rest of incurables and the last of immurables' or 'Lictor Hackett or Lector Reade'.

As time went on we sat nearer and nearer to each other. Now we had become a yoke of heads bent towards each other. The French translator presented the sentence first; it was easier because of the similarities between French and English. It took us longer. Czech, due to its unstructured nature, guarding itself like a virgin against rape, needed much more work.

Stuart Gilbert listed a whole dictionary in the Prolegomena *to* Work in Progress; *it is an attempt to interpret several words from the work, where each word is a work in and of itself. We forgot time because of the translation. Joyce is of course pleased with our interest in him. He apologized for his strictness and unyieldingness in matters of the translation and finally gave us permission to publish* Anna Livia Plurabelle.

Evening had already fallen when we left the high building on Square Robiac No 2. The Place des Invalides shone like the depths of the night. Blackly flows the quiet of Anna Sequanna. □

A note on the author

Adolf Hoffmeister (1902–1973) was a poet, novelist, translator and editor. He edited one of the main Czech daily newspapers, *Lidové noviny* (1928–30) and the main literary paper, *Literární noviny* (1930–32). He was also a talented artist and caricaturist, often illustrating his own work. Hoffmeister set up an anti-fascist magazine, *Simplicus*, in the 1930s after the German satiric magazine *Simplicissimus* was banned by the Nazis. He also wrote the libretto for a children's opera, *Brundíbar*, with music by the Czech composer Hans Krása in 1938; the opera was performed fifty-five times by children in Terezín concentration camp where Krása was interned. Hoffmeister emigrated to France in 1939, but moved on to Morocco when France fell. There, he was arrested but escaped from an internment camp and arrived in New York via Lisbon and Havana in 1941. He returned to Czechoslovakia in 1945 and worked for UNESCO. After the Communist coup in February 1948, Hoffmeister was named French ambassador by the new neo-Stalinist regime but was recalled shortly after. He worked then as a lecturer in fine art at the Academy of Applied Arts. After the Soviet invasion of Czechoslovakia, Hoffmeister emigrated to France once again in 1969, but decided to return in 1970. He died three years later in the Orlický mountains, judged by the regime to be a non-person.

NOTES ON CONTRIBUTORS

Desmond Barry is the author of three novels: *The Chivalry of Crime* (Vintage/Back Bay Books), *A Bloody Good Friday* and *Cressida's Bed* (Vintage). He is currently writing the screenplay for *A Bloody Good Friday*.

Tessa Hadley teaches at Bath Spa University College. *Everything Will Be All Right*, her second novel, is published by Jonathan Cape in the UK and by Henry Holt in the US. Her short story 'The Enemy' appeared in *Granta* 86.

Thomas Healy lives in Glasgow and is the author of a book about boxing, *The Hurting Business* (Picador), and two novels: *Rolling* and *It Might Have Been Jerusalem*. 'Martin and Me' is taken from his memoir, *I Have Heard You Calling in the Night*, to be published by Granta Books in 2006.

Isabel Hilton is the author of *The Search for the Panchen Lama* (Penguin/W.W. Norton) and is currently writing a book about Cuba. She is a columnist for the London *Guardian*.

Liz Jobey is the associate editor of *Granta*.

James Lasdun's books include a novel, *The Horned Man* (Vintage/W.W. Norton) and several collections of poetry. 'The Muse in the Cellar' is taken from his new novel, *Seven Lies*, which is forthcoming from W.W. Norton in the US in September 2005 and from Jonathan Cape in the UK in January 2006.

Andrew Martin grew up in York and now lives in London. His latest novel, *The Blackpool Highflyer*, is published by Faber. He first appeared in *Granta* with 'The Rollercoaster Champion' in *Granta* 79.

Joe Sacco is the author, most recently, of *The Fixer* (Jonathan Cape/Drawn & Quarterly) and is working on a book about the Gaza Strip. A longer version of 'In the Milk Factory' will appear in *I Live Here*, an anthology about refugees to be published in 2006 as a benefit for Amnesty International.

Luc Sante is the author of *Low Life* (Granta/Farrar Straus & Giroux) and *The Factory of Facts* (Granta/Vintage). He is currently writing a book about the picture postcard and prewar America.

Alec Soth is a photographer living in Minneapolis. His work was featured in the 2004 Whitney Biennial, and his first book, *Sleeping by the Mississippi*, was published by Steidl. In 2004 he became a nominee of Magnum Photos.

Neil Steinberg's most recent book, *Hatless Jack: the President, the Fedora, and the History of American Style*, is published by Plume Books in the US and is forthcoming from Granta Books in the UK in August 2005. He is a columnist for the *Chicago Sun-Times*.

Michelle Woods is acting director of the Centre for Translation and Textual Studies at Dublin City University. Her book, *Translating Milan Kundera*, will be published by Multilingual Matters in 2005.